T0330621

ROUTLEDGE LIBRARY EDITIONS:
SOVIET ECONOMICS

Volume 20

SOVIET MANAGEMENT AND LABOR RELATIONS

SOVIET MANAGEMENT AND LABOR RELATIONS

BRUNO GRANCELLI

Routledge
Taylor & Francis Group

LONDON AND NEW YORK

First published in 1988 by Allen & Unwin

This edition first published in 2023
by Routledge
4 Park Square, Milton Park, Abingdon, Oxon OX14 4RN

and by Routledge
605 Third Avenue, New York, NY 10158

Routledge is an imprint of the Taylor & Francis Group, an informa business

British Library Cataloguing in Publication Data
A catalogue record for this book is available from the British Library

ISBN: 978-1-032-48466-2 (Set)
ISBN: 978-1-032-49001-4 (Volume 20) (hbk)
ISBN: 978-1-032-49003-8 (Volume 20) (pbk)
ISBN: 978-1-003-39177-7 (Volume 20) (ebk)

DOI: 10.4324/9781003391777

Publisher's Note
The publisher has gone to great lengths to ensure the quality of this reprint but points out that some imperfections in the original copies may be apparent.

Disclaimer
The publisher has made every effort to trace copyright holders and would welcome correspondence from those they have been unable to trace.

Soviet Management and Labor Relations

BRUNO GRANCELLI

Boston
ALLEN & UNWIN
London   Sydney   Wellington

Allen & Unwin, Inc.
8 Winchester Place, Winchester, MA 01890, USA.
The U.S. Company of
Unwin Hyman Ltd
P.O. Box 18, Park Lane, Hemel Hempstead, Herts HP2 4TE, UK
40 Museum Street, London WC1A 1LU, UK
37/39 Queen Elizabeth Street, London SE1 2QB, UK

Allen & Unwin Australia Pty Ltd,
8 Napier Street, North Sydney, NSW 2060, Australia

Allen & Unwin (New Zealand) Ltd, in association with the
Port Nicholson Press Ltd
60 Cambridge Terrace, Wellington, New Zealand

Library of Congress Cataloging-in-Publication Data

Grancelli, Bruno, 1943–
  Soviet management and labor relations.
Bibliography: p.
Includes index.
1. Industrial relations – Soviet Union. 2. Labor and laboring classes –
Soviet Union. I. Title.
HD8526.5.G74 1987   331'.0947   87–11516
ISBN 0–04–497040–4

British Library Cataloguing in Publication Data
Grancelli, Bruno
  Soviet management and labor relations
1. Industrial relations – Soviet Union – History
I. Title
331'.0947   HD8524
ISBN 0–04–497040–4

Set in 10 on 12 point Sabon by Computape (Pickering) Ltd
and printed in Great Britain by Billing & Sons Ltd, Worcester

Contents

Acknowledgments

Many people have generously provided me with help and advice during the various phases of my research. The initial work of gathering data was greatly assisted by the financial contribution made by the Department of Social Policy, Trento University, and by the Kennan Institute for Advanced Russian Studies. I am grateful to these institutions and to their then directors, Antonio De Lillo and Abbot Gleason. I am also indebted to Marianna Tax-Choldin and the staff of the Russian and East European Center of the University of Illinois, Urbana-Champaign for their hospitality and assistance.

During my stay in the United States I had the opportunity to meet many Soviet specialists. To all of them I express my thanks for the fruitful exchange of ideas and for the useful information they gave me. In particular, I would like to express my gratitude for their support to Louise Shelley, James Millar, David Powell, and Blair Ruble.

This is a revised and updated version of a book previously published in Italian, and here I wish to thank all those who contributed in various ways to its rewriting. The work of translation was carried out with the highly professional assistance of Adrian Belton, to whom I am extremely grateful. Robert A. Lewis, Vittorio Mortara, Louise Shelley, and Peter Rutland read individual chapters and sections of the book, and I benefited greatly from their helpful comments and constructive criticism. In addition, I also owe thanks to an anonymous reviewer who, although his approach is at variance with mine, made a number of valuable observations that were of great help in clarifying my argument.

While drafting my research report, I had further opportunity to discuss it with scholars who have studied the less-visible aspects of Soviet society. Among them, I am particularly indebted to Gerald Mars, who also helped me in various ways; Gregory Grossman, who made me aware of the importance of the second economy; and Viktor Zaslavsky, who had the patience to read the Italian version, and who does not entirely agree with my arguments. Among my university colleagues I wish to thank Sergio Alessandrini and Bruno Dallago, with whom I worked on a comparative study of the unofficial economy in the West and the East. Finally, I would like to express my gratitude to those Russian friends of mine who told me of their experience of life and work, thus helping me in the attempt to understand better the human and social realities of their country.

Of course, none of the people quoted above is responsible for any errors or inaccuracies, nor for the ideas contained in this book.

Preface

Today the USSR is no longer "an enigma wrapped in a mystery." Indeed, an attempt is currently under way to lend "openness" (*glasnost*) to the working of the Soviet polity/economy. Supposing that this attempt continues, much time will be needed to produce significant changes in the relations between citizens and the authorities. Despite some recent progress, *glasnost* is still far from being dominant in Soviet society. Factory life, for instance, is by no means open, neither for the outside observer nor for planning authorities. Hence, the following warning from a Soviet analyst must still be kept in mind:

> Social phenomena are extraordinarily complicated and mysterious. The life of society has its underwater currents, its earthquakes and typhoons. To understand them we need not only statistics and cybernetics, but intuition, a subtle nervous system, acute political thinking and realism. (Shubkin 1978)

The image of "underwater currents" is an appropriate one because informal (or illegal) behavior is widespread in Soviet factories, and a "submerged" economy is thriving in the country. The puzzling problem then becomes one of gathering data and devising research methods suitable for an assessment of these phenomena and of the ways in which they shape labor relations. In other words, the issues to be addressed relate to the official framework of labor relations—its programs and regulations, and the differing degree of compliance with them manifested in the day-to-day practice of production units.

Existing Western literature on the subject offers exhaustive data on the first issue but does not deal satisfactorily with the second. Indeed, even those authors who have pointed out the lack of correspondence between the theory of labor relations and the practice in Soviet factories leave a set of questions largely unanswered (Brown 1966; McAuley 1969; Lowit 1971; Kahan & Ruble 1979; Ruble 1982). These questions include the variables influencing the reality of workplace industrial relations, their relative weight today compared with previous stages of industrial development, continuities and changes relative to the pre-Soviet history of labor and industrialization, and the influences of the national cultures on the factory regime. At present, the study of trade unions and labor relations seems to overlook two basic facts: First, the history of Soviet labor and industrialization does not begin with 1917 and second, the USSR is a multinational state (an empire to some) with striking diversities in culture and social life.

According to the official definition, the worker in the Soviet Union is the "Boss of the Enterprise" (*khoziain proizvodstva*), a term which should supposedly reflect a high level of political consciousness and a high rate of participation in the running of the factory. The abolition of private property as the reason for production is intended to prevent Soviet workers from being alienated—apart from a minority of "deviants." Unfortunately, the reality is quite different:

> It would be facetious to inquire whether the Soviet worker can recognize himself in this mirror which is held up to him on numerous occasions. It would be far more accurate to describe the basic attitude of the worker as one of realism and adaptability: he knows that he is not the boss of any enterprise, and he is well aware of who the real bosses are. (Kahan 1979:302)

According to Kahan, these basic attitudes are to be analyzed bearing in mind the "rules of the game" in the area of society and the workplace on the one hand, and in the area of personal autonomy on the other. This implies taking into account both the opportunities and constraints present in a social context and the "informal networks which are useful in the achievement of personal objectives."

The present study has taken these wise observations as its starting point, although the analysis of issues such as informal "rules" "social networks," and "personal autonomy" raises serious research problems. A non-Soviet student is faced with the dilemma of choosing between official sources or relying on an almost intuitive sense of Soviet reality. According to Kahan (1979:301), reliance upon Soviet sources biases interpretation, but the second approach implies drawing upon a multitude of hints and generalizations that may make sense in their inner logic but not in their evidential strength. Methods can be followed, however, to solve at least partially this dilemma.

First of all, when addressing this problem of bias it should be borne in mind that Soviet sources follow two basic laws. The first applies to the evidence and data released by the authorities. This is known as the "however" law; it applies generally to the Communist press, not just to the press in the Soviet Union:

> One begins quoting progress and advancements, data, new ferments.... Then one starts a new paragraph ... and one writes a good *however*, beginning to speak of what is going wrong. To spare time, the reader may look directly for the *however* and take it as the starting point. (Menduni 1986:133)

The second is called the law of "fragmentary criticism." This applies to working people and citizens, who can express their grievances concerning the behavior of powerholders without calling into question the system and its basic institutions (Miller 1967:279).

If Soviet sources are analyzed focusing on the "however" evidence and fragmentary criticism, the researcher is able to gather significant data on the less visible (but no less important) aspects of labor relations. But if the aim is also to move toward an interpretation supported by evidential strength, two further steps are needed. The first is to compare Soviet data on management and labor issues with evidence regarding these same issues in Tsarist Russia. Thus, one must determine whether indiscipline, informal practices, and corruption are actual residual phenomena or something else; the comparsion of sociological and historical data may be very helpful in this respect.

The second step consists of comparing "however" evidence and fragmentary criticism with the results of surveys of Soviet emigrées (Berliner 1957; Bauer et al. 1957; Ofer and Vinokur 1979; Mars and Altman 1983; Shelley 1984; Millar 1986; Linz 1986; Gregory 1986; Grossman and Treml 1987). This comparison is very instructive insofar as it provides insights into the evolution of informal/ illegal practices in Soviet factories since the Stalin years. It is also useful to read dissent documentation on the illegal behavior of managers and other officials; such documents often shed light on what actually happens to people who denounce illegality once the official inquiry has, according to the press, been concluded. This

documentation is also useful to a better understanding of the underlying sources of the collective conflicts that erupt in Soviet factories
from time to time.

Thus, data from Soviet and Western sources have been gathered
in order to test the following research hypothesis: Despite uniform-
ity of structures, programs, and norms, it is possible to discern
significant practical differences among the management and labor
relations of various Soviet enterprises. The actions of trade unions
play a strictly secondary role in the creation of these differences and
are to be seen as an effect rather than a cause. The most important
deciding factors seem instead to be those already important in
pre-Soviet history, namely the strategic importance and size of an
enterprise, the professional and relational skills of its management,
the availability of manpower and its sociodemographic structure,
and the cultural features of the environment.

Part I of this book outlines the main characteristics of labor
relations during Russia's three major industrialization drives: The
first was promoted by Peter the Great, the second was of the
capitalist type, and the third was imposed by Stalin. In Part I two
aspects of Soviet industrial relations are given special
consideration—the intended and unintended consequences of the
"external bureaucratization of enterprises"; and the attitude
toward work, entrepreneurs, and the state bureaucracy displayed by
workers with peasant origins and culture.

Part II describes the main aspects of the official model of labor
relations. Chapter 4 deals with labor legislation—not through
detailed analysis of laws, decrees, and resolutions, but rather by
focusing on the debate among Soviet jurists over two issues: "socialist legality" and the stability of labor relations. Information is
provided concerning improvements in labor legislation aimed at
reducing the social and economic costs of spontaneous labor
turnover and labor indiscipline (absenteeism, shoddy workmanship, pilfering, and so forth). The Soviet authorities do not seek
to attain these objectives only by improving economic and labor
legislation, however. They also resort to "social planning"—that is,
the Soviet approach to managing social and cultural services aimed
at improving the participation of working people in the "leadership
of production" and social work. Chapter 5 outlines in broad strokes
the main features of social planning at territorial and enterprise
levels.

Part III centers on Soviet management practices and labor relations. Chapter 6 examines the relationships between factory admin-
istrations and higher authorities, focusing in particular on "webs of
mutual involvement" (*krugovaia poruka*) and how they can work
in favor of the "plan" or in favor of the USSR's illegal "second
economy." Chapter 7 investigates industrial relations in the workplace and the dual functioning of Soviet trade-union committees:
their activities in defense of workers' rights and their participation
in the management of production. Chapter 8 addresses the strategic
behavior of different categories of workers: groups the Soviets call
the "vanguard of production," "individualists," and the "backward." Here attention is focused on workers' personal characteristics and the type of enterprise that employs them; this can explain
why certain workers choose to participate in the activities of trade
unions while others prefer to rely on moonlighting and various
informal-illegal dealings. Chapter 9 offers some evidence on collective actions that may occur when individual Soviet workers are
locked in undesirable working situations. The chapter also contains
personal testimonies from Soviet working people about their efforts
to create a "free trade union."

In general, the chapters comprising Part III contain findings on
such issues as the reasons why Soviet management either respects or
restricts the rights of workers; the role in running enterprises of
Party and trade-union officials; the powers and actual functioning
of trade-union factory committees; and the combination of
"command," "bargaining," and "dealing" in high-priority and
low-priority factories.

The accumulated data suggest that, in the Soviet Union, the
so-called survivals of the past in fact constitute informal mechanisms that regulate social and economic relations. In part they
compensate for the vicious circles and rigidities of the command
economy. But in the last fifteen years or so, they have also led to
the "crypto-privatization" of a large part of the production and
distribution of consumer goods and of the service sector. This
has enabled many workers, managers, and cadres to improve
their living standards by participating in (or protecting) underground economic activities. The "invisible hand" of the market
does exist in the Soviet Union, even if it mainly operates clandes-
tinely with the help of corruption. Other forms of bilateral
exchange are also important. *Blat*, for example, is Soviet jargon

for special relationships based on reciprocal trust, barter, and exchange of favors.

Marxist and functionalist categories are of little help in the interpretation of these phenomena. They entail approaches that emphasize the planning dimension of policy making and the role of formalized mechanisms in securing the functioning of the Soviet polity/economy. These approaches dull the sensitivity of the researcher to the actual implementation of official policies (Bialer 1980) and to the role of informal institutions, practices, and transactions in securing social and political stability. Chapter 10 outlines two cases of industrial relations located at the two extremes of the legality/illegality continuum—and puts forward some suggestions for their interpretation outside the Marxist and functionalist perspectives.

Soviet Management and
Labor Relations

PART I

Outlines of Labor History
in Russia

CHAPTER 1

Serf Labor and Early Industrialization

THE "EXTERNAL BUREAUCRATIZATION" OF ENTERPRISES

The models and paces of industrialization vary from country to country according to their history and social structures. The special nature of the process of industrialization in Russia has been vividly illustrated by Bendix (1956) in his comparison of that country with nineteenth-century England. He shows that whereas in England industrial growth was accompanied by the rise of an entrepreneurial class that concentrated its energies on the acquisition of political power and the legitimation of its hold over the productive processes, in Russia industrial growth was achieved as a result of government intervention. Socially the Russian entrepreneurs were heterogeneous, but all of them were in a position of dependence on the administrative and coercive measures issued by the tsarist government, designed to control economic activity and to promote industrial development.

The mindset and actions of Russian entrepreneurs were conditioned, on the one hand, by the principle of the absolute supremacy of the Tsar and, on the other, by the far-reaching control of the state bureaucracy. These two fundamental elements gave rise to the special nature of Russian industrialization and management. Tsarist autocracy had always endeavored to instill the principle that all social relations derived from sovereign will: If the actions of individuals and their mutual relations were subject to the authority of the Tsar, it followed that all social groups had to submit to his command and to be accountable to it. It was sovereign authority that interceded in the conflicts between social groups, and to do so it used the instrument of state bureaucracy.

In terms of the relations between entrepreneurs and workers, state intervention led to the "external bureaucratization of industry" (Bendix 1956:8), which presented quite different features from the "factory legislation" that developed in Western countries. In the Western system, the state concerned itself exclusively with defining the framework within which the autonomous interaction between workers and employers could take place. "External bureaucratization" went further:

> It stipulated the rights and duties of both parties, not only prohibiting certain actions, but also by ordering what should be done. And, in addition, the government superimposed on the authority relationship between employers and workers incentives and controls of its own. The purpose was to enhance the authority of managers over workers and the control of the state over managers, as well as to increase the obedience and productivity of the workers. (Bendix 1956:8)

In many societies of Western Europe, a general realignment of the functions of government was made possible by the historical presence of a relatively autonomous aristocracy and of communities with sufficient rights and prerogatives to obstruct the concentration of power in the hand of the sovereign. The sovereign, for his part, strove with the various means at his disposal to curtail any attempt at undermining his authority. The success of attempts to contain sovereign power varied from country to country and from period to period, but there is no historical instance where the success of the king was total. Generally speaking, in the West it was the balance between the impulse toward autonomy and the pressure toward centralized authority that prepared the ground for the creation of representative institutions and for the growing independence of economic activities from government regulation (Bendix 1980).

These historical conditions never existed in Russia. There, economic growth, as promoted by Peter the Great at the beginning of the eighteenth century, was founded on privilege and patronage. Many establishments were set up directly by the government and then transferred to private persons, generally ex-merchants. In other cases, the government granted interest-free loans to employers establishing factories or supplied them with workers and tools. Moreover, government buying power assured, in the main, a market for manufacturers (Tugan-Baranowsky 1970:8). The process of industrialization in Russia, therefore, even in its initial stage, had its own unique character:

> The industries were created by state plan and *ukaz*. Sons of the nobility were ordered to study science and technology; capital was invested by royal command; a labouring class was created by assigning state serfs from the crown estates. (Wolfe 1964:32)

Let us examine first the issue of the creation of a Russian laboring class. The grandiose schemes for the construction of industrial complexes and infrastructures, combined with military adventures, rendered the recruitment of manpower at local levels practically impossible. The employment of criminals, prostitutes, illegitimate children, orphans, and ex-soldiers only partially satisfied the demand of manpower (Tugan-Baranowsky 1970:18). Moreover, the introduction, in 1718, of a head-tax induced rural communities to keep as many inhabitants as possible within their boundaries. As a result, a system of compulsory labor was resorted to as the principal source of manpower for factories and work-yards. In this way, alongside the "freely employed workers," there arose two other forms of labor: the peasants from crown lands "ascribed" to the factories, and "possessional peasants"—a category originated in 1721, when individuals outside the nobility were also granted the right to purchase villages with serfs for use as labor in the "possessional factories" (Crisp 1979:388). The liberty of freely employed workers was only relative though, due to the fact that the employer, by paying the quit-rent (*obrok*) for the serf-worker, stripped him of his right to leave the factory. The abuses of the system were anything but infrequent, with the result that workers formally dubbed "freely employed" found themselves inescapably tied to their factories.

Here, a prime element in the special nature of labor relations comes to the fore. Russian society was dominated by a chaotic bureaucracy with scant respect for civil liberties. Nevertheless,

> this disorganization and disrespect for the law often worked in the other direction and made it possible to employ escaped serfs on a free contractual basis, or to adopt other recruiting methods, especially in the pri-

vately owned factories, where cash or similar incentives were used to
attract manpower—and skilled workers in particular. (Crisp 1979:338–
339)

Government policy toward escaped serfs was markedly ambivalent being the result of the conflict between two equally crucial
needs—for tax income, and for a steady supply of manpower to the
factories. To resolve this conflict, the government resorted to a
compromise: escaped serfs could not be returned to landowners if,
in the meantime, they had managed to obtain a certain degree of
industrial skill. In fact, the decree of July 18, 1721, stated that skilled
workmen and apprentices were not to be returned to their owners,
even if they were fugitives, "inasmuch as factory owners declare
that in such cases work stoppages would result in the factories"
(Tugan-Baranowsky 1970:17). This decree provided factory
administrators with an important discretionary power in their
handling of labor. The entrepreneurs acquired further advantages in
this direction when, in 1736, a decree announced that all craftsmen
were "permanently bound" (*vechno otdannie*) to their factories.
The effect of this decree lasted till the beginning of the nineteenth
century: In 1807, for example, the percentage of *vechno otdannie*
in the Urals was 5.8 percent of the active population in the crown
villages (Crisp 1979:389). Nevertheless, the shortage of manpower
remained a chronic problem for Russian industry, and to attract
workers to the factories and keep them there, various combinations
of incentives and restraints were employed for many years. On the
one hand, private entrepreneurs competed with state enterprises
over wages; on the other, the state monopolized craftsmen, who
were forced to work under conditions stipulated by the authorities.
For example, the authorities made the enticing of workers from one
factory to another before the expiration of the seven-year training
period punishable by heavy fines. The fines were paid by the factory
owner and the worker was returned to the factory he left and
subjected to corporal punishment (Tugan-Baranowsky 1970:19).
Generally speaking, it would be true to say that various forms of
compulsory labor predominated in eighteenth-century Russian factories (Crisp 1979:390).

The scarcity of manpower, especially skilled, was not the only
problem: Of equal seriousness was the problem of the quality of
production. This problem can be explained bearing in mind the

backwardness of the urban structure. At the beginning of the eighteenth century, Russian cities contained a minute fraction of the total population and were primarily military and administrative centers. Craft industries existed only in embryonic form, and it was this aspect that Peter the Great singled out as the reason for the low quality of work. Accordingly, in the period of 1720–1728, legislative acts were issued to promote the development of guilds (*tsekhi*) based on Western models; but the administrative and fiscal functions assigned to these *tsekhi* prevented them in practice from seriously performing their function of securing the supply of trained workers. Neither membership nor production was regulated, the inspection of product quality and of workers' training was haphazard, and production techniques remained relatively primitive. Thus the problems believed to be responsible for poor factory output were never dealt with (Crisp 1979:393).

In the eighteenth century, the Russian state, after intense efforts and the application of coercive measures on a vast scale, managed to set an early phase of industrialization in motion, but its patterns of development would have almost nothing in common with those of other European countries. The fundamental reason was that the driving force of industrial development was extraeconomic—that is, industrialization in the Western sense was overwhelmed by the need to transform Russia into a great military power.

In contrast with their English counterparts, the majority of Russian entrepreneurs participated in the process of industrial development more as instruments of the will of the Tsar than as free economic agents motivated by the consideration of profit. This was true in the nineteenth century as well. As Kaser (1979:547) has reported, in that period the rise of a powerful military apparatus not only created security for the entrepreneurs from the point of view of demand, but also ensured that

> the duty of defining industrial policy was concentrated in the hands of a civil or military bureaucracy, whose actions were governed by clear-cut legislative rules and who therefore did not depend on the contingencies of the world of business.

In the factories—which manufactured either under the direct surveillance of state functionaries or by governmental concession— decisions concerning company policy were taken by a small bureaucratic group, whose main objective was not so much profit as advancement up the "Table of Ranks" (Kaser 1979:547).

Bureaucratic decision-making processes at a microeconomic level were made within a macroeconomic framework that may have suggested some principles of mercantilism, but only in theory. In reality there was little effective interest in achieving a surplus in trade balance. Foreign currency earnings served mostly to pay for foreign technical expertise and to acquire military allies; the importing of foreign goods to compete on the domestic market was of secondary importance. Thus there was no reason why manufacturing enterprises that worked for the government should show a profit, and they represented a share that was by no means negligible. In 1725, for example, there were 336 industrial establishments, 43 of which belonged to the state; in 1750, 75 metallurgical and 50 textile enterprises were manufacturing for the government (Kaser 1979:549 and 626). It is worth adding that, as the factory owner, the Russian government had the monopoly for the production of vodka. Referring to the consequences of this monopoly, a traveler noted that the government should have tried to find "*de plus nobles sources de revenue que l'industrie des eaux-de-vie, dont il accapare le monopole en se faisant le premier cabaretier du pays.*" ["more respectable sources of revenue than those deriving from the production of aquavitae, a monopoly that has turned the government into the chief saloon-keeper of the country"] (Golovine 1845:92).

Finally, two more facts should be borne in mind. First, a system of bank brokerage still did not exist (Kushpeta 1978:17); decisions concerning industrial investments were not influenced by the cost of money, but by political considerations. Second, all production decisions were determined by physical factors rather than by economic accountability. Thus, as Wolfe (1964:32) has remarked:

> Long before Marxian socialism was so much as dreamed of, the Russian state had become the largest landowner, the largest factory owner, the largest employer of labour, the largest trader, the largest owner of capital, in Russia, or in the world.

This state domination was the result of a modernization that was intended primarily for the aims of state policy—a policy in which industrialization and militarization were strictly intertwined.

SERF-WORKERS: RECRUITMENT AND
WORKING CONDITIONS

Serf-labor has been analyzed primarily with reference to the metallurgical industries of the Urals. In the works of Soviet scholars the
conditions of the serf-workers are described in terms of the most
bestial exploitation. Gorovoi states, for example, that among
the most common features of life for the metallurgical workers in
pre-Emancipation Russia were

> the barbarous tyranny of the factory administration, the torment of
> workers, low rate of pay and long work day, the absence of any safety
> measures and the widespread use of female and child labour, disgusting
> medical services and almost total illiteracy among the workers....
> (Quoted in Esper 1978:661)

Moreover, any serf-worker who rebelled or sought to present a
petition to the Tsar risked being shot—or even being thrown alive
into the furnaces, as allegedly happened in Demidov's factories. For
less grave acts of insubordination, the guilty worker was punished
by being forced to run between two lines of his workmates; armed
with clubs, they were ordered to beat him (Kaser 1979:556). These
practices, however, do not give a complete portrait of the working
and living conditions of serf-workers in the eighteenth century and
first half of the nineteenth. Soviet historians tend to base their
research—as Esper has pointed out—not on archive data but only
on the few instances of industrial conflict to occur mainly during the
period 1820–1830 and 1856–1860. They make no mention of the
fact that these were years of depression for the metallurgical industry in the Urals, and they also neglect to mention that the workers
involved in the conflicts were only auxiliaries.

Documents from the period do not show that the conditions of
industrial workers were one of generalized degradation. On the
contrary, they indicate a correlation between the degree of prosperity of an enterprise and the conditions of the workers employed
in it. Besides, it should be remembered that the income of the
serf-worker families did not only consist of their wages and
payments in kind. Actually, all housing costs and the majority of
household food and clothing expenses were covered by the factory
in addition to wages. Each serf-worker had his own plot of land,

provided free by the factory, where he built his house and cultivated sufficient produce for his needs, improving his diet also by raising animals (Esper 1978:666).

The factories paid low wages but, at the same time—and in contrast with Western firms—they had to meet a series of extra expenses in their labor costs. They had, for example, to pay taxes on each serf-worker, regardless of his age and his capacity for work; other taxes had to be paid to exempt employees from military service. Employers were obliged by law to provide medical services, and even old-age and disability pensions had to be funded by the enterprise (Esper 1978:667). The cost of these social services varied from enterprise to enterprise, but they were by no means negligible anywhere. In the Nizhnii Tagil industrial complex, for example, in the decade 1850–1860, the funding of these services represented 42 percent of labor costs; in the Neviansk and Alapaevsk complexes they represented 27 and 16 percent respectively.

The law governing social services did not stipulate their quality, but the hospital at Nizhnii Tagil was described by a contemporary source as "excellent," and other sources relate that from 1828 onwards schools, hospitals, a library, a museum, and a botanical garden were built in the region. In 1819, in the hospital of Nizhnii, 6,617 patients were treated free of charge (Esper 1978:674).

The diet and living conditions of working families were minutely analyzed by Frederic Le Play in 1844, who based his findings on two typical families. These families owned their houses—as did most of the workers' families in the Urals. They enjoyed the right to cut timber and firewood and were entitled to sell their houses as long as the purchaser lived in the area. According to Le Play, these houses had satisfactory standards of hygiene (Le Play 1877:102). Most household provisions came from the vegetable patch and from the animals raised by the family—who also enjoyed the right to hunt, fish, and gather mushrooms on the entrepreneur's land (Le Play 1877:105). The enterprise also distributed flour to its workers or alternatively paid a bonus, as was done in Nizhnii Tagil (Esper 1978:676).

In Le Play's study, secondary activities all made a major contribution to the incomes of the two representative families: In one family wages represented 80 percent of their income; in the other, only 30 percent. The importance of complementary work to the family budget is underscored by the fact that the workload in the factories was not particularly heavy when compared with the situation in the West. In summer, the factory closed for four to six weeks to release workers for the harvest. The number of working days per year averaged approximately 250; the working day varied according to the season but usually lasted from 10.5 to 11.5 hours (Esper 1978:670).

Labor management for the serf-worker was markedly paternalistic, and this contributed greatly to the stability of community life. The social order was also strengthened from below by two other factors: the patriarchal structure, and the customs of serf families, who adhered closely to strict rules of public and private morality. Seen in this light, Le Play's observations do not strike us as strange:

> Most workers are happy with the benefits bestowed on them by the social organization of the country, but above all by the ties that bind them to their families, the community and their masters. (Le Play 1877:151–152)

This attitude can be understood when we take into account that—in contrast with their Western counterparts—Russian metallurgical workers counted on their factories to provide for their basic needs, regardless of the prosperity of their economic sector or factory. Furthermore, there is no evidence whatsoever to suggest that the serf-workers yearned for freedom in the Western sense of the word:

> On the contrary, while they at times complained of harsh discipline, they considered the assurance of their basic security to have been an inalienable right, an inherent aspect of the socio-economic system in which they lived. In none of the petitions sent by workers can one find requests or demands to be freed from serfdom; there are only protests against what the workers considered to be infringements by management of what one contemporary called "the mutual rights and obligations of the factory managers and the workers." (Esper 1978:671)

The previous discussion demonstrates that the serf-workers adapted quite well to factory life. In the nineteenth century, in fact, a shift in the character of petitions to the authorities became apparent. There were now increasingly fewer petitions seeking exemption from factory work in order to return to the fields, and many more complaints concerning wages, working conditions, punishments, and injustices. For example, the research of Tugan-Baranowsky (1970) into "possessional peasants" cites letters sent by workers of a factory in Kazan (and, in one case, by the owner) to the authorities and to the Tsar during the period 1796 through 1847. The petitions are relatively few in number, numbering only fourteen. From 1796 to 1800, the workers complained about their low wages and the cruelty of their employers. Subsequent letters only contain protests over harsh treatment: one was a case of whipping and deportation to Siberia; two others involved punishment that led to the death of several workers and unjust conscription into the army. The single petition from the employer asked for increased authority over his workers and greater freedom to employ female workers.

Except for the case of a senator who, on a local tour of inspection, granted a request for increased wages, the results of the petitions were poor. The rest of the petitions were refused as being "unfounded," the product of "deceit due to a quarrelsome nature," or as "fantastic requests" or "seditious fancies." In these cases the reply from authorities was accompanied by warnings of harsh punishment and orders designed to ensure the obedience of the workers; often this pledge to obedience had to be guaranteed in writing. Sometimes orders were issued to identify whoever had instigated the workers, in order to have him whipped, sent to forced labor in Siberia, or pressed into the army. In one case, the petition never reached the Tsar; the petitioners were imprisoned and tortured, and one subsequently died. A government official, sent to investigate, exhorted the workers to obey their master and abandon their "false ideas of freedom," but he also established a set of norms to govern labor relations to the factory. The only direct reference to emancipation is contained in a letter sent in 1834. After receiving a workers' petition against maltreatment and unjust military conscription, the Tsar appointed a commission of enquiry, whose object was to convince the workers that they were legally bound to their factories; but, as the commission later reported, "they insist in their demand for emancipation and in denouncing cruelty" (Tugan-Baranowsky 1970:116–120). By contrast, in 1861, the law for the abolition of serfdom was greeted by many workers in the Urals with disquiet, "for fear of losing their rights." In fact, in two large factories, the workers drew up a petition calling for the return to serfdom (Esper 1978:671).

It would appear, therefore, that the aim of workers' protests was not to call into question the autocratic pattern of labor relations. Confirmation of this is provided by data gathered in other factories, which show that low wages were the most frequent cause of complaint, especially when better-paid free workers were also employed. After low wages came protests over fines and supposedly unjustified wage deductions, protests over cases in which children and old people were assigned heavy work, and protests over the military conscription of workers instead of agrarian serfs. Another frequent complaint was the forcing of workers to undertake non-factory work of various kinds (Tugan-Baranowsky 1970:113). Nonetheless, factory labor was regarded as more attractive than working on the land—as demonstrated by protests over the sale of worker-families to landowners and the refusal by authorities to issue internal passports to peasants.

The conditions of the workers, and the quality of labor relations, depended not only on the sort of factory that employed them, but also on the personal characteristics of the entrepreneur. In the first half of the nineteenth century, a number of landowners built factories on their land and ran them personally. These cannot be described as capitalist enterprises, but rather as "off-shoots of the old despotic order" in the sense that they were protected, were subsidized and regulated by the state, and supplied the army in fixed quota at guaranteed prices (Blackwell 1982:22).

But the period saw also the rise of another, more modern type of entrepreneur: the serf-entrepreneur, whose activities provided the landowners with income in exchange for legal protection. These serf-entrepreneurs were usually craftsmen of great skill, who were ready to introduce technical innovations in production methods. They were most active in the textile sector, especially in the region of Ivanovo, but were also prominent in the leatherwork trade and in the manufacture of cotton articles (Kaser 1979:563).

A third entrepreneurial category comprised such religious dissenters as Old Believers and Jews. The former made a significant contribution to the development of the textiles industry in Moscow, and both groups seemed particularly adept at accumulating capital and at stimulating work productivity (Blackwell 1965).

In view of the fact that there was also a number of foreign entrepreneurs in the country, it is fair to assume that there was a significant degree of variation among the patterns of labor relations to be found in individual enterprises. And this was accentuated by another important factor: the ambivalent nature of government interference in labor relations.

The policies of the tsars have always had one overriding objective: to ensure the predominance of state interests over those of the individual enterprise and, at the same time, to ensure the supremacy of the aristocracy over all other social groups. Thus the exploitation of the serfs was limited by the state's interests. This is confirmed by the fact that the serf-workers had only one single right in their dealings with their masters: the right to denounce them in cases of violations of the laws of the state. This right was also a duty, and carried much more weight with middle-class entrepreneurs or those with serf origins: Their enterprises were subject to much tighter government control, and the power of master over worker was, in theory, strictly regulated. In practice, however, these entrepreneurs almost always behaved as if they enjoyed the same powers as the aristocratic factory owners, and the regulations imposed by the government were very often evaded, largely because of the widespread corruption of state officials, who "take by handfuls, do not wait to receive, but ask and peddle, accepting big presents without disdaining the small ones" (Golovine 1845:91).

In any case, no social group ever called into question the right of the government to regulate labor relations: The employers and the workers assumed that "the government and even the Tsar personally, would determine their rights and obligations" (Bendix 1956:171).

After the passing in 1826 of a regulation governing the "possessional factories," it became increasingly evident that workers were using the regulations to obstruct factory owners in their deployment and use of the workforce. Considerable uncertainty continued to exist over the precise nature of labor relations, due to the diversity of interests among the employers, the landowners, and the government functionaries. The employers wanted the government to create the best conditions for the use of the workforce, but the landowners tended to show a paternalistic-protective attitude toward their serfs. The government functionaries were either high bureaucrats or local administrators: The former generally tended to favor the entrepreneurs because they were primarily interested in ensuring uninterrupted output for the government. The latter, however, often paid heed to workers' protests because they had to maintain public order, but also because they were prejudiced against the entrepreneurs, who often were religious dissenters or foreigners. At the government level the least sensitivity to the employers' interests was shown by the Ministry of Interior, for two reasons. First, the minister was more concerned with the interests of the landowners, which were extraneous to those of the industrialists. Second, the minister was guided in his action by political considerations and the preservation of political stability. By contrast, the Ministry of Finance, as the body representing the interests of major industry, sided with the entrepreneurs. This tendency would remain constant: Even in the second half of the century, many labor protection laws would be supported by the Ministry of the Interior (Tugan-Baranowsky 1970:124).

This situation led to considerable uncertainty among the employers, and in turn gave rise to the conviction among serf-workers that the injustices they experienced were caused by the abuses of power committed by corrupt functionaries at various levels. This conviction was accompanied by the belief that only autocratic power could redress their wrongs (Bendix 1956:170). These contrasting interests and shared convictions contributed to create the basic patterns of labor relations in Russian industry in general, and not only for the pre-Emancipation period.

CHAPTER 2

Wage Labor and Guided Capitalism

AFTER EMANCIPATION: THE WORKER-PEASANT AND THE FACTORY SYSTEM

As early as the end of the eighteenth century, the importance of serf labor in Russia began to decline—if not in absolute terms, at least by percentage of the total workforce. In fact, the availability of labor increased during this period to an extent that rendered the use of serf-workers increasingly unnecessary, especially in enterprises situated in urban centers. Moreover, owners of "possessional factories" began to question the advantages of using serf manpower because they were unable to suit the composition of their workforce to the needs of their enterprises and market. In fact, they were legally obliged to keep those workers who were too old or too sick and to provide them with food at a low price. Besides, since the freely employed workers—whose wages were higher—worked side by side with the serf-workers, the latter felt that "their rights had been infringed and were permanently discontent" (Crisp 1979:397).

A decree issued in 1840 sought to emancipate serf labor in "possessional factories." Nevertheless, in 1860 one-third of industrial labor still worked in conditions of serfdom (Crisp 1979:398). The Act of Emancipation of 1861 did not alter significantly the character of labor relations in factories nor the social and cultural characteristics of the workers. The ties with the land continued to be extremely strong.

Even in a city like St. Petersburg, where in 1907 there was already a substantial population of industrial proletariat, more than half of the print workers (the most urbanized and professionally experienced) kept ties, if not with agriculture, at least with their villages of birth. Of this group, 20 percent helped in the running of the family farm, another 20 percent maintained ownership of their land and houses, and 14 percent—while not owning land themselves—sent money to their relatives in the villages (Crisp 1979:457). Generally speaking, the great majority of Russian industrial workers, were still undergoing a process of transformation from peasant to factory worker. The average worker still regarded himself as first and foremost a peasant and only incidentally a factory man. This is even truer when we look beyond the major factories to the industrial structure of the country as a whole.

During the nineteenth century, the industrial workforce was recruited in the villages by intermediaries or by agents acting for the factories. The contracts were signed in the presence of the mayor and often contained clauses guaranteeing the settlement of the workers' debts and the payment of their taxes owed to the community (Laverichev 1972:82). As a rule, peasants from the same locality who intended to work in a particular factory would organize themselves into a group (*artel*). One of the older members would act purely as an intermediary who negotiated with the management in the name of the group and who, in this capacity, would be paid the same wage as the other members of the *artel* who actually did the work. Further, he organized the supply of provisions to the workers housed in the factory's barracks. In certain economic sectors (mining, sugar milling, and seasonal work, for instance) the *artel* also functioned as a work squad. In these cases the intermediary assigned quotas, distributed wages, and kept the work books, which specified output and wage norms (Crisp 1979:464).

By the end of the nineteenth century, the *artel* decreased in importance. Group leaders and workers often quarreled; the former lined their pockets at the expense of the workers; the latter disappeared without repaying money advanced to them out of their wages. A further reason for the declining importance of the *artel* was the increasing tendency of the employers to provide lodging and services for whole families, or to recruit local labor—especially in winter (Crisp 1979:465).

In general, the major problem for employers was not the scarcity of manpower as such but rather labour turnover, which consisted in a movement from factory to villages during harvest time (Johnson 1976:56) and from factory to factory in search of better salary and working conditions. Consequently, employers insisted on long-term contracts that stipulated heavy fines for workers who left their posts between April and October; some offered bonuses to workers who stayed in the factories in summer. In some cases, the contracts stipulated that those who left during the summer had to arrange for a replacement worker. Summer wages were higher than those paid in winter. On the other hand, the employer found it difficult to dismiss workers or to reduce their wages in winter because this was often regarded as "unpleasant" by the workers—and often by authorities too (Crisp 1979:467).

Payment in kind was common, as in the eighteenth century. Also common was the granting of credit to the workers by the enterprise (Bonnell 1983:138–139). Moreover, wages were often paid only on completion of the contract. In consequence many workers ran away or absented themselves from the factory in order to earn money from collateral activities. Running away was often justified as the only way to protest to authorities over ill-treatment or injustices suffered at the hands of employers. These injustices were often not a pretext: Employers would sometimes keep back a considerable portion of a worker's wages as a guarantee against his running away, and sometimes these "deductions" were higher than the actual wages themselves (Crisp 1979:468). Reasons for discontent existed, therefore, especially in small industries and among unskilled workers (Bonnell 1983:77–81, 109–112), and workers reacted either by quitting their jobs, by petitioning the authorities, or, sometimes, by resorting to brief, violent outbursts of protest. As Bendix (1956:184) reported, the expression of workers' discontent "alternated erratically and dangerously between demonstrations of abject humility and direct threats to the life and property of employers."

By the beginning of this century, even if most advanced industrial sectors in Russia could rely on a stable workforce, the working day and the duration of the working year were still extremely erratic:

> Major and minor, local and national Saints' Days; historical and royal anniversaries; and various other occasions—all were cause for celebration, not to mention "Holy Mondays" and so on. (Crisp 1979:469)

Depending on the factory, the number of working days per year varied between 117 and 355; for industry as a whole, the average was calculated in 1900 as being 264 (Crisp 1979:469).

Moreover, the stability of manpower in the advanced industrial sectors was far from optimum: Many companies saw a 100 percent turnover of personnel in the course of one year. This high turnover in the factories was mainly due to the equally high percentage of unskilled labor. Employers tended to stabilize their workforce by insisting on long-term contracts, but this made it difficult for the company to adapt itself to suit market requirements and, in any case, there was no guarantee that the workers would in fact respect the conditions of their contracts. In order to satisfy their manpower needs employers also tended to resort to a further expedient—keeping excessive numbers of employees on their books.

Statistics underscore this worker turnover. It has been calculated by Olga Crisp (1979:470) that in 1904, in various metalworking factories in St. Petersburg, between 10 and 25 percent of the workers who had voluntarily left their job in the previous year had done so without giving notice; 30 to 50 percent had left at their own request or by "mutual agreement"; 10 to 45 percent had been dismissed for laziness, incompetence, refusal to carry out assigned work, or drunkenness; and the rest had either been called up by the army, had fallen ill, or had died.

Another major problem was factory discipline. Employers sought to enforce worker discipline by means of fines and punishment for the violation of production norms, absenteeism, and lateness. Managers also tried to exercise control over every aspect of their workers' daily lives. This was thought justified because many workers lived in lodgings provided by the factory, and also because tradition gave a strong authoritarian-paternalist flavor to labor relations. Thus, for example, a factory regulation stated:

> During the working hours it is forbidden to sing or to dance.... The workers must always assume a humble and decorous attitude and treat the women decently, without insulting them either by action or in words. After ten o'clock at night, every worker must remain in his room. (Bendix 1956:182)

In practice, however, management did not always insist on regulations being respected, and neither were fines always exacted. In certain enterprises the money collected from fines was set aside for social initiatives that benefited the workers (Crisp 1979:471; Bonnell 1983:145).

An important aspect of indiscipline at work was larceny. Entrepreneurs were plagued by pilfering in their factories which proved impossible to stop with normal disciplinary methods. So, a certain number of enterprises set up "workers' tribunals," forums that generally condemned the thieves to a good hiding. It is important to note that these punishments were seen as being meted out not by the management but by morally indignant workmates. Indeed, this expedient proved more effective than fines and was still being used in 1910 in advanced industrial regions such as that of St. Petersburg (Crisp 1979:471).

About enforcing discipline, two remarks should be added. First, workers used unofficial means to fight back against foremen. In the "wheelbarrow and sack treatment," for example, a group of workers would throw a dirty sack over the head of an unpopular foreman and tie the sack around him. If the workers were really angry, the foreman, after being bundled into the sack, could be "dumped into the wheelbarrow like so much cargo and then wheeled around to the accompaniment of hoots and whistles" (Bonnell 1983:107–108).

Second, there were also a variety of financial incentives designed to improve productivity, even if progress in this field was generally modest. For example, plant utilization in metalworking during 1901, 1904, and 1908 was 47, 39, and 46 percent, respectively. Per capita production quadrupled during the 1863–1913 period but still lagged behind that of other industrialized countries: The output of cast iron, for instance, was one quarter of that of the United States and little more than half that of Germany. The same was true of the textile industries, despite the fact that it is difficult to draw comparisons due to the varying quality of the output in different countries. In fine weaving in Russia, four to six workers were employed at each loom; in the United Kingdom, only two or three. Many Russian textile operations were still carried out manually, especially in preparation and carding, and many workers were employed in correcting errors committed during these operations. The low rate of output per worker was also due to the large number of supervisors and controllers, who increased running costs by 21 to 23 percent (Crisp 1979:506).

AUTOCRACY AND SOCIAL POLICY

In his analysis of managerial ideologies in the West, Bendix (1956) pointed out that entrepreneurs there were favored in that their values were largely shared by the rest of society (or, at least by the middle classes), and also by the fact that they enjoyed the support of law and constituted power. This is not to say that Russian entrepreneurs lacked this support. But the weakness of the entrepreneurial class and the widespread nature of anticapitalist values in Russian society combined to induce the tsarist government to assign—even if, ambivalently and indecisively,

> top priority to the preservation of stability and order, to ensuring the continuing loyalty of the masses rather than to general consideration of primarily economic issues, or to the specific satisfaction of the needs of the entrepreneurs. (Crisp 1979:473)

The government's basic attitude toward labor policy is clearly expressed in a statement by the finance minister, Witte, who in 1902 observed:

> Since Russia had embarked upon industrialization later than other states, her government could avoid their mistakes and draw all the social forces of the country toward harmony ... because the government was led by One Will which stood above partisanship and private interests. However, the government would support, not the profit motive, but the workers when they needed protection. (Von Laue 1962:135)

Minister Witte's statement clearly expresses the autocratic-paternalist principle of government. It is also clear that the legal existence of a labor movement was out of the question so long as this principle remained in force. This implied, however, that the defense of workers' rights was to be considered a concern of the government, which should intervene through labor legislation.

In reality, direct government intervention in the management of labor relations decreased significantly in the last two decades of the nineteenth century. A first reason for this was the development of the economic system along capitalistic lines. In the past the government had to rely on the "possessional factories" for supplies to its armed forces; now, with the general expansion of industry, it had a far wider choice of potential sources of supply. Before, the government had found itself forced to take responsibility for promoting industrialization since no banking sector—even if it had existed—would have been able to collect sufficient resources for industrial development on a wide scale. Now, as the nineteenth century ended, industry reached a stage of development which enabled it to act much more independently than in the past (Gerschenkron 1974a:20). A second reason for the reduction of government's control over industry and labor was that anyone who argued for more control was also aware that it could have an unwanted effect—causing workers to interpret the regulation of labor relations as tantamount to an official recognition of their claims (Bendix 1959:184). This is not to say that state control of the economy disappeared. On the contrary, Russian capitalism remained largely guided by the state. Industrialists continued to receive many kinds of privileges including loans and subsidies. Railroad and metallurgial enterprises were assured large state orders and the state also protected some industrial branches (Pushkarev 1985: 223).

This marked reduction in direct government intervention was matched by a corresponding improvement in labor legislation which, in the 1880s assumed significant proportions. The laws passed in those years were mainly based on proposals put forward by the Stakelberg Commission (1859–1864), which dealt with child and female labor, factory inspection, and the standardization of contracts. Eventually, laws were passed regulating employment of women and adolescents (1882 and 1885), the hiring of labor (1866), maximum working hours (1877), and the legal responsibility of the factory in case of industrial accident (1903) (Von Laue 1962; Laverichev 1972; Wagner 1976).

Government officials were divided between those who tended to give almost unqualified support to the employer and those who favored the subjection of both workers and entrepreneurs to detailed legislation from above. The former drew support from employers in charge of the more technologically backward factories, who needed to pay lower wages and exploit the workforce to the maximum extent. The latter were favored by more modern enterprises, whose owners hoped that tough labor laws would cause problems for their more backward competitors. The employers found their most active defenders in the Ministry of Finance, which, as the chief agent of the collection of taxes, was only interested in the economic success of the enterprises in order to increase the state revenues. Supporters of governmental control were to be found mainly in the Ministry of the Interior, whose officials—being responsible for public order—were primarily concerned with ensuring that tensions in the factories did not rise to a point where they could cause strikes and riots (Bendix 1956:177).

In 1906, permission was granted for the establishment of an organization which had many features in common with a trade union. This event merits a more detailed account. As the earlier quotation from Minister Witte indicated, the autocratic principle of government began to be mitigated during the 1870s by the "paternalist principle" (*popechitelstvo*), according to which the autocracy enjoyed a status above consideration of class. The Tsar's government had to act to prevent any excessive exploitation of the workers that might cause disturbances and threats to political stability, but workers were not to establish their own organization for the defense of their interests. Thus the government had to act as their protector and to guarantee—to a certain extent—their well-being. The task of applying the *popechitelstvo* and impeding the organization of a real trade union fell to the organs of the Ministry of the Interior, which attempted to do so by adopting a "complex approach," to use a term currently in vogue in that country.

The unionization question was dealt with at two levels. First came the steady building up of the police force. For example, in 1898 the Ministry of the Interior reported that the province of Ekaterinoslav had a policeman for every 482 workers and that of Ivanovo one for every 446; the ministry proposed that the ratio be reduced to a policeman for every 250 workers. The ministry also suggested an increase in the activeness of the police force, and, in fact, police "productivity" in terms of espionage, investigations, and arrests increased considerably over the next few years (Von Laue 1962:137). But this was not all: Regions with a record of labor disturbances were practically placed under siege (*usilennaia okhrana*). Full power was put in the hands of local authorities, who could ban public meetings, close down factories for a certain period, take "administrative measures" against agitators, and hold courts-martial (Von Laue 1962:138).

During this period officials of the Ministry of the Interior did not concern themselves only with improving the efficiency of instruments of repression, however. In their second strategy against unionization, they also sought to deal with the causes of workers' dissatisfaction. They carried out surveys into—and wrote reports on—wages, working hours, hazardous working conditions, and even the profits made by the entrepreneurs. For example, in his report to the ministry, the chief of police Sviatopolsk-Mirskii declared that workers had good reasons for complaint, especially regarding their pension and medical services. Above all, he deplored the workers' lack of opportunity to discuss their condition openly, and he condoned their resorting to the illegal press to air their grievances, given that they had no other means available. He concluded that the situation called for a government newspaper entirely devoted to workers' interests, one which could inform them of their rights and prerogatives—of which, he reported, they were entirely ignorant. Sviatopolsk-Mirskii also expressed annoyance over the tyrannical behavior of supervisors and the lack of arbitration procedures to deal with disputes between workers and management. Finally, he proposed the election of workers' representatives to act as spokesmen for their opinions and grievances (Von Laue 1962:139). Sipiagin, minister of the interior, regarded it as his duty to investigate personally the sort of conditions workers lived in, and he was convinced that the situation called for "a firm but just guardian to protect them from market forces." He was equally convinced that the workers should become "a conservative force, tied to the entrepreneurs by forms of savings and social insurance," and that every worker should be assigned his own plot of land to cultivate. Finally, the minister suggested that factory owners—like the workers—should be held legally responsible for every violation of the law, and that questions concerning the hiring and firing of personnel should be subjected to public control. It is no surprise, therefore, that the finance minister Witte called his rivals in the ministry of the interior "the real socialists in the government" (Von Laue 1962:138).

These reports were not without effect on the social policy of the government, as the increasing amount of labor legislation dating from the beginning of the 1880s demonstrates. This period also saw the growth of a new attitude among workers: From this moment forth, their dissatisfaction no longer limited itself to frequent job changes or to petitioning the authorities. This changed attitude was graphically described in a report prepared in 1884 by the St. Petersburg police. The report stated that factory labor was divided into two classes: permanent and temporary workers. The former were not as "backward" as the latter and very "mischievous," in the sense that they had

> a substantial amount of undesirable experience which consisted in reading half-understood books of doubtful content, in placing absurd interpretations on newspaper articles and in discussing problems with the agents of the anarchist party.(Bendix 1956:187)

After observing that these workers blamed their misery and impotence not on their own behavior but on "so-called social injustices," the report concluded:

> The relationship between manufacturers and workers leaves much to be desired. In most cases the masters try to pay the workers as little as possible, and have no other concern. And the workers have absolutely no respect for their masters. The question of wages often leads to discontent. It would be desirable to have a special organization carefully watching over the relationship between these two classes. (Bendix 1956:188)

These reports, as Bendix points out, reflect the basic dilemma of the autocratic regime in its regulation of labor relations. On the one hand, the authority of employers had to be maintained; on the other, action had to be taken to remedy the abuses committed by employers and by insubordination and unrest among workers. Since repressive measures by the police were no longer enough, and even counterproductive in that they led to increased disorders, a new form of protective action began to evolve. The paternalist principle acquired a concrete form in the shape of "police socialism," based on labor organizations supervised—or rather manipulated—by the police.

From 1902 onward the chief organizer of police-regimented unions was Sergei Vasilievich Zubatov, chief lieutenant of General Trepov, the head of Moscow police. In a report written in 1898, Zubatov based his arguments on the premise that Western-style labor movements, would not suit Russian conditions: If the workers were allowed to organize themselves autonomously, this would lead not to a reformist movement but to subversion. Such references to the incompatibility of Western ideas were a constant feature in the handling of labor questions by the government authorities.

Later Soviet historians have criticized these tsarist labor policies as a reaction against disorder that had become increasingly widespread against a background of the poorly organized labor movement, which, nevertheless, expressed fierce class antagonism. An alternative analysis of government actions in this period seems to be closer to the truth. In their handling of the labor question, government officials consistently tried to adopt legal models taken from more advanced countries. They hoped in this way to avoid excessive exploitation of the workers, which would lead to their rejecting the system of paternalistic guardianship in favor of the collective defense of their interests (Wagner 1976:393; Von Laue 1962:128). Thus, to defend the interests of the workers and to preserve public order at the same time, the government realized that it was worthwhile to create a labor organization and to ensure its moral and ideological supervision. Factory life, declared Zubatov, eroded the moral qualities of a person; to fight against this, the workers' leisure time and social life had to be carefully organized:

> The centers of all these activities were to be the unions, collective organizations like the village *obshchina*, attached to a given branch of industry, not hostile to the existing regime—as in the West—but closely identified with the ideal of Russian autocracy. (Von Laue 1962:140)

These worker associations would grant workers a freedom of action and an opportunity that, at that time, was beyond their reach, but it would also stoke "new spiritual fires in the urban-industrial society." As a corollary, the government would regulate bargaining over wages and working hours, thus limiting the capitalist enterprise's freedom of action and providing the workers with new guarantees of social security (Von Laue 1962:140).

In practice, the police helped to set up labor organizations in Moscow, Odessa, Kiev, Nikolaevsk, Minsk, and Vilnius. They also brought considerable pressure to bear on entrepreneurs, although the most important manufactuerers found support in the Ministry of Finance, claiming that the government, in order to protect itself against popular agitations, was sacrificing the interests of production. In their opinion, political rather than economic concessions were necessary if labor unrest was to be pacified (Von Laue 1962:141; Bendix 1959:185). The government, in fact, became increasingly aware that it could not go on encouraging collective action by workers to the detriment of the authority of the employers, and the experiment of "police socialism" came to an end. Before it finally disappeared, however, it played a significant role in precipitating the events that would lead to the revolution of 1905. Although, as far as the actual events that set off the insurrection are concerned, the situation was rather different from the one described by Trotsky in a pamphlet on the general strike written in 1904:

> Not Marxian socialism but one of the experiments in "police socialism" became the bizarre starting point for a general strike. Or perhaps we should say "clerical socialism," for its leader was a priest of the Russian Orthodox Church! (From Wolfe 1964:321)

Father Gapon (the leader of "clerical socialism") drew his inspiration from the ideas of Colonel Zubatov but, in contrast, believed that the workers of St. Petersburg, being more sophisticated than their Moscow counterparts, would take more readily to "spiritual supervision" than police control. Shortly before the 1905 Revolution he managed to have a "Trade Union of Russian Factory Workers" approved by the minister Plehve, which included among its aims the following:

> The sober and rational passing of leisure time, the elimination of drunkenness and gambling, the inculcation of religious and patriotic ideas, the development of a prudent view of the duties and the rights of the workers, and organized self-activity for the legal improvement of the conditions of labour and life of the workers. (Wolfe 1964:321)

It should be noted that this type of labor movement was at its strongest in the "Putilov workshops"—which would later become so famous in the 1917 revolution. Under Gapon's leadership, in 1904, the workers of this factory presented a series of moderate demands to the management, who responded in December of that same year by sacking all members of the trade-union committee. Whereupon, the factory workers asked Gapon to lead them directly to the "Father of the Russian People." The Tsar's reply, on January 21, 1905, was the massacre of "Bloody Sunday."

The experiment of "police socialism" ended in the tragedy of Bloody Sunday and this outcome leads to a final question: What were the conditions of labor in the absence of possibilities for unionization? Any attempt at an answer must refer—once again—to the distinction between real wages and the cost of labor. Although wages in Russian industry were low, labor costs were practically the same as those in other, more advanced countries. The reasons, as mentioned earlier, were the low rate of output per worker and a cost structure similar to those of the "company towns" found in the West (enterprises that included houses, schools, and hospitals, with high supervision and administration costs).

Labor costs were not so high for all enterprises, but certainly they were for major companies, and especially in the metallurgical, oil, and cotton industries. Around 1904, in the metallurgy industry of southern Russia, indirect expenditures on the workforce comprised 10 to 15 percent of wages; in 1900–1908, wages rose by 20 percent, while indirect outlay rose by 63 percent. In 1913, the maintenance of company schools, nurseries, hospitals, and so forth amounted to 3.7 percent of the total wage costs of the cotton, metallurgical, and oil industries, while another 4.5 percent was spent on social insurance. Total indirect expenditures, therefore, amounted to 8 percent of monetary wages (Crisp 1979:497).

On the whole, though, Russian industry, despite its growth, found itself unable to break out of the vicious circle of backward development, described as follows:

> The wages of the peasant-workers in the factories were low because their productivity was low; their productivity was low because their commitment to factory work was limited. If they refused to dedicate their lives exclusively to their future in the factory, it was because they could not afford to do so. (Crisp 1979:505)

Nevertheless, in certain sectors—such as the metalworking and printing and publishing industries—wages were considerably higher than average (although they were only a third or a quarter of workers' wages in Western Europe). Furthermore, workers in major industries benefited from a number of advantages that enabled them to live in the cities with their families. A 1907 study reports that approximately 16 percent of the total industrial workforce lived in accommodations provided by a factory and that a further 16 percent lived in the neighborhood of their workplace (Crisp 1979:506).

But despite such benefits, the majority of workers still had to supplement their wages with agricultural labor. On the basis of available data, it is difficult to precisely evaluate the effects of secondary agricultural labor on the industrial wage structure. However, the opinion of Olga Crisp—that the workers' ties with agriculture were one of the causes of the low productivity of industrial labor—sounds convincing. At the same time, she adds, by impeding an increase in the supply of manpower (thus making it difficult to keep manning levels stable), these ties with the land contributed to keeping wages higher than those that would normally have been permitted by the structural costs and marketing problems of Russian industry.

THE RUSSIAN LABOR MOVEMENT

The origins of the working class and the autocratic principle of government have been strong obstacles to the formation of a labor movement in Russia. Thus, in view of the highly ineffectual character of labor legislation (1880–1890), it was left largely to the individual worker to create his own "social policy." In other words, the absence of an organic labor policy on a national scale convinced the worker that his ties with the village were his insurance against unemployment and poverty in his old age. On the other hand difficulties in the implementation of labor legislation led to many instances of direct bargaining over "social wages" between employers and workers (Perlman 1980:71).

The lack of a labor movement in Russia at the beginning of this century is frequently explained by the fact that peasant-workers were too poor and exhausted to undertake the creation of cooperatives and self-help organizations, after the model of Western trade unions (Von Laue 1962:136). This is by and large true, but it does not imply that those peasant-workers had no means at their disposal to defend their interests at individual and group levels. At the individual's level, the most widespread practice was to move from one job to another in search of better pay and working conditions. But how does one explain the changes in workers' behavior in the years leading up to the Revolution? Undoubtedly, the oppressive living and working conditions of the majority of the Russian working class were crucial, as was the brief but painful life of the

Russian labor movement during the period from "Bloody Sunday" to the October Revolution.

There was no freedom of assembly under autocracy, and Russian capitalism was to a large extent controlled by the state. The actions of the nascent labor movement were conditioned, therefore, not by the ups and downs of the economic cycle but by the hardening and softening of the repressive policy of the state (although, of course, a certain correlation between economic cycle and wage level did exist). The most significant decreases of salaries, in fact, took place during years of recession (1878, 1886, and 1900), and the most significant increases occurred during periods of expansion (1878–1880, 1886–1890, 1897–1899), (Crisp 1979:503–504).

Until 1905, strikes and union activities were considered illegal; consequently, they were organized by revolutionary intellectuals. The turning point came after the events of 1905. In a law passed on March 4, 1906, the government granted legal status to the trade unions, albeit with many restrictions, and this led to a rapid increase in the trade union enrollments (Smith 1984:282). The erosion of the power of the Tsar had already led in the previous year to a relatively tolerant attitude toward the trade unions so that, by the end of 1906, there were already fifty unions in Moscow.

The city of Moscow provides an excellent observation point from which to describe the role of the working class in the Revolution (one which, according to Smith, enables us both to avoid a narrowly political point of view and to escape "the remorseless mythicization of contemporary Soviet historians"). Moscow industry, in fact, displayed a markedly different occupational structure from that of St. Petersburg, where large-scale mechanical industry predominated. In Moscow, alongside a massive concentration of textile industries, there were a large number of other factories, and a major part of the textile industry was distributed among small- and medium-sized enterprises. Moscow's social life was dominated by the middle classes, and the city contained the highest proportion of Russian entrepreneurs and capital. By contrast, social life in St. Petersburg, despite the economic preeminence of the city, was dominated by the Court and the bureaucracy.

The uprising of 1905 actually marked a turning point in the history of Russian labor. Before that date the predominant worker behavior could be summarized by a phrase of Hirschman's (1970): "fly instead of fight." The workers, we know, would often flee unfavorable working situations by changing jobs or going back and forth between factory and field. When occasions to fight came, they did so with terrible outbursts of violence that were very distant from the methods of disciplined strike action advocated by socialist intellectuals (Brower 1982). The question arises: Were the workers' riots of the 1890s the embryonic form of class consciousness which later grew rapidly with the events of 1905 and 1917? Did Marxist intellectuals have a lasting and widespread effect on workers' consciousness and activity? And did, in the long run, this effect overcome the influence of traditional Russian culture? In order to address these questions, some findings have been gathered from recent historical studies. These studies analyze the Russian labor movement and the October Revolution "from below," that is, focusing on the workers' behavior.

From a study by Diane Koenker (1981) it emerges that the driving force behind the strikes of 1905 were the artisans and skilled workmen in the factories. Thus the first unions to emerge during the subsequent period of relative tolerance were craft unions whose members were characterized by a high degree of professionalism and a parochial attitude which—however, did not necessarily preclude an awareness of class interests.

During this period, workers in the large textile, wood-processing, and metalworking factories played a comparatively less active role in setting up the trade unions. However, from the beginning of 1906 onwards, they formed their own industrial trade unions. Thus, in the space of a few months progress had been made that in other countries would have taken decades. In contemporary Russian history, the "telescoping" of the stage of trade union development had rapidly preceded the revolutionary phase (Smith 1984).

The climate of relative tolerance during the 1906–1907 period permitted the growth of a certain amount of industrial action aimed at obtaining wage increases and reductions in working hours. Many unions also tried to obtain the replacement of individual contracts by a negotiated collective contract, but the only success in this direction was that achieved by the print union. Progress was also made over issues such as unemployment and health insurance. Local trade unions consolidated during this period and also campaigned in the 1907 election for the Second Duma (Smith 1984:285–286).

The effort of trade unions to augment and strengthen their

organization and also institutionalize labor disputes suffered a series of severe setbacks under the Stolypin government. From 1907 to 1911, the combined effects of repression and economic crisis brought the trade union movement to the brink of annihilation (Bonnell 1979:287).

The trade unions regained a certain amount of strength in 1912. In that year, the Russian autocracy responded to renewed pressure from liberal and moderate forces and from waves of labor unrest following the massacre of the miners at Lena by permitting the limited restoration of the freedoms of speech, the press, and assembly. These liberalizing measures, however, were accompanied by frequent acts of repression. If one adds to this the Association of Muscovite Industrialists' refusal to recognize trade unions and accept collective bargaining, it is understandable why many militant trade unionists had less and less faith in the possibility that a legal labor movement (the objective of Mensheviks) might become a reality.

The other political current wielding a major influence over the trade unions was the Bolsheviks. By contrast, they thought that trade unions were to be used for the purposes of propaganda, recruitment, and the organization of clandestine political activity—and, in fact, this strategy began to achieve significant results from 1914 onward. During this period, the Bolsheviks gained control of the Moscow tailor's union and made major inroads into the print workers' union (Bonnell 1979:190). They had much the same success in St. Petersburg (Haimson 1964, 1965).

In his analysis of events in St. Petersburg, Haimson explains the Bolshevik hegemony over the labor movement emphasizing the importance of the new, youthful entrants into the working class. The political radicalism and support for the Bolsheviks among young recruits from an urban background is explained by the fact that these workers had not lived through the defeat of 1905 and had had no experience of trade union struggle. The uncompromising behavior of young workers from rural backgrounds, on the other hand, is explained by the sense of rootlessness and their bad working conditions (Haimson 1964:633–636).

According to Victoria Bonnell (1979), however, the thesis of generational differences does not hold in the case of Moscow, where the Bolsheviks also drew support from skilled workmen and artisans who—even if the majority were under age thirty-five—had a long experience of industrial work. Bonnell proposes a second type of explanation of the widespread revolutionary fervor among workers. From an analysis of Moscow's industrial structure during the first decade of this century, it emerges that there was practically the same number of industrial workers as craftsmen. The latter were faced with the progressive decline of their trades and social standing under the impact of the industrialization. Thus, we may observe a tendency that had already manifested itself in previous labor strife in other European countries. There, it had not been frustration arising from increasing expectations but the fear of an irreversible decline that had acted as an impulse behind the actions of a large portion of workers:

> Indeed it is striking that the Bolsheviks owed some of their strongest backing to artisans and skilled workers such as furniture makers, jewelers and tailors.... Ironically, the "vanguard" of the working class, the metalworkers, showed less enthusiasm for the Bolsheviks ... than did the tailors. (Bonnell 1979:293)

Naturally, the Bolsheviks also drew support from the workers in the great modern manufacturing plants, but insofar as small enterprises are concerned the role of the craftsmen seems more prominent.

Another distinction to bear in mind is the one between the more politicized workers and the rest of the workforce. As far as the "masses" were concerned, the primacy of a particular revolutionary party was far from clear. As a textile worker named Filippova reportedly said (Koenker 1978:41): "The SR spoke well, the Mensheviks spoke well, the Bolsheviks spoke well, but who of them is right we don't know."

In the evolution of political consciousness among the workers, a turning point seems to be July 1917. As Koenker (1978:42–43) claims, before that date three facts concerning the relationship between the working class and the revolutionary parties seems sufficiently proven. In the first place, the political-ideological differences among the parties were little understood by the vast majority of the workers, whose support for a particular party was determined by the orientation and personal qualities of those workers recognized to be the factory leaders. Second, for the Bolsheviks, this exploitation of the personal factor was particularly successful among young workers. Third, during the brief Kerenski Govern-

ment, the most popular party among the workers seems to have
been the Socialist Revolutionary Party (SRP).

From July 1917 onward, however, there was a shift of political
balance which becomes apparent in the election result of September
24. The main reasons for the ultimate political hegemony of the
Bolsheviks are to be seen in the behavior of the Kerenski Government. It was the lack of progress in the distribution of land and the
incapacity to deal with the economic situation that provoked dis-
illusionment among the workers. These facts—along with the feeble
organizational capability of the SR—contributed to a drastic reduction of the worker's support for the SRP. The Socialist Revolutionary Party, like the Mensheviks, was later eliminated.

CHAPTER 3

Socialist Labor and the Dictatorship of the Proletariat

THE STALINIST RUNNING OF ENTERPRISE AND PLANNING

In the mid-1920s the subjects of industrial relations were still the traditional ones of entrepreneurs, "bourgeois specialists," trade unionists accustomed to conflict, the employed worker, and the unemployed. But the politicoinstitutional scene had changed radically. In 1925 the Bolsheviks were firmly in power, and the Fourteenth Party Congress proclaimed industrialization as its objective. This industrialization, however, had to be achieved in a crippled economy and almost without the aid of foreign capital. The only resource that was abundantly available at the time was labor, but this consisted mainly of unskilled laborers poorly socialized to industrial work.

In this context of scarce capital and abundant "semirustic" manpower, the various campaigns for economic efficiency and "rationalization" came increasingly to signify the dependence of productivity upon individual effort (Carr & Davies 1974:36). Given the kind of workforce at industry's disposal, an increase in production was possible only after a concerted campaign against indiscipline and absenteeism. Among peasant-workers, drunkenness and absenteeism (when workers returned to their rural communities for the harvest) were rife; and skilled workers, who were in short supply, fully exploited their bargaining power (Carr & Davies 1974:37). The influx in the factories of this kind of workforce with the introduction of new technology produced a huge gap between the expected and the real productivity of workers. The crucial question became control over the pace and methods of work. Skilled workers, fearing lost demand for their skills resisted technological innovation. Among the new workers recruited, many belonged to *arteli* in which jobs were rotated and tasks allocated by an "elder." Despite official efforts to disband them, *arteli* survived in many factories till the mid-1930s, often under the guise of brigades (Siegelbaum 1984:52). A leading role in the battle against indiscipline was played by the trade unions, who were ordered to combat "the anarchic methods employed by some groups of workers" (abandonment of their workposts, strikes) and their widespread "absenteeism, slackness and irresponsible attitude to their obligations" (Carr & Davies, 1974:41). In practical terms, this situation rapidly led to the setting up of a "triple alliance" among the Party, industry managers, and trade unions. Put simply, each of these three components had to collaborate with the others, each having at its disposal a specific area of monopoly: political power and state institutions belonged to the Party, the running of industries to the (bourgeois) managers, and the labor market to the trade unions.

Planning was still an ill-defined project during this period. The fulfilling of the plan targets was not yet a problem for the state's enterprises: Their major preoccupation was finding the best combination of productive factors. "Rationalization," therefore, meant increasing the workrate and getting rid of excess manpower. The trade unions were prohibited from organizing strikes and demonstrations at this stage, but were allowed to monopolize the recruitment of manpower. Accordingly, labor contracts included clauses stipulating that workers could only be hired through employment exchanges controlled by trade unions. At the same time, however, restrictions were imposed on union enrollment, which was a necessary condition for employment.

In other countries recognition of the unions led to the system of "closed shops." But in the USSR, the existence of a "worker state" and a labor market where the supply of manpower exceeded demand, created a sort of "closed industry." For a certain period, the unemployed found themselves prevented from working by the trade-union monopoly—not just in a single factory, but in industry as a whole. At the level of the individual enterprise, however, managers tended to take a free hand in their hiring of manpower, and in some cases would dismiss union members in order to make room for workers coming in from the countryside. In fact, in the Ukrainian Party Conference of 1926, the trade unions were attacked because they tolerated the practice of direct hiring of labor by enterprise managers. At the conference of the following year "paternalism and nepotism" in hiring were also condemned (Carr & Davies 1974:12).

This collaboration among the three members of the "alliance" was therefore highly ambiguous; an ambiguity that led to a divorce between theory and practice that would become a constant feature of labor relations in Soviet Russia. During this period, however, the contrast between words (resolutions, directives, regulations) and deeds acted in favor of enterprise managements and the unions, even if their room for maneuver was limited and would diminish further in the second half of the 1920s.

In a brief period many changes came rapidly. Stalin continued to consolidate his power; and by the end of the decade accelerated industrialization and coercive planning had become a reality. All this brought far-reaching changes in both factories and the labor market.

Until 1928, Party policy toward enterprise management had been a mixture of official declarations of confidence and acts of mistrust, because the technical and cultural inferiority of Communist managers was considered a serious problem by the Party. This inferiority often took the form of *komchanstvo* ("Communist conceit") coupled with a lack of faith in the possibility of exerting political hegemony over "bourgeois specialists." The practical result of these contradictory attitudes was more often than not "specialist-baiting" (Kuromiya 1984:187). But from that year onward a decisive change took place. So far debate in the Party had sometimes emphasized the "supremacy of production by means of the hierarchical form of organization" and sometimes "the transformation of production relations through mass initiative." With all power concentrated in the hands of Stalin, official Party policy followed the second line. Stalin now insisted on "criticism and self-criticism" and on the "cultural revolution":

> What does it mean if the workers take advantage of their chance to criticize openly and freely the defects of production, to improve and advance our work? It means that the workers take an active part in the running of the country and industry. And this strengthens their awareness that they are the masters of the country; it raises their activity, their vigilance and their cultural level. (Carr Davies 1974:159)

Thus the question of the cultural revolution was put on the
agenda. The existing regulations were accused of "placing nearly all
administrative power in the hands of the technical manager" and of
"blocking access to the administration of the enterprise for managers coming up from the ranks of the working class" (Carr &
Davies 1974:159–162).

Stalin's appeal helped overcome the fear of sanctions, and an
increasing number of workers began to criticize their managements.
And there was no lack of reasons for dissatisfaction (increased
production rates, lack of supplies, shift work, and so forth). As in
past years this criticism was not only verbal. The section of the press
biased toward economic authorities and managers talked of "cultural and technical backwardness of the workers," of theft, and of
physical violence against the "specialists." Even *Pravda* felt obliged
to censure "destructive criticism" (Carr & Davies 1974:167).

Thus, the new Party line, in the early 1930s, was to restore
managerial power through *odinonachalie* (one-man management),
which was to be controlled, however, from below by workers and
their organizations "to prevent the unlimited despotism (*svoevlas-
tie*) of management" (Kuromiya 1984:193). According to Kuromiya, control from below was a deliberate mechanism which,
together with "control from above," had to replace "spontaneous"
market control on management. The political leadership, in that
period, had two kinds of worries. The first was the possibility of a
special combination between the controller and the controlled in the
factory, or "collusion" (*sgovor*). The second was concern that "the
bureaucrats and red-tapists (*kantseliaristi*) have long been past
masters in the art of demonstrating their loyalty to party and
government decisions in words, and pigeon-holing them in deeds.
(Kuromiya 1984:195). It was precisely this side of *odinonachalie*—
control and accountability—that became the dominant concern of
Stalin, and he used all possible means to make management strictly
accountable to political power, and the same for trade unions.

The first blow to unions was the campaign for increased productivity. When the trade unions had to pledge themselves to the
"regime of economy," Tomsky, their president, declared that the
interests of today should be subordinated to the class interests of
tomorrow. But, as has been justly observed, Tomsky's sophisticated
argument "was much more likely to please the Party Conference to
which it was addressed than the workers, who faced a bitter struggle

for survival" (Carr & Davies 1974:98). However, in 1926–1927, the question of the ratio between wages and productivity was still the subject of fierce debate between the Supreme Council of the National Economy and the trade unions, and the latter were still able, to a certain extent, to protect the jobs of their members.

The final blow to the independence of unions came from the increasing pressure of the first five-year plan, which began in 1929. In theory, the planning of economic growth should have enabled workers to participate in the management of production through their unions. In practice, as the president of the food-industry union said,

> The trade unions cannot play the part that they should in the drafting of the broad lines of the plans because everything is done in great haste, the figures are not checked and sometimes are simply made up. (Carr & Davies 1974:99)

The representatives of the workers, therefore, only participated in a *pro forma* manner in decision making. At the same time, they were no longer able to put forward their members' demands. On the contrary, they had to act swiftly to forestall strikes (the number of which, in fact, dropped sharply). At the trade-union congress of 1928, Tomsky talked of "strikes that develop from time to time without the knowledge of the trade unions." He blamed this on the inadequate attention to the needs of the masses and on contempt for the small details of the workers' life (Conquest 1967:51). He demanded real union elections and added that rank and file dared not speak their minds for fear of being labeled Mensheviks or counterrevolutionaries. The last reported strike of the 1920s took place in 1929 (Carr & Davies 1974:115–116).

With the advent of central planning and "accelerated industrialization" the trade unions found themselves in a difficult situation. They could not oppose these policies because they could potentially increase employment, but the price they had to pay was the loss of their bargaining power in exchange for a subordinate role in the government structure. This caused severe conflict between the central unions' structure and the local levels which Carr and Davies (1974:100) define as battles between major and minor bureaucrats.

At the same time, the unions were subjected to a series of attacks in the Party newspapers and by the Komsomol, which culminated at

the Eighth Trade Union Congress in the removal of all the old
leaders. The internal struggles in the party also played a role here, in
terms of which Tomsky was actually considered a "rightist"
(Deutscher 1968).

The most significant sign of the political changes under way came
in the final resolution of the congress, where heavy emphasis was
placed on the cultural and educational functions of the trade unions.
This topic had already been discussed in depth at the previous
congress (1926), where Stalin defined the "Dictatorship of the
Proletariat" as a "mechanism with a directing force (the party),
levers, and 'transmission belts' (the trade unions) which connect the
mass of the workers to the vanguard of the working class" (Conquest 1967:151). But now the aims of cultural activity and political
training became much more directly linked to the overall aim of the
industrialization drive. This objective, however, entailed the
absorption of an enormous number of new workers from rural
areas, who were said to have "extremely poor class consciousness"
and "consumerist tendencies," and who had been "exposed to the
influence of petty bourgeois elements." These new workers were
also described as showing "a tendency to keep themselves aloof
from the mass of the proletarians, from their interests and social
life." Hence, the task of the trade unions was to prepare these
workers "to play an active and conscious part in the building of
socialism." Steps were to be taken to raise their cultural level, to
defend their economic interests, and, above all, to reduce inefficiency and indiscipline. This educational activity was also to take
place outside the factories. In a section of the final resolution
devoted to the problems of daily life, the union was exhorted to
battle against "drunkenness, gambling, uncivilized conduct, the
violent treatment of women, and other survivals from the old way
of life, including religion, xenophobia, and antisemitism (Carr &
Davies 1974:110).

The rapid decline in the trade unions' function as the mouthpiece
for workers' grievances was accompanied by the centralization of
decision-making processes concerning labor norms and wage levels.
The procedure was now this: The Politburo of the Communist Party
set the following year's increase for productivity and wages in
consultation with the Supreme Council of the National Economy
and the trade unions. Collective contracts were signed between an
industrial trust and the corresponding trade union, which had to

follow the wage-productivity ratios previously laid down by the central authorities (Bettelheim 1978:117–18).

In accordance with the demands of rapid industrialization, fundamental alterations occurred not only in the managerial structure of factories but in labor policy too. The tendency toward differentiated wage scales became more accentuated. The central authorities' decision to increase these differences among basic pay rates can be explained by the persistence of an attitude that distinguished between skilled workers (those that were well socialized to industrial labor) and unskilled "occasional workers"—"impregnated with a peasant mentality." It was the former class of workers that was primarily regarded as the "true proletariat" and the sure foundation of the Soviet power. Its material interests had to be safeguarded (Bettelheim 1978:179–181).

This rift between the "true proletariat" and the others persisted, but was accompanied by a change in the method employed to defend the interests of genuine proletarians. In previous years there had been a short-lived attempt to protect union members on the labor market, but now that the nature of the trade unions had changed and every worker could (indeed had to) enroll, the protection of the "true proletarians" was assumed directly by the political authorities through the means of wage policy.

A series of not wholly unsuccessful mechanisms for social integration were introduced for the other class of workers—the "semi-proletariat." Their material interests were safeguarded to a certain extent by placing the management of the "social wage" (especially after 1933) in the hands of the trade unions, while the tautness of production plans was accompanied by the increasingly common practice of paying for piecework, enabling even the unskilled to increase their earnings. Consequently, if in 1925 the percentage of workers paid at piecerate was 50 to 60 percent in large industries, in 1928 it came close to 90 percent. The piecework, however, was considered a temporary measure:

> Unlike the capitalist regime, in the USSR these are purely provisional measures. Production norms and piecework will become superfluous as the socialist education of the worker eliminates his ingrained individualistic tendencies. (Bettelheim 1978:177)

For those semiproletarians who wished to join the vanguards and become "front-rank workers," evening courses were organized, followed by their participation in the various forms of "mass initiative" that were becoming increasingly institutionalized at the time. These mechanisms were reasonably effective in stimulating the productive and social activism of a certain proportion of workers; but, if one takes into account the relations between the working class and the Soviet regime as a whole, the picture is rather different. In the first place, the various institutions for workers' participation in running production set up during this period (production conferences, socialist competition, Stakhanovism) played only a minor role in improving productivity in that they were introduced in the wider context of centralized planning, restored power of factory directors, and of political campaigns for the imposing of discipline and hierarchical relations (Granick 1961). Besides, front-rank workers were used to bring pressure on the mass of ordinary workers and to impose penalty on those who violated labor discipline through the "comrades' courts" (Conquest 1967:77). In this environment, where the plan targets had to be fulfilled at any price, output increased but brought with it two unexpected consequences. The first was the inability to govern the movement of wages and productivity, despite the subordination of company bargaining to the decision making of central authorities (in subsequent years, factory contracts practically disappeared). The second was the widespread violation of labor legislation and contract clauses, which brought with it a further deterioration in the material conditions of the great majority of workers (Smith 1937). In this way we recognize the onset of a series of phenomena typical of a "command economy." The first is the inability to regulate effectively the relations between productivity, wage volume, and the availability of consumer goods. The second (closely connected with the first) is the persistence of indiscipline and poor quality of work, deriving to a large extent from the dissatisfaction of the workers and from the so-called "survival of the past in the consciousness of the individuals."

The question of Soviet workers' dissatisfaction entails a short description of some of the main features of working conditions at the time. From the beginning of the 1930s gross output became the key success criterion for Soviet enterprises, and the negative consequences in terms of working conditions were not slow to follow. Among the most frequent occurrences in the factories of the period, one can point out the following.

Restrictions on overtime and weekend work practically disappeared. To cover up these violations of labor legislation, overtime
was sometimes disguised as "socialist competition":

> Socialist competition and shock work ... are considered easy ways of
> filling the gaps and veiling every "little sin" in the organization of work.
> Ah, well, the shock workers, they'll get the job done! After all, it's in their
> own interest to fulfill the production plan, as nonfulfillment would
> disgrace the whole plant. So they're going to work—and it won't be
> overtime either. Oh no, this will be just plain socialist competition.
> (Schwartz 1951:286)

Sometimes plant managers would take preventive measures to
protect themselves, for example, by passing off requests for
overtime as having been approved by a workers' assembly which in
fact had never been convened. The laws governing female and child
labor were also violated with increasing frequency. Factory safety
standards declined generally—because of inefficiency and because
of unqualified factory inspectors who, in any case, were ignored by
plant managements and regarded as alien by the trade unions
(Schwartz 1951:286, 288, 294–298).

The gross output principle, as a feature of coercive planning,
entailed not only a deterioration in working conditions; it also
implied the linking of the social wage to increments in productivity,
to tightening up discipline in order to confront the task of
industrialization and the building of socialism. However, jointly
with these new principles of social policy, there still persisted the old
idea that the type of workers labeled "the principal cadres of the
proletariat" should be the main beneficiaries of social services
(Schwartz 1951:309).

The end of the 1920s saw the culmination of two processes: By
now all political opposition had been eliminated, and the trade
unions had been transformed into mere "transmission belts" for the
Party. The workers thus found it impossible to put forward their
claims in an organized and collective manner. The unions' loss of
control over the use and remuneration of the workforce was not
total however: They still kept some control, but only by employing
means that were very different from those provided for by the laws
and decrees of the Soviet regime.

The radical changes that came about in labor relations during the
early 1930s can be better understood if we bear in mind that Soviet

industrialization, precisely because of its extensive and accelerated character, brought a sudden change in the labor market—one which had already made its presence felt in 1929–1930 in the form of severe shortages of manpower. From the last months of 1930 onward, these shortages, which were to become chronic, brought about a complete reversal of the labor policies in force during the 1923–1927 period.

After a further, brief attempt at introducing the compulsory hiring of manpower through the employment exchanges controlled by the unions, it was now realized, because of the development priorities of the various sectors of industry, that this was not the best system for the allocation of the workforce. Consequently there was a trend toward leaving the hiring of manpower—like other aspects of labor relations—to the economic bodies and plant managers. These would now take on new labor directly by means of contracts with collective farms (Brodersen 1966; Conquest 1967). Thus in practice, industry took on manpower in exchange for machinery and industrial goods. According to Deutscher (1968:134), 24 million people were transferred from agriculture to industry in the period 1926–1939.

Trade unions now changed their role in the labor market completely and began to play a leading part in this system of "organized recruitment" (*orgnabor*). The plant's management would sign a contract with the *kolkhoz* (collective farm), but it was the Factory Trade Union Committee that acted as the recruiting agent and sought to make the idea of industrial work as attractive as possible to potential recruits (Conquest 1967:25). The factory union organization was also responsible for the training of new entrants and their socialization to industrial labor; it was also responsible for the living and working conditions of the workers—housing, social services, health safeguards, and so on (Deutscher 1968:136).

These functions proved to be far too many for the factory committees to handle properly and were only manageable in theory. In practice, in order to defend and improve their material conditions, workers resorted to the only legal means at their disposal: moving from one job to another in search of better living and working conditions. In fact, labor turnover—which had already been high in tsarist and early Soviet Russia—now assumed incredible proportions (Schwartz 1951:88–89).

Once all political debate within the Communist Party had been eliminated and the trade unions transformed into a docile instrument for the Party's policies, the major problem became one of disciplining the workforce—one of the main requisites for the smooth running of a planned economy. To do so, the Party used well-tested methods: the combined use of government agencies, political agitation, and "mass initiative." Now, however, it was not "class enemies," political opponents, or trade unions to be caught in the cross-fire, but the new proletariat that was massing under industrialization.

This new labor policy developed in the form of a pincer movement: On the one hand, to pursue the objective of an adequate supply of manpower and its most efficient usage, tougher disciplinary measures were introduced; on the other, to crush the widespread resistance to intensified work rates, "shock workers" were utilized in the factories (Conquest 1967: Schwartz 1951). These workers, like those with a good service record, enjoyed a series of privileges. Among disciplinary measures adopted were the following: "Shirkers" were brought before the "comrades' courts" and could be expelled from a trade union—thereby losing their rights to certain social services—or even sacked. Workers who, changed jobs more than once (or habitual absentees and disruptive workers) were branded as "disorganizers of production." A worker's employment book became a sort of "production passport," in which everything concerning the worker's political and working behavior was recorded so that "birds of passage, grabbers, and disorganizers could not enter the factories" (Schwartz 1951:97).

In December 1938 a further revision of the labor laws provided for even harsher penalties against "floaters" and disruptive workers and granted greater privileges to those workers who undertook to remain for a long period in the same factory. Only a minority were actually sacked, but fear of dismissal became widespread because the new laws also provided for severe penalties against those managers who tolerated undisciplined behavior in their factories (Schwartz 1951:100).

The real militarization of labor began with the war. The Supreme Soviet's decree of June 26, 1940, on hours and working conditions laid down prison sentences or forced labor for those who canceled a contract or for absentee workers. It is significant that the latter category also included workers who refused to do overtime. Moreover, according to an interpretation of the law by the Central Council of the Trade Unions, any worker who was punished under the terms of the decree lost all his seniority (Schwartz 1951:106–109).

In effect, the militarization of labor managed to cut the size of labor turnover and undisciplined behavior, but it certainly did not create an efficient, well-planned, productive organization. With the end of World War II and the relaxation of coercive measures, turnover reappeared along with a series of unofficial practices which would lead to the formation of a system of mutual coverup (*krugovaia poruka*) among the organizational elites in the factory enterprises. One such unofficial practice was "labor piracy"—especially of skilled workers—whereby enterprises with gaps in their personnel would entice workers away from other factories by various means (Schwartz 1951:106–109). This practice naturally involved violations of "financial discipline," which was condemned by trade union hierarchies and condoned by factory trade union committees. The situation reverted, therefore, to that of the early 1930s, when the company contract was replaced by an informal system of give-and-take between managers and the workers.

LABOR MANAGEMENT UNDER AUTOCRACY AND STALINIST RULE: CONTINUITY AND CHANGES

Between the industrialization process imposed by Peter the Great and the forced industrialization of the 1930s, there had been two revolutions in Russia and a war, followed by radical changes in politics and society. The preceding historical analysis of Stalinist rule had the aim of giving some answers to the following issues: What were the real changes in the behavior of workers, managers, and higher authorities? What changed only on paper?

In Russia there had been a revolution in 1917 based on Marxist doctrine. But knowledge of that country and its history invites us to take into account other influences. As Nove has observed:

> Russia's past is in many ways more relevant than Marxism to an
> understanding of Soviet political and economic structure, because the

phraseology is Marxist, but the one-party state, the bureaucratic controls over movement and the printed word, and much else besides, owe nothing to Marx's ideas. (Nove 1979:42).

Thus, if we focus on the early industrialization in Russia, we must mention at least four aspects that will play a decisive role in future developments. The first is the attitude of both workers and employers toward production, seen as a service rendered to the state. The overmanning of factories that was imposed on the entrepreneurs by public powers was linked to this idea.

> The workers believed that the Government would force those that possessed money to open factories and construct barracks for those that had to work in them; both were convinced that the employers had no right whatsoever to close down the plant, and that if the workers could not manage, the Government would take over the factory. This mentality had been inculcated in the "possessional factories"; memories of which were still alive in the minds of the generation that had witnessed the take-off of industry during the last decade of the 19th Century. (Crisp 1979:400)

A second aspect was the workers' attitude toward the belongings of factory owners or the state:

> In the daily life of the peasant villages the produce of forests and orchards were commonly regarded as *res nullius* ["belonging to no one"] ... the workplaces also offered ample and fully exploited opportunities for deceit and for evading orders and regulations. It was a long time before Russian workers of serf origin shed those habits that had become so deeply formed in their minds during adolescence in the villages. Not dissimilar were the beliefs and behavior of businessmen ... whether large or small. (Gerschenkron 1974b:782)

A third important aspect to bear in mind concerns the quality of work performance—that is, the habit of shoddy, negligent work acquired during labor in the fields of the landowner (*pomeshchik*). The Russian climate, with its short summers, forced the peasants to concentrate their activities into brief bursts of heavy work (*sturmovshchina*) followed by long periods of idleness:

> It is not at all surprising that in these conditions regular steady application was sneered at as being "German," as "not Russian," while excep-

tional feats of hard work, which perhaps involved a certain amount of
risk and bravado on behalf of the worker, were regarded with great
admiration (Gerschenkron 1974b:817)

A final aspect linking past and present has been traced to the *skvoz-
naia barshchina*—that is, to the fixing by the owner of the serf's work
obligation for a certain period of time. In the relationships between
the two it was tacitly assumed that the laborer depended entirely on
orders he received and that he had no autonomy whatsoever (Kaser
1979:463). Most laborers were organized into work groups, and
group responsibility was used for centuries by the Tsars and the
owners as a form of mutual coercion among the subordinates (Blackwell 1982:174). The laborers, however, constantly sought to transform this system of mutual coercion into a system of mutual complicity (*krugovaia poruka*) in order to deal as comfortably as possible
with the impositions and controls from above.

The tradition of bureaucratic interference in factory life had
long-lasting effects on the behavior of entrepreneurs. They were
usually reluctant to take risks in the running of enterprises and
tended to rely on tried managerial practices instead of pursuing
technical and organizational innovation. Thus modernization of
industrial management was generally possible either by direct order
from the Tsar or on the initiative of foreign entrepreneurs, at least in
big firms (Kaser 1979:532).

From the 1880s onward, however, direct state intervention in the
economy began to decline and Russian society began to express
signs of more autonomous development. Actually, the period saw a
growth of entrepreneurism while, on the other hand, new forms of
organized action began to emerge among the workers. Nevertheless,
this does not imply that labor relations underwent radical changes.
The autocratic principle did not cease to apply; it merely assumed a
more paternalistic character which led, at the turn of the century, to
the establishment of labor organizations run by the Ministry of the
Interior through the police apparatus. Thus one can observe, in this
period, the growth of new forms of industrial action with the
organizational support of socialist intellectuals, alongside the rapid
spread of "police socialism," while rioting still persisted in which
the behavior of workers resembled that of "primitive rebels" (Hobsbawm 1959; Brower 1982).

In subsequent years, especially from 1912 onward, the influence of the socialist *intelligentsia* over workers increased, despite repression, and one of its representatives—Lenin—led the party that was to climb to power in the October Revolution. For the most part, literature on Leninism and the October Revolution elaborates on the relation of Lenin's thought and political actions to Marxism. Recently, for example, Carmen Sirianni (1982) discussed in detail the links of Lenin and Marx via Plekhanov. What has been overlooked, however, is the influence exerted by Russian history over Leninist political thought, and the role played therein by the relationships between autocracy and intelligentsia. This topic has been brilliantly discussed by Marc Raeff (1984). His observations apply mainly to the nihilists and the radicals of the 1870s but fit well also for later generations of revolutionary intellectuals.

Raeff emphasizes that the radical intelligentsia coincided with that section of the educated or semieducated elite that refused to integrate itself with the civil service or the liberal profession. He adds that this refusal derived, among other things, from a kind of university teaching which was divorced from reality and opposed to the prevailing currents of European culture. At the same time, the government obstructed the development of civil society and the formation of a body of professionals that might have engaged in economic activities independent of the control and regulations of state bureaucracy. Thus, the radical intelligentsia waited in the wings for a revolutionary upheaval and—both because of its professed doctrine (populist, Marxist) and (more rarely) because of its awareness of the miserable conditions that the rest of the country lived in—continued to oppose any compromise or program of reform. Given these conditions, it was inevitable that these radical and alienated intellectuals regarded the imperial regime that imprisoned and persecuted them as their mortal enemy. Among this social group hatred against the regime was

> unremitting, violent and total. Only the complete destruction of the regime, at any price, can placate it. Thus its thought, more than its actions, has an incipient totalitarian slant. Intolerance and inflexible dogmatism characterize the collective mentality of the radical *intelligentsia* and make it the *pendant* of the shabby, brutal autocracy it fights with such a stubbornness and self-sacrifice. (Raeff 1984:184)

Confirmation of this thesis—that similarities exist between the mentality and actions of the revolutionary intellectuals and autocratic logic—may be found in Bendix's (1956) analysis of the role assigned to Soviet trade unions at the beginning of the 1920s. As noted earlier, in the last years of the nineteenth century the autocracy was faced with a dilemma: whether to increase its repression of growing industrial unrest or to take measures to prevent it by setting up para-trade unions controlled by the government. The autocratic regime no longer intended to limit itself to organizing social consensus from above; it now sought also to organize it from below. This shift in emphasis was an historical antecedent which influenced the conception of labor relations in Soviet Russia:

> Tsarist autocracy had aspired to a principle of rule which was not to be abandoned even after the Revolution of 1917. According to this principle, all relations among men in society are an outgrowth of a sovereign will—that of the Tsar or that of the people "represented" by the Communist party. (Bendix 1956:186)

According to Bendix, analysis of Lenin's writings reveal the same principle of government. Under the autocracy, the subjection of the workers had been justified by the ideal of the equal subordination of all subjects to the supreme authority of the Tsar. In Lenin's writings the ideal of equal claim to ownership and managerial function was used to effect the greatest subordination of all citizens to the control of the party (Bendix 1956:188).

The legacy of the autocratic principle in its most explicitly paternalist form appears in Lenin's idea that the unions, as representatives of the workers, should participate in management and, at the same time, criticize managers and defend the workers' rights. This idea was not basically different from the previous idea that an agency of the government should participate in the labor movement to direct its protest into officially approved channels:

> For Lenin insisted with extraordinary forcefulness that all policies, including the policies of trade unions, should be directed by the same central organs of the Communist Party in much the same way the Tsarist police was subject to the Ministry of Interiors and to the Tsar himself. Thus, autocratic as well as Communist rulers on occasion call upon the people to participate in the formulation of policies, while the police as well as the trade unions see to it that these demands and this participation remain within "proper" bounds. (Bendix 1956:191)

The tsarist managerial ideology survived in Soviet Russia in a modified form. Bendix points to an important difference, however. In Soviet Russia the revolutionary leaders found themselves faced with the task of developing self-discipline and the spirit of initiative among workers of peasant background. This is an important change. But the revolutionary task of creating a new type of worker has had intended and unintended results. Studies of the October Revolution centered on workers' collective behavior demonstrate that the period—albeit brief—of political participation helped in significant measure toward creating a more advanced form of collective action and political consciousness among the workers. These studies also emphasize the rational nature of the workers' reaction to economic and political pressures. In other words, it is fair to suppose that in the short period in which there was a certain political freedom in Russia there had consequently been development in worker's consciousness. Between the last decade of the nineteenth century and the October Revolution there had been a break with traditional patterns of attitude and behavior and a stratum of worker intelligentsia actually emerged (Suny 1982:441). Unfortunately, almost none of them remained in the ranks of the working class in the 1930s. The overwhelming majority became officials of the new Soviet state and disappeared later in the civil war, or were eliminated by Stalin's purges.

It was another category of people that began to predominate among Party members in the early 1920s. These were "the petty-officers of the old society." Neither workers nor intellectuals strongly motivated by ideology, they were persons who—already under the *ancien régime*—were upwardly mobile, even if in narrow limits (Malia 1984:172).

Thus, the Soviet approach to the political and professional education of workers was carried out by means of political and organizational devices, managed by the Party and social organizations like trade unions and Komsomol. This was undoubtedly a new approach which offered, during Stalin's rule, opportunities for social and professional advancement for a lot of working people. But if we focus on implementation of this policy in the workplace, a more balanced view of continuity and changes in labor management can be elaborated .

Before an assembly of metalworkers in 1922, Lenin made an insightful reference to Oblomov, the quintessence of sluggishness:

Russia has passed through three revolutions, but the Oblomovs are still with us, not only because the landowner was an Oblomov but because the peasant was one too, and not only the peasant but the intellectual, and not only the intellectual but the worker and the communist as well. You only have to look at us, see how we meet, how we work in the commissions to be able to say that old Oblomov is still alive and that we must wash him, comb him, shake him, beat him in order to turn him into something good. (Linhart 1977:175)

These directives were actually implemented by the "petty officers" who imposed their "booty" style on a working class made up of new recruits from the countryside and ex-petty bourgeois. Thus many old patterns appeared again in the organizational behavior of workers, managers, and officers. For example, whoever dared to voice dissatisfaction with working conditions or salary levels, or protested over some illegailty, was labeled with politically or morally insulting epithets and threatened with severe sanctions. Shock workers and "vanguards" were called upon to play an active role in counteracting workers' demands for salary improvements. And they performed the task in various ways, including appeals to the press of this kind:

When collective contracts come up for renewal, backward groups of workers, stirred by counter-revolutionary Trotskyites, rightist opportunists, kulakophiles, and initiators of whispering campaigns, will start presenting their non-proletarian and greedy demands.... We appeal to all workers of the Soviet Union to put up the most active resistance against the sorties of grabbers and whisperers, and actively fight the class enemy who has infiltrated our plants. (Schwartz, 1951:186)

Yes, the language had changed since the Tsar's times, but the "moral indignation" of some workers toward others was again encouraged. No more did grabbers risk getting a good hiding from workmates, but they still risked forced labor.

But the achievement of shock workers quite often were far from sufficient for fulfilling impossible plan targets, not to speak of the times when they were an obstacle to the regularity of the production process. In this frantic situation the careers and personal security of plant directors and Party and trade union officials were very often at stake. To avoid punishment, organizational elites of an industry resorted again to informal defenses against higher authorities, ones which were already widespread in the past regime. In other words there was a reemergence, on a mass scale, of the *krugovaya poruka*, which Stalin denounced in the following terms:

> Sometimes, in our country, not only in the outlying provinces, but also at the center, problems are solved "at home" within the family circle so to speak. Ivan Ivanovich, member of the managerial staff of some organization has made, for example, some gross blunder and has ruined everything. But Ivan Fiodorovich doesn't want to criticize him, denounce his mistakes or punish him. He wants to avoid "making enemies." ... Today I, Ivan Fiodorovich, save his skin. Tomorrow he, Ivan Ivanovich, will save mine.... It is obvious that we will cease to be proletarian revolutionaries, and that we will certainly perish, if we do not stamp out this Philistinism, this way of resolving the vital problems of the building of Socialism "within the family." (Bettelheim 1978:236)

The transformation of Soviet trade unions to "transmission belts" of the Party caused ordinary workers to adopt patterns of behavior very common in the past. If in Imperial Russia finding a better job was a matter of personal initiative and "family connections" (Bonnell 1984:84), in Soviet Russia the situation *for ordinary workers* did not change too much. The disappearance, after a short and tormented life, of a claimant union able to organize collective action and the new Soviet industrialization were the main causes of the reemergence of spontaneous labor turnover on a large scale:

> The peasant, who was accustomed to laboring in the fields, ... to toiling from dawn to dusk in the summer and to sleeping for most of the winter, was now forced to adapt himself to a completely different way of life, against which he rebelled by moving incessantly from one place to another. Nor was there any threat of unemployment, which often keeps the worker from abandoning even the most unsatisfactory work.... On the other hand, the Soviet worker was not free to fight to improve his conditions of life. Unlike workers of other countries who had fought under the leadership of their trade unions, the Soviet worker could not go on strike. The Soviet trade unions energetically discouraged strikes, and behind the unions stood the political police. The fluidity of labor became the substitute for striking (Deutscher 1968:138)

In the late 1930s the repressive machinery and the militarization of labor succeeded only temporarily in reducing the scale of these traditional aspects of workers' and managers' behavior. These aspects reappeared on a larger scale at the end of Stalin's rule and are continuously criticized by Soviet media, as will be shown in the third part of the book.

PART II

The Official Model

CHAPTER 4

Legislating Labor Relations

The years from the death of Stalin to the present have been marked by a series of important changes. Politically, a process of "de-Stalinization" was inaugurated at the Twentieth Party Congress, although its results have been partial and contradictory. Economically, the 1960s saw the beginning of the "phase of intensive development," accompanied by attempts at decentralization and economic reform—designed to encourage state enterprises to strive for greater efficiency in production. But these attempts, too, have been only partially successful, and laws and decrees are still periodically issued with the dual purpose of urging decentralization while improving centralization.

If the evolution of the official conception of labor relations during the thirty years since the death of Stalin were to be summed up in one sentence, one might say the debate involves, as in the 1920s: (1) those who emphasize the importance of scientific management accompanied by increased managerial autonomy and (2) those who insist on perfecting the machinery of centralized planning accompanied by increased "mass initiative."

This chapter contains a description of the main legal aspects of labor relations, although it should be made clear that the intention is not to provide an exhaustive examination of labor legislation. This has been done elsewhere (Joffe & Maggs 1983; Lowit 1971; Bartocci 1980; Carlini 1975; McAuley 1969; Ajani 1986; Ruble 1977). Chapter 4 addresses instead some of the most significant aspects of current legislation as they relate to what has always been, and still remains, the fundamental management problem: the stability of labor relations. In fact, those aspects of workers' behavior that have always preoccupied management and the Soviet authorities still remain high turnover and bad discipline in the factories. Because of the adverse effects of these two phenomena on the planned economy and on the system of participation in management of production, Soviet authorities have insistently declared their firm intention to come to grips with them. Accordingly, the issues addressed in this chapter are: (1) the main legislative measures designed to regulate the voiding of contracts caused either by actions of management or workers; (2) those sanctions (positive and negative) regarded by the authorities as necessary to combat labor indiscipline; and (3) the moral and material incentives introduced to stimulate the participation of workers in the management of production. The chapter concludes with a brief summary of the main issues involved in the debate over "socialist legality" and the measures designed to ensure that workers' *legal* rights become real rights.

STABILITY OF LABOR RELATIONS

One of the guiding principles of Soviet labor legislation is the "universality of work" (*vseobshchnost truda*). This principle, it is claimed, could never be accomplished under capitalism because of unemployment and the exploitation of wage labor. Under socialism, the opposite is the case, because it has eliminated private property and exploitation. Hence, work can become the moral and legal foundation of the citizen's life (Smirnov 1977:81).

The principle of universal work presupposes that citizens' right to work is guaranteed by the existence of planned recruitment and distribution of labor resources. The labor recruitment and distribution process assumes a variety of legal forms: individual contracts draw between workers and enterprises; the system of vocational schools; the planned distribution of young people with specialized training; the organized recruitment of workers and technicians for special projects and for service in certain regions. The common feature of these specific forms of labor distribution is that they are all centrally planned in accordance with current Party policy.

At the level of individual enterprises, the quantity and composition of the workforce is directly decided by the factory administration, which is offered special incentives to ensure that the workforce is utilized in the best possible way. An enterprise's plan comprises three sections, each containing indices relative to labor productivity, number of employees, training of personnel, and average wages to be paid to different categories of workers. Composition of the workforce is established by the factory's Office of Labor and Wages, in which the trade union is also represented. The documents drawn up by this office are legally valid at a local level and are drafted on the basis of the norm guidelines laid down by the ministries, although these are not legally binding. This does not mean, though, that these norms are totally without regulative force; the mere fact that the ministry drafting them regards them as the optimum level to be aimed at lends them an obligatory character (Smirnov 1977:103). The other means at a ministry's disposal to exert influence over quantity and composition of workforce at the enterprise level is the wage fund.

Plans governing manpower exist at other levels and are managed by various state organs. In every republic of the Soviet Union, a ministerial committee draws up a three-month directive concerning the organization of recruitment and training of manpower for industry and construction. These directives are then worked out in more detail for the territorial units that make up each republic. Plans for organized recruitment take the form of legal administrative acts comprising specific, binding "duty-norms" (*normi zadania*), (Smirnov 1977:111).

Legal norms regulating work assignments to graduates of the secondary institutes are mostly contained in the decree of the Ministry for Secondary Education of March 1978. The assignment of young high school graduates to a certain job for the two years set by law is administered by a commission composed of functionaries from the Ministry of Secondary Education and from other ministries concerned in accordance with the requirements of the national economy (Smirnov 1977:112).

A second guiding principle of Soviet labor law is the creation of working conditions that are "favorable to the maximum degree" (*maksimalno blagopriaten*) to working people. This principle is expected to acquire concrete form when the legal apparatus controlling working conditions is perfected; it provides a balanced combination of generally applicable normative acts and others that are designed to deal with three different variables: (1) the specific nature of local and branch variations; (2) the sociodemographic features of the working population concerned ("subjective differentiation"); and (3) the geographical location of the enterprise ("geographical differentiation") (Baru 1971).

The actual application of labor laws are laid down by Article 106 of the Foundation of Labor Legislation and pertain to such subjects as labor contracts, working hours, the incentive quota of wage packets, discipline, and factory safety. By drawing a distinction between generally applicable norms and those that refer to specific situations, the state is deemed able to resolve problems arising in the local context by applying, on the one hand, state regulations and, on the other, those formulated at the enterprise level by management and trade-union committees (Smirnov 1977:119).

Increasing importance is attached to the latter kind of norms, especially as far as two of their aspects are concerned: their use as a means to plug up the gaps in regulations emanating from central authorities, and as a method for trying out new variants to be subsequently incorporated into labor legislation.

The norms issued by the central authorities continue to be, however, of fundamental importance, since they arise from the monolithic economic base of socialist society and from the uniform, undifferentiated direction of Party and state policy over the organization of production.

Further progress toward the achievement of ideal work and life conditions will depend on the rapid and balanced development of social production. A fundamental precondition of this development is seen to be the rational deployment of the labor force and the best possible management of the problems arising from its mobility by the instruments of planning and "social prognosis" (*prognozirovanie*) (Molodzof & Soifer 1976: 3; Tikhomirov 1978:250–260).

The problem presently of uppermost importance to Soviet labor legislation is the stability of labor relations; two aspects of this problem currently are concentrated upon (1) the breach of contracts by workers and (2) the arbitrary firing of workers by enterprise managements. The first case brings to the fore the massive problem of labor turnover (*tekuchest kadrov*), and the second the problem of discipline at work.

As we will see in Chapter 8, Soviet sociological research has repeatedly demonstrated the important part workers' dissatisfaction over material conditions plays in high job turnover. Indeed, it is a generally held opinion among Soviet researchers that, in recent years, dissatisfaction over the physical workplace and methods of production has come to predominate significantly over traditional workers' grievancies such as low wages and housing shortages. Consequently, authorities see one of the most important tasks of labor legislation as the judicial regulation of problems arising from the introduction of new technology in the production process.

The relationship between labor law and technical progress today proceeds in two directions: first, toward a more precise definition of the reciprocal obligations of labor and management; second, toward a consolidation of the rights and guarantees pertaining to both parties of the labor contract (Molodzof & Soifer 1976:53–54; Avakov & Glozman 1971:24–57). The defining of contractual rights and obligations within the framework of productive modernization, however, is regarded by authorities as a necessary but not sufficient condition. The second area in need of legislative reform is the organization of productive processes and the psychological climate in the collective. In other words, the goal of stable labor relations is to be pursued by taking action not only over technical and economic aspects but also over the psychophysiological situation of the worker (Ivanov & Livishits 1982). This latter aspect must be dealt with on the basis of a "scientific organization of work," the models for which are drawn up jointly by the Central Bureau of Statistics and the state committee for labor (Molodzof & Soifer 1976:56).

A principal problem involved in drawing up these models of "scientific organization" is conflict between job descriptions and the changing requirements of actual job responsibilities. According to Molodzof and Soifer, a major source of these difficulties is the heterogeneous nature of sociological and legal approaches to the problem. In the first place, only the three following forms are dealt with: job enlargement (*sovmeshchenie professii*), job rotation in the "brigade," and the performance by workers of other tasks related to their job (Molodzof & Soifer 1976:59). Not provided for, however, is the performing of a number of dissimilar jobs. As far as the legal aspects of the problem are concerned, the Labor Code of the RFSSR (Article 87) does in fact cover "professional polyvalence," but this clause is not included in the contracts of employment. For this reason, the management of an enterprise does not have the right to ask a worker to perform a number of other tasks if these are not similar to those formally stipulated in his contract.

The diversified use of time is regarded as another important element in the "scientific organization of work." The question of part-time work is regulated by Articles 15 and 49 of the Labor Code. According to the terms of these articles, management of an enterprise is authorized to sign labor contracts that provide for part-time employment, with a corresponding reduction in wages. However, the spread of part-time work is impeded by the relatively haphazard organization of work and by the imprecise nature of current legislation concerning the mobility of part-time labor. According to Article 33 of the Code, management does not have the right to move a worker on a part-time contract to full-time employment. Thus, a worker who refuses to obey an order to work full-time cannot be dismissed. If production requirements in the factory should change, the management is legally obliged to find the worker concerned another part-time job (Art. 15), or to hire a second worker on a part-time basis. The law in this respect is most felt in small- and medium-sized enterprises, where managements are unable to offer a choice of similar jobs to workers on part-time contracts (Molodzof & Soifer 1976:71).

Health protection is another area given wide coverage by Soviet legal literature:

> The best possible health and safety protection for Soviet workers is one of the fundamental principles of the legal regulation of the Socialist organization of work....
>
> In a society where the principal rule of behavior for Party and State is "everything in the name of the individual; everything for the good of the individual," the lives and safety of the people cannot be endangered by the pursuit of high economic indices. (Smirnov 1977:185)

This principle of health and safety at work—"the best possible protection"—has the following features in the law: It is general in character; it imposes the maximum vigilance in especially hazardous situations; it presupposes a particular concern for women, adolescents, and the handicapped; and, finally, it mandates the duty of workers and trade union representatives to ensure that norms are respected (Smirnov 1977:186; Avakov & Glozman 1971:195–212).

Health-protection norms are issued for every industrial branch by the Council of Ministers, in agreement with the central council of trade unions. At the branch level, responsibility lies with the ministry and branch organization of the trade union. At the level of enterprise, management, jointly with the factory committee, must implement Article 57 of the Labor Code regarding the introduction of the most up-to-date safety installations and the creation of the hygiene conditions required to guarantee full health protection for the factory personnel.

An enterprise's plan and the collective's contract also contain clauses governing accident protection and work-related diseases. Thus, each management has a dual responsibility: toward the state administrative organs and toward the production collective (Smirnov 1977:188). Under the terms of Article 147 of the Labor Code, the managers must, jointly with the factory committee, conduct appropriate enquiries into accidents in the factory (to be presented in written form). In the most serious cases, other organs such as the trade union's Technical Inspectorate and the Procurator's Office are to be called in. Article 61 of the Foundations of Labor Legislation and Article 145 of the Labor Code oblige employees to respect the safety measures, adopted by the factory administration jointly with the factory committee of the unions. "Standard norms" (*tipovie*) may also be issued for the main industrial jobs by the branch ministries, jointly with the central council of trade unions of the relevant category (Avakov & Glozman 1971:195–212).

The safety norms designed to protect women, teenagers, and the handicapped are specially defined by Soviet legislation in three different ways. There is first the "supplement-norm" (*norma dopolnenia*), which provides special advantages and concessions for certain categories of workers. Second, the "exemption norm" (*norma iziatia*) recognizes the nonapplicability of general norms to certain individuals. Third, there is the "adaptation norm" (*norma prisposoblenia*), that is, the particular application of the general norm to suit specific cases (Smirnov 1977:191)

The question of health and safety protection leads naturally to a discussion of the ways in which the general conditions of Soviet work and life are being improved. In the USSR this is primarily a problem of broadening and improving public services—both sociocultural and those concerning the provision of housing.

Here, too, the problem is directly related to the stability of labor relations: The gross regional differences in the standards of public services have caused migratory movements, which the authorities have only partially been able to control (Musatov 1967:112–121).

Once a worker signs his contract and joins an enterprise, the worker acquires the right to the satisfaction of his social needs—a right which is financed by the social funds set aside by the state and by the enterprise's budget. First, centralized funds pay for those social rights guaranteed by the Soviet constitution: the right to education; the right to material sustenance in old age, illness, or incapacity; the right to rest from work; and so forth. At the same time, decentralized funds are allocated to individual enterprises according to their size and productive merits, that is, on the basis of Lenin's direction to grant "vanguard" enterprises a great quantity of resources for social and cultural services. These latter funds are to be utilized (1) to provide sociocultural services and, (2) to construct housing for employees. They are jointly administered by management and the Factory Trade-Union Committee (FZMK).

In general, the social funds for consumption possess both general and specific characteristics. The former derive from the basic premise governing distribution under socialism, that is "it is the direct, continuous concern of Socialist society that every individual is fully guaranteed his complete welfare and unrestrained multilateral development" (Molodzof & Soifer 1976:177)—a concept that, according to the official doctrine, finds concrete form in the free provision by the state of sociocultural services to all citizens. The latter characteristics of the social funds derive instead from differences that exist among social interests and relationships, and are specific to the decentralized social funds. These are administered directly by the enterprises proportionately to the workforce's degree of involvement in the management of productive processes.

In the exercise of its managerial rights over social funds, the enterprise is authorized to issue local regulations (*localnaia reglamentatsiia*) in agreement with the FZMK. These regulations set out two types of normative acts: the first are "local normative acts" (*localnie normativnie akta*) such as, for example, the collective's contract or measures designed to provide supplementary material incentives based on seniority in the enterprise.

"Individual legal acts" (*individualnie pravovie akta*) are the second class of normative acts. These regulations concern not only legal relations in one particular area of sociocultural services but rather constitute the "means of individual regulation" of legal relationships from the point of view of subject, object, and content. In concrete terms, this signifies that the enterprise management and the FZMK, under the terms of "funds of social consumption," take into consideration not only the worker's particular needs and their urgency, but also his personal contribution to the common productive output. Thus, by means of the "individual legal acts," the enterprise lays down the criteria for the concession of goods and services on the basis of work performance. In fact, labor contracts in many enterprises contain clauses that define conditions under which deserving workers may be awarded vouchers for holidays, convalescence in rest homes, and other special privileges (Molodzof & Soifer 1976, 181). Actually, the special funds of consumption are essentially *incentive funds* (Article 55 of the Foundation of Labor Legislation).

MORAL AND MATERIAL INCENTIVES

The various incentive schemes provided for by Soviet labor legislation are not only directed toward the reduction of labor turnover; they are also designed to stimulate participation in the "leadership of production." Such participation can be subdivided into "direct" and "indirect." The former concerns participation in general meetings, where questions dealing with output plans or the drafts of the collective's contracts are discussed. The latter concerns participation through the social organizations operating under the supervision of the Party and the trade union; this would include such groups as the Permanent Production Conference, the Society of Rationalizers and Inventors, Popular Control, and others. The purpose of these social organizations is to participate in solving major problems of management, to help find better use of material resources, and to increase efficiency. The FZMK performs two important functions in its participation in production management. First, it is called to act in the interests of the working people when they concern the factory's organization of work or its environmental condition. To protect the workers' interests, the FZMK uses the instruments of "inspection" and "social control" to enforce observance of labor legislation by the enterprise's management (Smirnov 1977:125). The second major function of the FZMK is the management and planning of all "rationalizing" activities by workers and technicians, as comprised by the "scientific organization of work."

One form of mass participation with strong traditions is "socialist competition" (*sotsialisticheskoe sorevnovanie*). This "creative initiative by the workers" is not a legal obligation as such, but its organization displays significant legal features. It is regulated by norms which reflect a fundamental principle: that socialist competition should be wholeheartedly supported by the state organs (ministries and enterprise managers) on the one hand, and by the Party and trade unions on the other. The ministries and managers are urged to give all necessary institutional support; the Party and unions must constantly develop the creativity of the masses by means of education and political mobilization. Consequently, the general regulations governing "socialist competition" are issued jointly by the central committee of the CPSU, the Council of Ministries, the Central Council of Trade Unions, and the central committee of the Komsomol. These regulations have a dual aspect: On the one hand, they serve as *legal acts*; on the other, as *social directives*. They are therefore obligatory for all levels of trade union and Party, and their legal bases are provided by agreements made between the trade unions and enterprise managements, and by all regulations issued with the aim of creating the best organizational framework for "socialist competition."

Of direct relevance here is the passing on January 1, 1971, of the Foundation of Labor Legislation. This law granted greater legal powers to the trade unions in terms of participation in the "leadership of production." Some legislative functions of state organs were delegated to the trade unions, whose powers to specify working conditions were now on a par with the state's. The legislative activity of the trade unions displays a "state-social" character in the sense that (1) the normative acts issued by the trade unions are binding on all state organs and (2) this activity enables the workforce to be represented directly. However, unlike that of the state, the trade unions' power of legislative initiative is limited both in form and in content. Generally, the legislative initiatives of trade unions must be previously sanctioned or subsequently authorized by the competent state organs. The Central Trade Union Council enjoys autonomous powers of legislative initiative only as far as a limited series of legal acts are concerned (the control of environmental health hazards, social services, and so forth) (Karinsky 1975:37–44).

In the past ten to fifteen years there has been a concerted effort to relaunch the movement of socialist competitions, in an attempt to remotivate workers' participation. One such example are the "counterplans" (*vstrechnie plana*)—pledges by individual workers to a certain level of production over a certain period of time. These forms of worker initiative, unlike those of the past, stress the qualitative aspects of performance. "Counterplans" are seen as being the point at which the principle of central planning blends with the principle of "mass initiative"—the correction of the official plan by increasing its output and enhancing the quality of products.

The management of an enterprise, by virtue of its legal obligation to give full support to socialist competition, must create the necessary conditions for the counterplans and other initiatives "from below" to be able to mobilize all existing production reserves. This obligation is not absolute: It depends on the technical, organizational, and financial capacity of the enterprise. Moreover, not all Soviet jurists think that counterplans constitute a legal obligation for the management, even if the necessary production capacities do exist in the enterprise (Smirnov 1977:125).

Whether such forms of socialist competition are compatible with the requirements of an enterprise is contractually established. In fact, the company contract (renewed annually) stipulates both the legal responsibilities of the management and the ethical-political responsibilities of participants in competitions for improving production standards.

SOCIALIST LEGALITY

Labor relations in Soviet factories also have their dark aspects. As Smirnov (1977:140) points out, there exists "elements of bureaucratism and formalism, the disguising of the ways things really are, fraud and so on—against which we must wage a resolute campaign."

Behind remarks such as this (repeated by the Soviet press for decades) there lies the major problem of "socialist legality." Officially, class antagonism has been eliminated in socialist society. Consequently, objective conditions for breaking the law are no longer supposed to exist. And when laws are broken—by managers or workers—the blame is placed on the "survival of the past in the consciousness of individuals." As former Soviet leader Leonid Brezhnev declared:

> It is no secret that there still exist among us those social evils which we have inherited from the past and which are inimical to Socialism— unconscientious attitude to work, laxity, lack of discipline, greed for money, and the various ways in which the norms of Socialist society are violated. The Party sees it as its duty to focus the attention of society on these evils and to mobilize the population in a resolute campaign against them. If they are not eradicated, Communism will never be built. (Tadevosyan 1980:11)

The campaign against these "survivals" is being conducted in two principal ways. The first and most traditional is the practice of "criticism and self-criticism," in which those responsible for violations of "socialist legality" go before the masses to acknowledge their responsibility. The second—of growing importance—is the improving of economic legislation.

In the past fifteen years, a series of steps have been taken in the Soviet Union to improve economic legislation. Among these, of particular importance was a June 1972 resolution of the Council of Ministers. The resolution established guidelines for the observance of contractual obligations between enterprises, for state arbitration, and for the introduction of the *iuriskonsult* (legal consultant) and legal offices in enterprises and other state organizations. These legal offices are faced with a difficult task, however, given the unsatisfactory level of codification in labor legislation and its unsystematic nature. In fact, it is often the case that different laws apply to the same identical situation—and many of these laws are antiquated and mutually contradictory (Tadevosyan 1980:99).

One question at issue in the debate among Soviet jurists is the way in which economic relationships are to be defined. According to some, they are to be understood in a narrow sense; according to others, in a broad sense. Proponents of the broad conception would include labor law as part of economic law, insofar as the enterprises, in their economic activities, enter not only into relations with other enterprises but with the workforce and the labor collective as well. However, it is not within the scope of the present analysis to develop this issue.

The aspects of labor law of interest here are those concerned with the improvement of "socialist legality" in industrial enterprises. According to Article 52 of the Foundations and Article 128 of the Labor Code of the RFSSR, the methods that may be employed to ensure discipline on the job are those of persuasion (*ubezhdenie*) and "stimulation" (*pooshchrenie*). If necessary, social and disciplinary measures may be applied to individual, "unconscientious" (*nedobrosovestnie*) workers. These disciplinary measures are set out by the foundations and the codes of the various republics, by the Code of Labor Standards, and by a factory's disciplinary regulations. The social-disciplinary measures are stipulated by "comrades' courts" or by the social organizations (Party, Komsomol, trade union) operating at the enterprise's level.

Judicial sanction against indiscipline derives in practice from a broad interpretation of Article 55 of the Foundations. This article grants "conscientious" workers privileged access to valuable social services. Disciplinary measures (cancelation of bonuses, transfer to lower-paid jobs, and so forth) are usually included in the enterprise's regulations or in the factory collective's contract. In some enterprises, norms establishing collective responsibility for breaches of discipline have been introduced. This does not imply material responsibility, as set out by Article 49 of the Foundations and by Articles 118 and 119 of the code of the Russian Federation; rather, it implies moral responsibility by the work collective and the sanctions that may be applied consist of reducing or removing altogether any individual bonuses and privileges previously granted by the management. Nevertheless, Soviet labor law continues to be based on the relations between the enterprise and the individual worker; this is partly due to the fact that the problems of collective "stimulation" and responsibility still have not been satisfactorily dealt with by legal and economic literature, even if some attempts have been made (Molodzof and Soifer 1976: 116).

The most extreme disciplinary measure is dismissal, and in this regard Soviet scholars have divided into two camps. On one side, there are sociologists like Aitov (1975:200) who see no sense in sacking a worker who the collective has been unable to educate and who—after a period of unemployment lasting an average of one month—soon starts work again in another enterprise. In practice, this amounts to a system of exchanging undisciplined workers from one factory to another. On the other side, many argue that disciplinary dismissal is justified because it is prescribed by the law, the various classes of offense indicated in the resolution of the Central Council of Trade Unions of January 1965. Molodzof and Soifer share the second view because they claim that the social conditions have not yet evolved to a point where the work collective is able to carry out its educational function to the fullest extent (1976:129).

Present legislation provides that the decision to dismiss a worker is to be taken with the assent of the FZMK (Article 18 of the Foundations and Article 35 of the Code). The agreement of the FZMK is always necessary, even when the dismissal is ordered or sanctioned by the higher organs, and must be unanimous—that is, the assent of only the chairman of the factory committee is not enough. At least two-thirds of the members of the Committee must be present at the meeting where the decision to dismiss the worker is taken, and the reasons for the decision must be minuted. Assent by the committee must precede the formal act of dismissal. If this assent is withheld, then management has no choice but to withdraw the dismissal; it cannot appeal to the courts (Nikitinsky & Panyugin 1973:31–34).

The management of an enterprise may only resort to disciplinary dismissal in cases of systematic violations of factory regulations, the law, or labor contract. It is not empowered to dismiss employees for undisciplined behavior outside their working activities, or for their refusal to carry out social activities or duties not included in their job specifications, except in cases prescribed by the law (Nikitinsky & Panyugin 1973:50).

The enterprise has the right to cancel the contract unilaterally if it goes into liquidation, or in cases of cutbacks in production or technological innovation. In the event of legal controversy, the motives of dismissal are adjudicated by the courts on inspection of the output plans, directives of higher organs, and documents relative to the workforce and wage funds. This does not imply that the tribunal is entitled to pass judgment on the opportunenness or efficacy of the restructuring decided upon by the management, but if the enterprise should subsequently take on workers that have not previously been employed by it, the dismissed worker has the right to be reinstated to his formal post. An enterprise that dismisses workers because of reorganization is obliged first to find alternative employment for the workers who will lose their jobs. In cases where the workforce is to be reduced in numbers, priority in job security belongs to those workers ranked at the top of the productivity and qualifications scales (Nikitinsky & Panyugin 1973:43).

In determining worker rankings, it is not the rating of experts that count, but the documentation supplied by the management and the social organizations of the factory relative to the extent to which the workers involved have fulfilled their output quotas and carried out their duties, and relative to their educational level, experience, and so on. If two workers receive the same ratings, then the decision is based on their family responsibilities, length of service, and any possible work-related diseases they may be suffering from (Nikitinsky & Panyugin 1973:45).

There are also rules for dismissing a worker who otherwise possesses the formal requisites for the job—if he is unable to carry out the tasks assigned to him either because he lacks the skills or because of the state of his health (Article 17 of the Foundation, and Article 33 of the Code). His unsuitability for the job must be demonstrated by persistently substandard performances both quantitatively and qualitatively. Here, in case of legal controversy over dismissal, the court must ascertain whether the enterprise has effectively provided normal working conditions—that is, machinery in good working order, necessary technical documentation, suitable tools and material, and adequate safety protection (Article 108 of the Code).

A worker on sick leave is entitled to keep his job until he has been absent for a total of four months. For longer absences the enterprise has the right to reach a decision on the basis of its production requirements. As for work-related diseases, the decision must be postponed until the worker is either fit to return to work or has been officially declared disabled (Article 33 of the Code).

TURNING LEGAL RIGHTS INTO REAL RIGHTS

According to the Soviet viewpoint, the basic characteristic of Soviet labor law is that—unlike "bourgeois" labor law—"it rests not on the formal proclamation and protection of the rights of the citizen, but on the guarantee that they will be effectively implemented" (Smirnov 1977:199). Article 5 of the Foundations decrees the non-validity of any employment contract which contains clauses setting conditions substandard to those stipulated by law. This norm provides the guiding principle for a further series of norms which instill in the worker the belief that his rights are being respected (Livsic & Nikitinsky 1974:32).

Soviet labor law also defines the extent to which it is possible to diverge from the norms that regulate labor relations; but, in doing so, it also regulates the function of control with respect to these divergences (Molodzof & Soifer 1976:220).

Workers' rights are guaranteed by granting to various organs the right to exercise the function of control. In particular, trade union officials are empowered to inspect factory premises and to demand all necessary documentation and explanations from an enterprise's management. Moreover, under the terms of Article 231 of the Code, they may call in competent authorities to take suitable disciplinary measures against officials guilty of breaches in labor legislation (Molodzof & Soifer 1976:221).

Overall, the guarantees provided by Soviet labor law form a system of *organizational-judicial instruments* distinguished from one another by their contents and their range of application. On the basis of content, these labor laws may be divided into (1) *judicial-material* content—that is, those provided by the Foundations and the Code of Labor Legislation; (2) *judgmental* content—that is, those pertaining to the composition of labor disputes; and (3) *judicial-social* content—concerning, for example, the rights of a trade-union factory committee. With respect to range of application, organizational-judicial instruments break down into categories of (1) those that define the limits of subjective rights and duties—these actually, are, guarantees of the *exercise* of rights, that is, pertaining to holidays, special leaves, and transfers; and (2) instruments for the *protection* of individual rights—the numerous norms that oblige enterprise managements to come to an agreement with factory committees over all decisions touching the rights of their employees (work standards, overtime, mobility, dismissal, and so forth (Smirnov 1977:200–205).

In conclusion, the fundamental principles governing labor relations emanating from the Soviet legal system include the following guarantees to workers: the right to work, freedom from exploitation, participation by working people in the "leadership of production" and in deciding working conditions, freedom to negotiate the labor contract, renumeration according to quality of output, and the maximum safeguarding of health and safety of working people.

Now it remains to verify how well these labor principles are implemented in the day-to-day reality of labor relations. First, however, a brief outline is needed of what the Soviets call the "new mechanism for the regulation of the social labor"—that is, social planning, an issue that has been widely debated and experimented with in the Soviet Union during the last two decades.

CHAPTER 5

Social Planning

Lenin found in "scientific management" as elaborated by Frederick W. Taylor a series of positive features that could be usefully incorporated into an efficient system of work organization. Lenin's idea was to transform what under capitalism seemed to be a refined instrument for exploitation into a body of new methods of work organization typical of the great mechanized industries. Thus "Taylorism" was regarded as being the most rapid and economical way of teaching a largely inexpert labor force how to work (Linhart 1977:108).

During the 1920s, this was a question of teaching the rationality of industrial labor to workers of predominantly rural origins. This process was effectively suspended during the thirty years of Stalinist rule. But, at the beginning of the 1960s, the debate reopened over what should constitute "scientific management" in Soviet enterprise. In this new phase of "intensive development" the problem for political leadership was not so much the training of worker-peasants as the instilling of new principles for administering human and material resources—to managers and functionaries who, so far, had been concerned only with the fulfilling of plans at any cost. Social planning and its connection with economic planning were to help attain the "superior forms of the organization of social labour" (Podmarkov 1969:130).

The aim of this chapter is to outline the Soviets' approach to social planning and the ways in which it materializes in the plans for the social development of production collectives.

THE "COMPLEX APPROACH" TO SOCIAL PLANNING

Since the early 1970s, the duties of the Soviet social sciences—and of Soviet sociology in particular—have been laid down by a series of resolutions issued by the Party and commented on in editorials of the journal *Sotsiologicheskie Issledovania*. The fundamental task of the social sciences now is to provide new mechanisms for the regulation of social labor within the framework of the "scientific management of developed socialist society"—to be implemented by means of a series of operations grouped under the heading of *social planning*, defined as

> the scientifically based determination of objectives and indices of social development, and the definition of the basic means for the practical implementation of this development in the interest of the working class and the whole working population of socialist society. (Toshchenko 1981:118)

At a conference on socioeconomic planning and ideological work, held in Leningrad in 1975, it was emphasized that social planning

> resting as it does on a solid scientific base, and strengthened by capable organizational work, becomes the principal factor in efficient management, optimizes relations in the collectives, and orients the social activism of working people towards the performance of the technical and social tasks of the moment. (Podmarkov 1979:21)

We can summarize all this by saying that in the "developed socialist society" three requirements are currently regarded as being fundamental: improved methods of management, the utilization of new reserves in order to enhance production efficiency, and the development of the social activism of workers. Various authors have emphasized one or another of these objectives. However, judging from the most recent Soviet literature, the theoretical and practical tendency seems to be in favor of a "complex approach" (*kompleksni podkhod*) oriented toward the simultaneous optimization of all three requirements.

The complex approach to enterprise management was sanctioned by the Twenty-Fifth Congress of the CPSU, and its experimental

implementation began during the tenth five-year plan (1976–1980).
In practice, this approach addresses all sociotechnical aspects of
management in a planned economy, and it has as its objective the
surmounting of the traditionally negative consequences of the older
fragmented approach. The complicated problems involved require
the coordinated effort of various economic branches and territorial
bodies. Apart from this approach there are two others. The first
concentrates on objectives; in it organizational structures, plans,
and incentive schemes must be oriented toward the final results of
the five-year plan rather than toward monthly results, as in the
current practice. In the second, long-term approach, problems such
as technological innovation, economic experiments, environmental
protection, and so on, which cannot be solved within the framework of the five-year plan because enterprises and ministries are
mainly concerned with plan fulfillment, are dealt with in a wider
perspective (Popov 1977:10).

The complex approach to social planning is justified by the needs
of scientific-technical progress and the greater organizational complexity of today's Soviet enterprise. Thus, in management practices,
a distinction is drawn by social planners between technico-organizational and socioeconomic aspects, the latter being regarded as
crucial to the development of efficient production in the interests
not only of the plant but of the whole society as well. A further
distinction is then drawn between economic planning and social
planning, with the added requirement that both the interconnec-
tions and the specific area of application of the two types of
planning should be carefully defined (Rudich 1980:78–79).

Despite their diversity of function, the various forms of social
planning are guided by a set of common principles: "democratic
centralism," objectivity, concreteness, optimality, scientificness,
and their application "in the interests of the working class and the
entire working population of socialist society" (Rudich 1980:79).

But, apart from these common principles, the various types of
social planning under the heading "complex approach" possesses
their own specific characteristics. The first type comprises the planning of socioeconomic processes, the principal goal of which is the
planning of scientific-technical progress and the introduction of
technical advances in the productive processes. This type of planning is addressed to all the economic and technico-organizational
indices. They have also contained social indices, that is, indices

pertaining to sociocultural development. Attempts have also been made to forecast the social consequences of plan fulfillment (Kerimov & Pashkov 1975:27–28). Other attempts have been made to identify the social means most useful for the fulfillment of economic plans (Toshchenko 1970:132).

Another element of social planning concerns the regulation of sociopolitical processes. Here, the fundamental objectives are "unity between working class and peasants" and development of "socialist democracy." Socialist democracy, however, remains subordinate to the corresponding development of "socialist discipline." In the planning of sociopolitical processes, extreme importance is attached to the direction in which the efforts of the population, the Party, and state are oriented. This means that, once again, political considerations take precedence over the economy. Any desire to give priority to economy over politics must wait—according to Lenin—until "there are no more political dangers and political errors" (Toshchenko 1970:133).

The final aspect of social planning concerns the planning of the spiritual life of society (*duckhovni zhizn obshchestva*). Here Soviet writers imagine the reactions of the "representatives of bourgeois science" to such a strategy. Western sociologists would certainly ask: "How can such an outright attack on spiritual life, on the *sancta sanctorum* of human liberty, be possible?" Toshchenko answers:

> Communists believe that, with the creation of socialist society, the decisive factor in the formation of a spiritual culture in the individual lies in the new forms of social life which render impossible the existence of a "lonely crowd" or of "mass loneliness." In socialist society, the individual is not only the object of planning, but also the subject. (1970:140)

Under socialism, the spiritual life of the masses coincides with the objective needs of social development for a series of "well-known" reasons: "the liquidation of private property, the elimination of exploiting classes, the sovereignty of the social ownership of the means of production and the victory of Marxist-Leninist ideology" (Sergeev 1970:57). Thus, the subjects, purposes, and content of "spiritual planning" are quite different from the social planning that exists in capitalist countries. And, in fact, this form of planning in the Soviet Union is intended to act upon the "internationalist and patriotic awareness of the workers." It must be capable of removing from their consciousness any vestigial traits from prerevolutionary times (survival of the past) and ensure that workers are not influenced by the "enemy's ideology" (Toshchenko 1970:143).

In these terms, it is not only quantitative indices that are important (number of courses, lessons, conferences and so on): The development of spiritual life must be regulated not only by organizational measures, but also by indirect socioeconomic instruments.

PLANNING THE "SOCIAL DEVELOPMENT OF PRODUCTION COLLECTIVES"

The "complex approach" to social planning is elaborated in the so-called plans of social development applied at enterprise and regional levels. At present, the emphasis is on the generalized application of these plans, understood as instruments for the improving of "socialist democracy," social control, and participation from below in the "leadership of production." The measures employed in these sorts of plans are designed to reduce or eliminate a series of negative features that have traditionally characterized industrial relations such as indiscipline, high turnover, and unsatisfactory working conditions.

The implementation of "social relations" requires the provision of measures for the improvement of work conditions, and here responsibility lies principally with the enterprise management. The trade unions play a leading role in the rational use of leisure time—or that use which encourages the "multilateral development of the personality." The ideological conditions that favor the further development of socialist society in accordance with the marxist–leninist doctrine are created by the propaganda and agitation activities of the Party, Komsomol, and the trade union.

The "plans for social development," for their part, entail a change in the methods employed in the organizational and educational work of the Party, inasmuch as they equip the collective with a "social passport" (*sotsialni passport*). By this is meant that they provide a portrait of the sociodemographic features of the different labor groups, thus permitting the combining of the individual approach with the mass approach in the politico-ideal-moral education of the working population.

The drafting and implementation of "plans of social development" proceeds in three stages. The first involves research into the social interactions to be found in a particular production collective, followed by the elaboration of a plan of action. The second stage comprises the drafting of the plan itself and its consideration by the collective. In the third, operational stage, before the actual implementation of the plan, management, Party and trade union officials verify that the plan is compatible with similar plans at that level of industry and region.

Plans are not all equally complex. The simplest—and most common—comprise a list of measures to be adopted in order to improve the working and living conditions of employees at an enterprise. In general, the commitment of managers to the implementation of these provisions is set out in the company contract. These are plans whose peculiarities are very far from those proposed by social planners, insofar as preliminary research is not carried out and a plan of action is not drawn up. Very often, in fact, this sort of plan is drafted by commissions or soviets, the members of which are not equipped with sufficient practical experience or theoretical training (Khokhlyuk 1976:27).

A second, more sophisticated model allows sociological research into questions such as the causes of high turnover, the socioprofessional composition of the collective, the relations in the work group, productive activism, and so forth. This research may be conducted by sociologists either employed in the enterprise or commissioned from outside.

Lastly, results from preliminary research must be checked. This operation is conducted by the enterprise's sociological services, the trade-union committee, the Party, and Komsomol, each of which reports on a single section of the plan. The employees are kept informed in various ways during each stage of the plan by conferences, seminars, meetings, and factory radio broadcasts.

PART III

The Operational Reality

CHAPTER 6

Red Executives Today

THE SOVIET

The fundamental problem facing Soviet management may be stated as this: How can Soviet managers create the organizational slack necessary to meet the requirements of the planning system when they are faced with the uncertainties of input? More specifically, since the introduction of central planning, Soviet enterprises have had to create maneuvering room for themselves to cope with two sources of uncertainty: (1) the quantity, quality, and delivery terms of supplies and (2) the quantity and quality of manpower available.

The causes of industry's uncertainties over input are embedded in the planning process whose functioning may be summarized as follows. The central political authority has the prerogative of issuing directives and establishing priorities. Enterprises must supply information concerning their production capacity and make applications for the supplies and manpower required by their subsequent production. The State Planning Committee (GOSPLAN) must handle these applications in such a way as to give balance and overall coherence to the five-year economic plan. The method GOSPLAN uses is called "material balancing"—that is comparisons are drawn between the resources required by a particular kind or sector of production and their availability. Resources are allocated or reallocated on the basis of input coefficients derived from previous experience and modified according to forecasts of technological change (Nove 1977:31–59).

The fundamental difference between present-day planning and

that of the Stalin period lies in the fact that, then, directives from above were regarded as "legally binding" and the basic index was gross output. Today, greater attention is paid to economic account-ability (*khozraschet*) at all levels of the planning system.

The reality of planning and production, however, still falls short of the optimization criteria currently under discussion. The price system is far from assuring effective and rapid comparison between costs and results and the process by which priorities are drawn up has little or nothing to do with the price mechanism (Nove 1977:172–198; Conyngham 1982:138–141, 148–149). Con-sequently, the planning bodies manage to reconcile their basic priorities with the availability of resources only by resorting, empirically, to what has been defined as the "Ratchet principle" (Berliner, 1957:78–79; Dyker 1985), which roughly translates as: "Whatever you did last year, do more of it this year, and better" (Nove, 1977:105). The planners adhere in practice to this principle because their knowledge of the productive capacity is often incom-plete and distorted. As a result, the degree of planning efficiency falls below a level deemed tolerable by the political leadership. Thus, continuing efforts to reorganize the system of industrial planning and management are being carried out, but an effective methodology for establishing the criteria of economic account-ability is still in embryonic form. Since relying on market forces arouses strong ideological opposition, attempts to reduce waste and inefficiency are made which try to preserve the logic of the centra-lized bureaucratic model, concentrating at the same time on its computerization (Conyngham 1982). A resolution issued in July 1979 is significant in this respect. It mandated elements of decentral-ization (accountability based on sales volume and net production, for example) combined with elements of centralization (increase in the number of centrally planned commodity groups, emphasis on physical indicators). The reasons for this ambivalence may perhaps be found in the planners' confidence that computerization will eventually solve most planning problems. But the persistence of a centralized system stems above all from two basic principles of action which seem to resist any attempt at *perestroika*: (1) preserve centralized planning, trying to use computerization for that purpose; and (2) aim at getting things done through "trouble-shooting" and "chivying people up" (Dyker 1980:1–3).

In short, despite a succession of economic reforms in the last twenty years, and despite the continual organizational reshuffling and establishing of ever-newer indicators of efficiency, there has been no fundamental change in the "command-based" system of planning. In fact, three traditional principles continue to apply: The first holds that it is not the absolute volume of production that counts, but rather whether and by what percentage the plan's goal has been fulfilled. The second is the "Ratchet principle": once a plant has managed to meet a certain plan target, it finds it difficult to obtain a reduction of its targets in the future. The third principle gives priority of resource allocation to heavy industry, to the military, and to the space programme. Of course, in recent years there have been attempts to readjust planning priorities in favor of more consumer goods, but these efforts seem not to have substantially altered the functioning of the "command economy." Consequently, the fact remains that the planning process is a general source of uncertainty for the great majority of enterprises (Nove 1977:99).

Soviet enterprises, however, must not only cope with the unreliability of material supply: Their second major source of uncertainty is the availability of required labor, both in terms of quantity and quality. "You can't supply a factory with manpower to order, as you can with coal and metal," wrote a *Pravda* correspondent (Nov. 26, 1977:2). Remarks such as this indicate the intricate complex of factors that make regulating the labor market in a centrally planned economy so difficult to accomplish. Today, the difficulties faced by most plants in finding manpower (especially qualified labor) result from the impact of the falling birthrate on a system of economic management still unable (or insufficiently motivated) to use human and material resources efficiently. In other words, the reduced intake from the labor market increasingly highlights the irrationality of the present distribution of labor resources, when compared with the demands of intense economic development and the officially proclaimed target of the "scientific-technical revolution." That this state of affairs continues to exist is not just the fault of planners and central authorities: The special interests of enterprises and individuals also make a substantial contribution, as various examples taken from the Soviet press will demonstrate.

When it comes to the responsibility of planning, frequent complaints are made concerning the lack of housing, shopping facilities, and cultural amenities—and this despite the emphasis of recent years on social planning (Mochalin, 1977:10; Manevich

1978:5–6). The industrial ministries make their own contribution
to the distribution imbalances by concentrating their energies on
the expansion of existing enterprises, or on constructing new ones
only in major centers where there is an already-existing infrastructure. If these ministries are among the most powerful, they
have ample funds to spend on social services and housing; thus
their plants attract labor away from other industries located
perhaps in small centres, but with good potential for development
(Drobnys 1977). These ministries are also able to keep the best
workers to themselves and, if forced to release manpower to new
industries, will make available only those workers least suited to
their needs (Sonin, 1978). Another cause of the labor shortage
lies in the preferences of young people, who are reluctant to take on
heavy and monotonous work (Skarupo 1978; Kotlyar and Talalai
1977). Further, job-training centers do not provide an adequate
supply of skilled labor, or their training programs do not reflect
needs of the local labor market but rather the preferences of train-
ees (Vorinin 1977). Finally, the labor shortage is exacerbated
by the policies of the enterprises themselves, which—because of
competition on the labor market—tend to keep excess labor on
their books.

Central planning and the labor market, therefore, are the chief
sources of uncertainty for enterprises. How do Soviet managers
deal with these difficulties that in theory should not exist?

According to official doctrine, one of the superior features of
socialist economy is that considerations of "microprofitability"
must yield in favor of choices that guarantee the satisfaction of
state, enterprise, and individual needs. Official theory requires that
both individuals and organizations adjust their behavior to suit the
interests of the socialist society. That this turns out to be impossible
is due to the "trivial" fact that resources are scarce and poorly allocated. Hence the emergence of a "centralized pluralism"—that is,
the dividing of a centralized economy into semiautonomous units,
each guided by its own needs and priorities and in competition with
all the others for the resources from the center. Local political
bodies, industrial ministries, production associations, and enterprises can all be understood in these terms (Nove 1977:60).

In this context, the steps plant managers commonly take to cope
with the uncertainties of planning are various, but in general they
can be regarded as employing three fundamental principles of

action. The first is the creation of a "safety factor"—an expression deriving from the term *perestrakhovka* ("overinsurance"):

> It conveys the idea of holding back a reserve, of preserving "slack" in the drafting and execution of plan targets, so that if anything goes wrong management will have untapped resources to fall back upon in order to meet its targets. (Berliner 1957:76).

There are at least five important stages in the creation of a "safety factor," ranging from the moment when the plant's targets are defined to their final concrete realization.

Chronologically, the first step is the practice of inflating requests for supplies. Industrial managers are often obliged to resort to this practice because they know that, in all probability, their request will be cut by the ministry. Managers know the reason behind this: that the ministry itself will likely not obtain all the material requested from GOSSNAB (State Supply Committee). Added to this is the ever-growing lack of confidence in the efficiency of the official distribution network, which encourages managers to think that "One ton in the warehouse is worth ten tons on paper" (Berliner 1957:109).

The lack of confidence in the official channel of distribution stems also from two other factors. The first is a consequence of the "Ratchet principle": Enterprises fear that a reduction in their materials consumption over a given period will lead to a downward adjustment of the procurement plan for the following period. The second reason is the fact that, by inflating its requests, the plant strengthens its hand in its negotiations with the ministry; this enables it to avoid overburdensome plan targets, which cannot be refused outright.

It may happen (and does frequently) that an enterprise will find itself in difficulties over the quantity, quality, and delivery schedule of its supplies, despite its practice of inflating requests. The reason for this may be found in the system of priorities: Heavy industry takes precedence over light industry; military-production over civil manufacture; plants where economic experiments are in progress over others; and large plants over small. In general, high-priority industries are in the minority and the others (the majority) are left to cope with the problems caused by the uncertainties from the input side.

Managers lost with the majority in such low-priority industries resort to informal exchange arrangements with other enterprises. And here, a second principle of action comes into play: the *blat*. This term was originally underworld slang, but today it indicates the use of personal influence to obtain something one is not entitled to—or conversely, to something one *is* entitled to but that is unobtainable through official channels. *Blat* is different from corruption in that it does not involve the pay of "kickbacks"; it is rather a system of mutual familiarity, trust, and exchange of favors between individuals. The bartering of materials between enterprises—or "arm-twisting" to obtain the plant's supply requirements from official channels—is arranged by the so-called *tolkachi* ("pushers" or "expediters"). Generally speaking, these unofficial dealings involve the low-priority enterprises, who use the system to compensate for their disadvantaged situation. However, larger or more strategically important plants also resort to *blat* and *tolkachi*, perhaps because it is easier to manipulate a certain large quota of materials and articles, or because they may have problems not in their main product, but in obtaining supplies for auxiliary production.

Blat is also influenced by structural factors. The nature of the product is one of these: It is easier "to make deals" in raw material than in finished goods because the latter are manufactured in fixed quantities. Another important factor is the nature of the demand for a given output: the more widespread the demand (that is, the more customers), the easier becomes the *blat* (Berliner 1957:195).

Once a "safety factor" has been created, it must be preserved—that is, steps must be taken to ensure that subsequent ministerial (or Party) checks do not reveal the existence of unused stocks. This is done in a variety of ways. One of these is to introduce technical innovations at every opportunity. In fact, in the absence of innovation the ministry will increasingly be able to ascertain the production capacity of the enterprise. In this case, the "safety factor" dwindles dangerously, badly impeding the fulfillment of the plan targets. Improved technology, together with a certain underestimation of the new production potential, will assist the management in regaining logistical maneuvering room. This does not mean, however, that enterprises are generally in favor of new technology. Reorganization also make it difficult to fulfill current plan targets and, very often, innovation is in fact the result of legislative measures or of pressure from above (Richman 1965:158–159). The most common practice is the maintaining of a certain organizational slack. This is done in two ways: first, by trying to keep machinery-utilization norms low, and then by reducing them still further by making the decline in machine productivity appear even greater; second, by accumulating capital assets. The second option is possible because prior to the economic reform of 1965 no interest had to be paid on the credits for the purchase of machinery (Richman, 1965:152). Today, of course, interest rates do exist, but they still remain quite low.

The safety factor can be preserved by acting on input and on "throughput." Now it remains to be seen how the same can be done by acting on output.

For the last two decades, a succession of new measures have been introduced, all aimed at regulating production by the logic of economic efficiency. Today, therefore, alongside the gross output required by plan directives, enterprises must also hold to indices that govern the reduction of production costs. Since, in the Soviet economy, the manufacturer holds the advantage over the customer (unless this happens to be a military body) firms tend to pursue a reduction in cost by imposing a high cost-price differential on the customer while, at the same time, ensuring that this margin is not easily detected by the authorities. This strategy is especially common if the client industry belongs to a different ministry or in cases of nonstandard or experimental manufacture, where there are frequent changes in the specification of products. This provides enterprises with room to maneuver on prices as well, because, in the case of new or nonstandard articles, the enterprise can propose interim prices to buyers. The interim prices are "set" by inflating to a certain extent the elements that have contributed to their determination. In addition, firms often manage to prolong this interim period—that is, the period that precedes the large-scale manufacture of the articles in question. A further device of an enterprise's disposal is to take advantage of the delay in the lowering of prices to reflect the increased output made possible by technological innovation (Richman 1965:156–158). In cases where all these strategies prove inadequate to fulfil the plan, managers still have some cards left to play *in extremis*. A part of future production can be "lent" to the present period through a reshuffling of accounts. The chances of being discovered depend on whether or not the purchasing company makes any complaints concerning the so-called finished product. Hence it is necessary to be fully informed of work progress in the purchasing company and, if need be, fall back on the *blat* principle.

The third main principle of action managers use to cope with uncertainty is the manipulation of reports. This manipulation is rarely total in the sense, for example, of exaggerating accounts of overall production. Most commonly, it is a question of partially transferring the cost of one product to another that belongs to the target as defined by the plan directives (Berliner 1957:160–170).

These three fundamental ways of coping with planning uncertainty followed by Soviet managers have been described in detail by two American authors: J. Berliner and B. M. Richman. In the early 1950s Berliner conducted a series of interviews with Soviet emigrés who had worked in prewar years at various levels of responsibility in Soviet industrial enterprises. Richman based his research on both existing literature and on interviews conducted—in the USSR in 1960–1961—with a hundred planners, plant managers, economists, workers, and trade-union and Party officials.

Readers may question the validity of these principles after twenty-five to thirty years in which the constant Soviet emphasis has been on management organized according to economic accountability and the "scientific-technical revolution." To verify continuity and change on the matter we can first find out how these arguments are today covered by the Soviet press.

As far as Soviet sources are concerned, mention has already been made of the plan decree of 1979, and of its mixture of decentralizing and centralizing elements. The same features appear to be present in subsequent official resolutions. In November 1982, for instance, the central committee of the CPSU introduced new measures for the further development of "democratic centralism" in industrial management. The aim of these measures was to stimulate labor productivity, raise qualitative standards, and provide incentives for enterprises to intensify their programs of technical and organizational innovation. Official sources immediately pointed out, however, that these measures, although designed to increase the rights and responsibilities of enterprises, should really serve to strengthen centralized management of the economy. The president of GOSPLAN, N. K. Baibakov, for example, wrote:

In taking steps to expand the rights of the enterprises ... we are not setting ourselves the task of weakening the centralized management of the economy. On the contrary, we are taking steps to improve centralized management and to enhance its scientific character and effectiveness. (*Izvestia* August 18, 1983:3)

However, in an article published two weeks earlier, the economist Kulagin reported that the economy was still only making slow progress toward intensive development, and added:

Although supposedly a good deal is being done in this field, in practice the independence and responsibility of enterprise executives and collectives has perhaps even decreased somewhat in recent years. (*Pravda* 1983)

The author cites various examples to support his argument. At the Sverdlov Association in Leningrad, during the late 1960s, eight to ten annual plan indices were subject to confirmation from above; today, this number has doubled. He further cites the extremely complex nature of the incentive fund—which lacks any correlation between the work results of a collective and the bonuses it receives. He adds that the rise in indices imposed on a firm, far from strengthening plan discipline, broadens the field for the manipulation of reports and ultimately leads to "adjusting the plan" to fit actually achieved results.

All the other practices described above are still very much alive. In fact the new measures, as periodically announced by the central authorities, provide fresh opportunities for the old, well-established, unofficial practices to persist. Let us take as an example the practice of bartering between enterprises, which is still reported in the press. Managers have to resort to this practice because the ministry assigns them targets without providing the necessary materials. How do they justify this practice? "Let he who is without sin cast the first stone," one manager has said: Another added: "If you wanted to, you could bring the same charge against any director" (Spiridonov 1983).

In the last decade or so, experiments are periodically conducted which should pave the way for the spread of economic efficiency and organizational innovation in industry. The end of the 1960s saw the Shchekino experiment, the most important attempt to manage an enterprise according to the criteria of profit (Rutland 1985; Norr 1986), and economic experiments are now under way in the ministries of heavy machinery and electrical equipment in the Ukraine, and in the ministry for food and light industry in Belorussia (Gorlin 1985; Bornstein 1985). On the basis of the Shchekino experiment, one can predict that these experiments will be difficult to generalize because, as Soviet analysts observe, they are "deviant with respect to generally accepted norms and laws." In other words, the experiments run counter to the bureaucratic system of industrial management (Kroncher 1977:3).

The most effective summary of this state of affairs is still Richman's:

> The Soviets have not been able to design an incentive system that encourages managers to pursue with equal effort and effectiveness all of the objectives of their enterprises. Each incentive scheme tried has had the unintended consequence of inducing managers to engage in a wide variety of practices contrary to the state's interests; each has precipitated its own type of distortions and patterns of undesirable behavior. (1965:175).

Thus, at least in many cases, managers do not choose the most efficient combination of production factors to fulfill their plan targets but rather rely on hoarding as has happened in the past.

In concluding his analysis of the behavior of Soviet managers, Berliner posed a nagging question: How is it possible that "in a totalitarian regime, sturdily propped with all the murky paraphernalia of a police state, managers go blithely about hoarding materials, engaging in *blat*, and systematically evading the intent of regulations?" (1957:231). This question can be answered bearing in mind two facts. The first is the mentality still dominant among the Party and state officials (*apparatchiki*), who tend to concentrate on the political control of working people and of the entire population, at the expense of a more efficient allocation of economic resources (Dyker 1981). That is to say, despite the earnest requests of top leaders, priority is given, *in practice*, to the political stability of the regime rather than to economic efficiency. The fact is, however, that although the economic cost of political stability has reached impressive levels, the "treadmill of spurious reforms" (Schroeder 1979) has produced a lot of unintended consequences. A very good opportunity to verify continuity and change within the context of Berliner's remarks is offered also by the Soviet Interview Project (SIP) led by James Millar (1986a).

The issue of managerial autonomy has been addressed by SIP's Susan Linz (1986), who interviewed fifty-three expert informants involved in some aspect of planning, production, or distribution decision making in the second half of the 1970s.

Beginning with the question of material input requests, it emerges that managers have more success in negotiating for additional materials than for lower output targets. The degree of success appears to depend on factors such as personal relations between directors and the ministry and geographic location, in the sense that firms in Moscow and other big cities are privileged. Also important is the technical documentation which sustains input requests (Linz 1986:8–9).

Linz's study differs from Berliner's and Richman's in that interview information suggests that ministry officials have sufficient technical expertise to effectively prevent managers from significantly overhoarding inputs (Linz, 1986:10). This does not necessarily imply that ministries and other planning bodies take into account the calculations that enterprises send "upstairs": Planning from the "achieved level" has by no means disappeared (Schultze & Livermore 1985:73).

The SIP study includes other surprising findings: Increased expertise of ministries—combined with problems of labor discipline, turnover, and aging machinery and equipment—allow enterprise managers little opportunity to grossly understate productive capacity. This means that directors, in priority or nonpriority sectors, are unable to maintain substantial hidden reserves or hoard labor (Linz 1986:12–13). Paul Gregory (1986:22–23), on the basis of interview information from the whole SIP sample (2900 respondents), reports low levels of redundant labor among blue-collar and skilled white-collar workers. Redundancy seems instead high among engineers, planners and administrators, and unskilled white-collar workers.

It is worth noting that this information has been confirmed by an *Izvestia* article. It reveals that the number of administrative personnel in 1983 has increased by 3 million in comparison with 1975. One figure is particularly striking: 31 percent of administrators are chiefs, managers, and deputies—in other words "there are [only] two subordinates for every executive" (Schultze & Livermore 1985:73). Other Soviet sources report that labor reserves hidden in industrial enterprises range from 10 to 20 percent of personnel (Porket 1985:24).

Good personal relations with planning authorities and good documentation are also important during plan implementation. If these conditions prevail, managers can get "corrections" of monthly and quarterly—and even annual—plans when deadlines get closer. In light industry, however, respondents reported great difficulties in winning reductions in either volume or value of output targets, or in wresting control over product line, a power exerted not only by planners but also by trade organizations. This is another divergence from data gathered by Berliner and Richman (Linz 1986:16–17). A strong continuity with the past remains instead the persistent inability of planners to solve supply problems, a fact that is underlined in the Soviet press. For example, articles in *Voprosi Ekonomiki* and *Sovetskaia Rossiia* (1979 and 1980) reported that the clothing industry was receiving only 69 percent of the equipment it required, the leather industry 38 percent, and the footwear industry 29 percent (Kroncher 1982b:6). Hence the continuing reliance on *sturmovshchina* ("storming") because nonfulfillment of plans would imply nonpayment of bonuses, an essential condition to maintain a stable workforce (Linz 1986:21). Enterprise directors, who despite "storming" do not fulfill the plan, revert to old tricks such as reshuffling of accounts, a practice which continues to be denounced in the Soviet press (Kroncher, 1982b:3; 1985:6). But new ways out are also available. The origin of the change here can be considered the behavior of working people—that is, their decision to quit jobs over problems with salary. In the SIP interviews, managers did report negotiating with planning authorities to increase the size of wage funds. But success seems hard to achieve: "If you could prove funds for salary were insufficient, they added, with tears and scandal, but they did add funds" (Linz 1986:27). Thus, it is understandable why directors who run into difficulties with wage funds generally try to avoid the ordeal of such negotiations, tending instead to use bank loans and repay them as soon as possible.

The role of the central bank—and its implications on the discretionary power of managers—appears at variance both with the findings of Berliner and the economic theories of Agambegian. The latter advocates more independence for enterprises, which should be controlled more "by the ruble" than by higher authorities, i.e., make a profit (Schultze & Livermore 1986:78–80). Actually, in many instances such control has the unintended consequence of helping to cover irregular production patterns (Linz 1986:28).

Berliner's question about the circumvention at local levels of the orders from the center can be addressed by taking into account another traditional feature of the management of Soviet enterprise. In the Soviet Union, officials responsible for the smooth running of the economy are frequently dissuaded, by a combination of forces, from strictly adhering to formal rules in the exercise of control.

It should be remembered that the managing director of an enterprise is formally a state official, and as such has been given the responsibility of running the production process. In this guise the managing director is directly answerable to the state and government for all aspects of company policy. Alongside the director, there are other functionaries who are also equipped with the necessary powers to ensure that company activities conform with the interests of society as a whole. The most important positions in this respect are those of the chief accountant, the head of quality control, and the chief mechanical engineer. The former is in charge of all financial transactions, must draft all plan reports, and sign all contracts and all wage and salary documents. He is empowered to refuse all orders that he believes to be illegal but, in such cases, must report the matter to authorities (Berliner 1957:232). The head of quality control is responsible for ensuring that products meet quality standards and that, especially, inferior products or rejects are not allowed to pass on to the market place. The chief mechanical engineer is legally responsible for the correct use of machinery and equipment. Consequently, he is expected to safeguard the state's long-term interests in this respect against encroachment by product-oriented members of management.

People in these three managerial positions may find themselves in an invidious position. Many enterprises, in order to fulfill their plan targets, must violate to a greater or lesser extent various of the multitude of regulations and directives that reach them from higher authorities. If, however, one of these control officials decides to report illegal behavior by management to the higher authorities, life will not be made easy for him in the plant. And this is why the Soviet press frequently accuses the managers of various organizations of seeking to "live peacefully":

> For, despite the ever-present danger of prosecution, in the reality of Soviet economic life the man who seeks to avoid trouble feels that the best course is to go along with his immediate superior and his colleagues even in their unlawful actions, rather than take the unpopular course of informing on them to the state. (Berliner 1957:241).

It should be added here, however, that a manager responsible for monitoring the enterprise's activities is not entirely defenseless against his superiors. If he finds himself with his back to the wall, he can cause severe problems for the enterprise. Consequently, there exists a series of compromises and accommodations which enable this official to reach an understanding with the rest of the managerial staff, rather than enter into open conflict with them. The following account shows graphically how this comes about:

> Sometimes the molds were badly made, and this resulted in a certain part being too heavy. Therefore the final product will weigh fourteen tons instead of ten tons. I have to explain this error, but I cannot say that it is due to bad work. I must say that tests show that this added strength was necessary. The director will call in the chief design engineer to confirm this or everybody will get into trouble, and he is too small a man to object. If he should refuse to do it, the chief engineer and the director will remember this and he will never get a premium again. If he ever gets into any minor trouble, they will make it very hard for him. The chief design engineer often gets into trouble because his work is difficult and experimental, and he makes many mistakes.... This mutual relationship is called *krugovaia poruka*. It is very hard to free yourself of it. You can get out of it only if the ministry transfers you to another factory. (Berliner 1957:243)

Krugovaia poruka ("the web of joint complicity") is the set of forces that induce plant controllers to turn a blind eye (or both eyes). It must be added, however, that even if an enterprise's managing director wields considerable authority, his power is far from absolute. Consequently in the typical situation, where the "web of mutual involvement" exists, the three functionaries we described immediately beneath him do not passively submit to the wishes of the director—nor do they grant him complete license to take whatever measures (lawful or unlawful) necessary to fulfill the plan. Evidence would indicate that most such officials provide only qualified support for the actions of their director. Officials normally yield to the pressure of *krugovaia poruka*, but they avoid becoming completely defenseless. They will often insist on countersignatures on all potentially compromising documents (at times there may be more than ten signatures), or they make formal but vacuous protests, and so on. The director, for his part, does not blindly trust his colleagues: He keeps them under constant pressure, but he makes prudent use of bonuses and favors to keep the joint complicity system functioning smoothly. Thus:

> When a small group of officials have succeeded in establishing this atmosphere of a cautious mutual confidence, the system of *krugovaya poruka* flurishes and life is easier for all. The managerial group supports each other in their strivings for plan fulfillment and on occasion for their personal advantage. (Berliner 1957:244).

This raises an interesting question: It is well known that the Soviet system possesses a tight network of interlocking controls, and that harsh penalties are meted out for activities engaged in for personal profit—defined as "speculation"— the only exception being certain individual activities permitted in the service sector. How is it possible, then, in such a system, for production quotas of greater or lesser size to be siphoned off and sold on the market by groups of persons who share the profits? In other words, how can a "crypto-private enterprise" system (Grossman 1979a) take root and grow?

THE GEORGIANS

The unofficial practices described in the last section amount to various devices that are resorted to when lawful means are insufficient to fulfill the plan—the officially sanctioned objective. But there is also evidence that, in many cases, these practices are accompanied by considerations of personal interest. In other words, in the management of Soviet enterprises a shadowy area exists in which private interests do overlap company ones in various ways. However, often it is the company's interests that force this illegal behavior. In the words of one of Berliner's informants on the subject of *blat*:

> Sometimes this sort of activity was done for the sake of the enterprise and sometimes for the pocket of the one who sold the commodities. But in fact we were often compelled to do illegal things not for our own benefit but simply so that the enterprise could function. (Berliner 1957:197)

Nonetheless, often it happens that production for the plan is no longer the major concern; the main aim becomes the organization of a relatively substantial part of production for the personal profit of the member of the *krugovaia poruka*.

Several cases of illegal production camouflaged as production for the plan have been reported in various parts of the Soviet Union (Feldbrugge 1984; Simis 1982; Kroncher 1982a; Grossman 1979, 1981). On the bases of the evidence, it is fair to say that a "second economy" based on illegal activities and "crypto-private enterprises" is working in that country (Grossman 1979a; 1981). Of interest here is the question of how a "crypto-private-enterprise" operates, and what is its relation with the planning system from one side and the "second economy" from the other?

The only known empirical research on the organization of Soviet private-profit manufacturing has been conducted by Mars and Altman, who investigated the "second economy" in Soviet Georgia. The authors knew they were investigating unlawful activities in a society where sociological research is under strict political control. Thus, since their data could not be gathered *in situ*, they had to use a sample of Georgian emigrants living in Israel. Socioanthropological research techniques were used in an attempt to reconstruct the functioning of unofficial Soviet economic institutions and their underlying cultural base (Mars & Altman 1983:546–548).

In their study of the role played by industrial enterprises in the "second economy," Mars and Altman took as their initial point of reference the function of the *tolkach*, as described by Berliner, a plant's expert in under-the-table bartering. Their goal was to explain how the desire for personal enrichment can transform itself from a secondary drive into an overriding one—and one which will in fact become institutionalized in the presence of a favorable cultural context (Suny 1979).

Their data concerned three factories situated in different areas of Georgia: a bisquit factory with 200 workers, a textiles factory with 1000 workers, and a metalworking plant with fewer than 100 workers. The most significant features to emerge from Mars and Altman's reconstruction of the structure and function of "crypto-private enterprises" can be summarized as follows (Mars & Altman 1983; Mars 1987).

An indispensable precondition for the setting up of illegal production is the obtaining of the most "indulgent" plan possible, in order to accumulate sufficient spare capacity for illegal production. However, illegal production can be obtained by various other means. The first is winning a plan allowing for a higher level of production rejects. These rejects (which are such only on paper) are then used as the input to illegal production. The second is the obtaining of surplus raw materials from the official supply network, or from other enterprises.

It appears that the vast majority of employees are unaware of the existence of crypto-private production, even though they can guess what is going on behind the scenes. The reason is obvious: The fewer people in the know, the better the chances of not being discovered. Only when the quota of illegal output is high, and the involvement of a certain number of workers becomes necessary, are they chosen on the basis not of professional qualification but of their family's trustworthiness.

In other cases, as the study learned, not only were workers aware of what was happening, but they also took an active part in illegal production. In Georgia two managers (subsequently arrested) ran an illicit raincoat factory. One of these was the director of a state enterprise. This illegal factory was able to fulfill its plan targets by working only in the mornings. In the afternoons the workforce was ferried by taxis to an illegal operation, where raincoats of better quality than the official ones were manufactured. The raw materials, the machinery, and the building had been fraudulently obtained through official channels. The raincoats were sold in Georgia and other republics by traveling salesmen, who paid kickbacks to the managers in the state shops (Bukovsky 1979). In other areas of the USSR private production is most widespread among owners of private farming plots, who, being often workers, manufacture various type of tools and also minitractors. Crypto-private enterprises are usually set up on *kolkhoza* under the cover of ancillary enterprises (Kroncher, 1982b:4, 10).

Members of an illegal production scheme are usually very limited in number, and their working relations are characterized by a high degree of cooperation and informality. This close cooperation is necessary because, unlike illegal distribution, in illegal production it is impossible for one person to run the operation single-handed, however powerful and far reaching his collusion network might be. Illegal production, in fact, requires a well-established organization which can handle all the production and distribution stages.

The degree of complexity of the decision-making processes in an illegal organization depends on various structural variables, such as the ratio between the legal and illegal production, the degree of continuity of illegal production, and the number of suppliers and customers. For example, the organizers of the illegal biscuit-manufacturing scheme decided to keep illegal output at 25 percent of the total official amount, in order to maintain continuous flow of illegal production and to limit the number of suppliers and customers. Their illicit production thus became a matter of routine and required no complex decision-making procedures.

Mars and Altman apply the concept of "open sociotechnical system" to both legal and illegal organizations insofar as both interact with the same external bodies and deal with the same officials, the only difference being the form that these interactions take.

Apart from its dealings with customers and suppliers, the formal organization has contacts with the chief of the industrial association and the branch ministry, the plan authorities, and the local politicoadministrative organs. Among other groups, an official enterprise has only very rare dealings with two other bodies: the police and the Komsomol.

In order to understand the relationship between an illegal organization and the police and Komsomol we must refer to an observation made by all of Mars and Altman's informants: that the impetus toward illegal activities may be either from inside or outside the enterprise. The director's administrative superiors, the local political authority, and the police all expect to be paid off, not necessarily because they have positive proof of illicit activities in the enterprise but—knowing as they do how Soviet enterprise works (and how to profit from it)—they assume that illicit activity will take place as a matter of course (Mars & Altman 1983).

Mars & Altman make a prior distinction between authorities who are formally responsible for official management of an enterprise (planning bodies, ministries, industrial associations) and those who are not, such as the police and Komsomol. Among the first set of officials are authorities who "grant licenses" to operate and supply the official resources that will subsequently be used partly for private ends, or are those who simply "turn a blind eye."

Payments to these officials are defined as "licensing fees." In the second case, payments are made to those authorities who have no direct links with official management. The most important are police officials, who are bribed to block inquiries into administrative irregularities or—in cases where investigation is already under way—to arrange for a coverup. In these cases the payments are defined as "hush money" (Mars & Altman 1983).

The first set of authorities enjoy "obstructive" powers. They exercise control over the availability of resources which may be used in illicit activity. The second set exercise "reactive" powers insofar as they have the option of reacting or not in cases of unlawful activities (Mars & Altman 1983). The total amount of these payoffs is in proportion to the hierarchical level of the recipient within the two power structures. This is because the higher one goes in the hierarchy, the more diversified are the personal interests and aims compared with those of the local authorities. This means that when dealing with the higher authorities the risk factor is greater than when dealing at a local level, where cultural conditioning and the working of social networks is pervasive.

THE GOGOLIANS

The joint complicity system known as *krugovaia poruka* does not necessarily have as its objectives the fulfillment of certain planning targets nor the setting up of a crypto-private enterprise and distribution network. Yet a third goal exists: the obtaining of material and financial gain for production that exists only on paper. This case will be described largely from an account in a book by Soviet writer Shatunovsky (1970:82–85).

The episode took place in the 1960s, not in some outlying province but 250 kilometers from Moscow in a small factory making combs, soap dishes, and other toilet articles. The factory employs ninety-three workers who, judging from the fact that their warehouse is empty, seem to know their trade well:

But what is strange is this: of the 93 workers, 84 turn out to be on the managerial staff, and their number continues to grow. A few months ago a small section was closed. The machinery was removed and its place was taken by office furniture .... The office equipment is left untouched by the managerial staff: all they do is lounge around chatting and telling jokes.

The puzzled writer wanders the corridors of this strange building. The doors bear nameplates announcing "The Vice-Director for General Affairs," "Chief Construction Engineer," "Chief Mechanic," "Vice-Director of Personnel," and so forth. He decides to knock at a door—the door of Vice-Director P. R. Elkinson, who, when asked what the factory actually produces, hesitates and answers:

> "Well, to tell you the truth, this year we aren't producing anything."
> "Can I see then the production figures for last year?" Elkinson hesitates again. "We didn't produce anything last year, either. ..."

It turns out that no production is foreseen for the following year. All the same, three other persons work in the Production Vice-Director's section: an engineer and two technicians.

> "Well, what do your subordinates do, then?" Elkinson continues to dither. "Er, well, ... you sometimes wonder how you are going to keep your people busy tomorrow. But tomorrow comes around and there's always something for them to do. We don't sit around here doing nothing."
> "Tell me what they do, then. For example, what did your engineer and two technicians do yesterday?"
> "Engineer Grochotov is the president of the local section of the Red Cross. His name has also appeared on the roll of honor for his excellent work performances. Technician Kuravlev has been ill recently. Technician Zolotareva sings in an amateur choir. But she is not often at work—she's got a small child."
> "Yes, but I'd like to know what Engineer Grochotov actually does—apart from his voluntary activity."
> Elkinson hesitates again. ...

Interviews with the other "executives" continue in the same vein. For example, the "Internal Transport Manager" has only one crane operator in his section.

> "So you are managing?" asks the interviewer.
> "Yes, I am managing ..." he answers, blushing.

The "Vice-Director for General Affairs," however, does not bat an eye when he declares that his work consists of doing nothing in particular:

"But what are these 'general affairs' that you handle?"
"Well, it is like this.... What the director tells me to do, I do. Yesterday I went to the Post Office to send a letter. Last Saturday I met his mother-in-law...."

"But how could this 'old folks home' (*bogadelnia*) have been established and classified as a state organization?" asks Shatunovsky, whose astonishing experiences led him to entitle his book *Layabout Worker* (*Trudiashchisia Tuneiadets*). The following is a distillation of his findings.

Several years before there existed a certain production association with four member companies, one of whom had been the company in question. Subsequently, two of these enterprises changed their production profile and were moved to a different ministry. The third was transformed into a training workshop for a *tekhnikum* in the machine-building sector. Thus, a large association had to administer one small factory. Then someone had the bright idea of moving the administrative apparatus closer to production. So, much to their displeasure, the office workers found themselves transferred from the regional center to the district center, and then to the factory. Of reductions in administrative personnel, there was not a sign.

In the years preceding the account of Shatunovsky the factory had been subjected to at least fifty inspections and checks by local, republic, and national organs. No one, however, had shown the slightest surprise at the wildly disproportionate ratio between managers and workers.

Certainly, admits the writer, it is not always easy to recognize immediately that a certain organization is completely useless:

Take a look at a certain organization and you will see all the staff sitting so hunched over their desks that they seem glued to them. Nobody is lounging around doing nothing. They are all busy writing and making business telephone calls. They fix appointments, juggle with statistics, send off messages. The typewriters rattle like machine-guns. People tip-toe past the director's office. Inside, a special meeting is in progress, to which comrades from the local organs have been specially summoned.

In a word—Shatunovsky adds—everybody is busy, but it is all an elaborate pantomime:

> The messages leaving the offices are pointless. Nobody will read the forms that have been so dutifully filled in. And the meeting of local officials is discussing issues of no practical significance whatsoever. In this way, it is not just one individual that is wasting time (*bezdelnik*) but an entire organization—which is receiving money from the state but giving nothing in return.

This case represents a rare example of *gogolian management* in its purest state. A story that could have come straight from the pen of Gogol, it shows how a combination of *krugovaia poruka* and dramatic flair can give rise to a truly theatrical performance. Here only the input of the organization was real; the production process was *acted* and the output was immaterial. There exist, however, a certain number of organizations which can be defined as *partially gogolian* in the sense that the gogolian features show themselves only in personnel policy. A classical example, reported sometimes in the Soviet press, is the practice of placing fictitious workers on the payroll. These "dead souls," if they happen to correspond to real persons, receive a small part of their salary to keep them quiet. The rest goes to the enterprise, which needs cash for various reasons: either because it is involved in illicit production and needs payoff money, or because it must resort to the black market in order to overcome deficiencies in supply. In other cases the management makes a deal with some of its employees. The bookkeeping is rigged so that these employees receive extra rubles in their pay packets, which are then handed back to management (Simis 1982; Grossman 1979:842).

In reality, how frequent are such "gogolian" and "georgian" cases? Why do they take place?

A point to be considered is that the legal sector of the Soviet second economy (private farm plots, for instance) has become the springboard for a wide range of activities, ranging from the dubiously legal to the outright illegal. In fact, the legal part of the second economy appears to be a "visible tail wagging an invisible dog" (Feldbrugge 1984:530). Actually, the same can be said of the official economy and the system of central planning, as a few examples may demonstrate.

A garment factory received from its ministry new 1984 plan

targets which exceeded the capacity of the plant by 13 million rubles. The protests of the director were of no avail, and he was forced to follow the same creative bookkeeping of the ministry itself—that is, spread around the workshops of his enterprise the nonexistent 13 million rubles of the unrealistic plan. "Zero" (*nulevie*) units were created on paper. A corresponding number of fictitious workers were also hired. The result was that the enterprise had 71 mythical workers who were supposed to produce 168,000 men's shirts and 43,000 pairs of trousers in a year. At the end of the year, the ministry corrected the plan and canceled the original unrealistic targets. The case was reported by *Sotsialisticheskaia Industria* (April 8, 1984); the newspaper stressed that this is normal practice and not an exceptional case (Kroncher, 1985:6).

In Feldbrugge's article he reports several cases of "georgian" management that have been judged by the courts. The first was the running of a private factory which involved 2 million rubles; the second was the collection of "ghost workers" for a construction firm which involved only 12,000 rubles. Another case involving a huge amount of money occurred in the Caucasus: Some people were running a private fur workshop with a profit of 475,000 rubles.

Much more common than crypto-private enterprises are the cases of thieving and report padding. Sometimes the sums involved are really high, such as in the case of the cotton industry in Kazakhstan—a million rubles—or in a case concerning the railways, which involved 2.5 million rubles (Feldbrugge 1984:536–537). The origin of these phenomena can be traced back to the mechanism of planning "from the achieved level." The problem is that the level *has not been achieved*, so any added target for the next period becomes quite unreal. But, as the plan has to be fulfilled anyhow, the need for false additions is constantly reinforced. Thus enterprise managers "drive themselves even deeper into the trap" (Kroncher 1982:3).

CHAPTER 7

Workplace Industrial Relations

This chapter introduces the main functions of Soviet trade unions. These functions can be grouped under two headings: The first is organizing workers' participation in the leadership of production; the second is defending the material interests of working people and the safeguarding of their legal rights.

In the last ten to fifteen years, the question of legal rights of workers and trade unions has received increasing attention from the Party and the government. The result has been a series of resolutions all having two general aims. The first of these aims is to grant greater legal powers to trade unions in the handling of labor disputes and in checking the application of labor law. The second is to strive for a more global and "scientific" approach to social planning, that is, the preparation and distribution of all the social services that Soviet enterprise traditionally provides for its employees.

In this chapter the legal provisions and the programs of social planning, described in the previous section, are seen in the context of their impact on factory life. Some data are provided on issues such as "socialist competition" and other forms of worker participation, labor disputes, types of bargaining, and "plans for the social development of production collectives."

PARTICIPATING IN THE "LEADERSHIP OF PRODUCTION"

To describe the forms of shop-floor participation—and of joint administration by management, Party, and trade union—it is useful to refer to both the drafting and executive phases of production plans.

Both individual and collective participation in the drafting of a plan are provided for. The forms of collective participation are outlined throughout the chapter. Individual participation involves the rather peculiar system of individual plans, also known as "counterplanning" (*vstrechnie plana*), which means that, during a production conference, an individual worker will pledge himself to a certain quota of work for a certain period of time.

An idea of how such conferences went in the past is provided by the testimony of one of Berliner's informants—worth quoting in its entirety, despite its length:

> All the workers, all are called to the production conference. And then begins the so-called "counterplanning" in a very crude form, which quickly ends in a fiasco.... "I hope that some of the workers"—this is said by some engineer or a representative of the party organization— "will bring forth a counterproposal." Now, everyone wants to manifest his "activity." Some "butterfly," some "milkmaid," gets up from her place and says, "I think we should promise Comrade Stalin to overfulfill by 100 percent!" She takes no account of materials, no account of supply, nothing at all, but she just blurts out "100 percent!" Then a second stands up and says, "We all should promise 100 percent and I personally promise 150 percent!" In short, it piles up higher and higher, and the engineers and the economists scratch their heads. Nevertheless, this is called "counterplanning," a manifestation of the new socialist morality and higher socialist enthusiasm. All this goes up to the top and there, you understand, there is confusion, downright confusion, a complete muddle. (Berliner 1957:275–276)

Has the situation changed nowadays? The answer is yes, but only in the sense that the high-sounding bombast has gone. Production requirements have become more complex: Today attention is given not only to the gross-output indices, but to product quality, efficiency, and cost-effectiveness as well. However, with respect to these new indices, the inadequacies of production conferences (PDPS) and of counterplanning are frequently apparent.

As far as PDPS are concerned, three major deficiencies emerge: lack of PDPS members' experience with problems, insufficient time for discussion, and imprecise definition of the function of the conference. In a letter to a trade union journal, one author came to the following conclusion:

A conference can recommend this, a conference can recommend that, but the administration does whatever it likes. (Ruble 1983:93)

This does not seem a hasty judgment, but rather a correct synthesis of the effectiveness of the production conferences. Confirmation comes from the conclusion of two Soviet sociologists who, after ranging widely over the positive aspects of the system of workers' participation, add:

However, in a number of factories the picture is completely different. The administration and the social organizations take little notice of the conference work. Consequently, these conferences are convened infrequently—or not at all—and they function in a purely symbolic manner, playing no positive role whatsoever in the involvement of the workers in the management of production. (Volkov & Cherviakov 1977:30)

Other authors reach similar conclusions. After the obligatory praise for the great opportunity afforded by these forms of participation they report that—in a certain number of enterprises—the PDPS are feeble, many of their suggestions are never taken up, and they are often unable to discuss questions related to production efficiency (Gusakov 1972:187).

The conferences' members themselves are critical of the functioning of these bodies. At a chemical works in Sverdlovsk, only 3.4 percent gave a completely positive opinion of production conferences, 62 percent were not very satisfied, and 34.2 percent judged them as unsatisfactory (Volkov & Cherviakov 1977:130). Still in the region of Sverdlovsk, other research showed that 47 percent of the PDPS members interviewed thought that the conferences were effective in enhancing production. But when asked for detail, only 23 percent claimed that they had any influence over productivity, and even fewer (20 percent) that they had any influence over production quality or over cost-effectiveness (15 percent) (Iovchuk & Kogan 1972:198).

On the basis of these findings Soviet researchers drew up a scale showing the amount of influence exercised by various bodies in the management of production. The most influential turned out to be "Popular Control," although this in fact represented only 35.2 percent of the positive responses. The PDPS were regarded as influential by 20.4 percent; the Social Bureau of Planning by 14.4

percent; the Social Bureau of Economic Analysis by 12.6 percent, and the Social Bureau for Labor Standards by 11.7 percent (Iovchuk & Kogan 1972:204).

An idea of what informants mean by scant influence of these participatory bodies is provided by the writer Gelman, screenwriter for the film *The Prize* (referring to a production bonus)

> Initiative and critical thinking are much valued nowadays, but sometimes persons who do not really possess these qualities pretend that they do. Pseudo-specialists in criticism deal only with trivial matters, things that are easily spotted and corrected: the kind of criticism that executives are pleased to hear. (Gelman 1977:16)

As for individuals' pledges to increase production, recent articles in the Soviet press reveal that they are not taken too seriously by the workers concerned, and that the checks on individual production performances are perfunctory. In effect, the chronic problem of "formalism" (*formalnost*) is far from being overcome because the setting up of work standards for the fulfilling of personal targets is not taken seriously, more often than not.

The work brigade is nowadays regarded as one of the main devices for introducing the logic of economic efficiency at shopfloor level. The brigade should raise the individual sense of responsibility toward work on the one hand and facilitate the development of industrial democracy on the other (Malle 1984; Rutland 1984). To achieve efficiency, the awarding of bonuses is conducted by the brigade as a whole on the basis of a "coefficient of work participation" ranging from zero to 1.4. To achieve democratization, the leaders of the brigade are set up to deal directly with the plant administration (*Sovetskie Profsoyuzi* 1981:6).

However, distinctly contrasting situations are reported by the Soviet press, even for the same factory. Thus, for example, at the Baltic Yards of Leningrad, the objectives of individual responsibility and industrial democratization were only achieved by the ship-launching section. In other sections, workers were still employed to do piecework. Where brigades were operating, however, the "coefficient of participation" was not applied and premiums were distributed equally or according to the level of qualification. In total, only 17 percent of the existing brigades were judged on their final results. Many brigades only existed on paper because of the

TABLE 7.1 *Assessment of Work and Labor Relations by Workers in a Machine Factory*

| | Departments | | | |
Answers	Automatic Machinery	Instru- mentation	Engines	Assembly
You have no chance of improving your qualifications.	3.4[a]	4.2	10.8	9.4
I do not see any great social significance in my work.	6.9	4.2	3.1	9.4
You can do the work without thinking.	6.9	4.2	10.8	3.7
Heavy work.	10.3	12.1	23.1	3.7
Repetitive work.	23.8	16.7	13.8	26.4
Irregular supply of work materials.	48.3	16.7	18.5	15.1
Obsolete machinery.	48.3	20.8	27.7	3.7
Poor organization of work.	65.5	45.8	35.3	–
Poor accident prevention.	17.2	4.2	27.7	3.7
Inconvenient shifts.	3.4	12.1	9.2	5.7
Relations with workmates not always good.	6.9	4.2	–	3.7
Relations with management not always good.	48.3	20.8	32.3	20.7
No answer.	3.4	12.1	–	15.1

[a] Percentage of workers responding.
SOURCE: Dmitrik (1982:42).

"passive attitude towards innovation" in the workplaces (*Sovetskie Profsoyuzi* 1981:7).

Any attempt to understand the problems involved in the generalization of the brigade model must take into account the chronically vulnerable points (*uzkie mesta*) in Soviet planning and production: the uncertainties in procurement of human and material resources, the bad organization of work, the often inadequate technological level of machinery. Table 7.1, which contains the workers' self-assessments of their work situation in a Minsk machine plant, can be taken as an example of a state of affairs quite common in Soviet factories.

According to Stolyar, the relations between workers and administration are psychologically conditioned by the work organization in the shops and by the behavior of management. Workers justly claim that it is the administration's responsibility to provide favorable working conditions:

> But, in many factories a whole series of problems remain to be solved in this area. The great majority of workers are satisfied with their work in their brigades, but not with the work organization: they report irregularities in the supply of raw material and pieces, frequent stop-and-go in the production cycles, "storming", overtime, bad working conditions, and the persistence of many manual operations that could be mechanized. (Stolyar 1973:83)

All these problems have been reported for decades, in many factories and in diverse regions, to such an extent that they can be taken as a summary of all the difficulties faced by plant management in the country. All these difficulties, in turn, cause tension and conflicts among working people, between the members of the brigade and its leader, and between brigade and management. Stolyar correctly diagnoses the root of the problem when he writes:

> The road towards the elimination of these deficiencies of production management is strewn with obstacles, whose overcoming in many cases does not directly depend on either the workplace or the plant administration, but on action to be taken by top management as well as ministerial and district party organization. (Stolyar 1973:84)

If the plant administration cannot deal with these problems upstream, then it may be tempted to intervene downstream by either widening or narrowing the brigades' rights and duties with respect to regulations. For example, the administration can delegate certain technico-administrative duties to the brigades, such as the setting up of performance indices. But the administration can also act in the opposite direction. In the case, for example, of insufficient manpower, the management can decide on premiums and upgrading, ignoring the brigade's recommendations. Consequently:

> The ignoring of individual's competence sometimes brings excessive isolation, and results in the *krugovaia poruka* (covering up for absentees and for damages, slowing down of the pace of work, hostility towards new brigade members, etc.). In many cases, *krugovaia poruka* is the *workers defense strategy* against the administration's failure to manage

the production process and labor relations properly [italics added]. (Stolyar 1973:85)

Here, clearly, the same defense mechanism adopted by management is used by the work brigade to cope with uncertainties and problems unloaded onto it by higher authorities. Thus, informal practices and defense mechanisms are adopted not only by management against planning authorities, but also by work groups at the shop-floor level against management.

So, what has been the real impact of all those participatory instruments (both old and new) designed to guarantee the intensive development of production and the spread of economic accountability in the production units?

The statistics on workers' participation in the leadership of production are impressive. To give only one example: At the end of the 1970s the total number of "shock workers" (*udarniki*) was approximately 24 million. Berliner has shown long ago that the reason why the figures are so impressive is because the quantity of "mass participation" is one of the main indices used to judge the performance of Party and trade union officials. But what does this participation really consist of? Let us take first an example from the past:

> With management's help a Stakhanovite "show" is put on. One young worker is selected for the starring role, and he is set to work on the best machines, provided with the best materials, and aided in every way to break a production record. Similarly, a large number of rationalization suggestions are formally accepted and paid for, which satisfies the party and trade union, and most of them are filed in the waste basket, which satisfies management. The former can report great success in stimulating mass participation, and the latter can keep mass participation under control. (Berliner 1957:274)

These scenes refer to the 1940s and 1950s, but what is the situation today? The "shock workers" still exist. And how does one become a "shock worker"? An example is given by N. Morosov and V. Prokushev in a *Pravda* article entitled (Sept. 6, 1983:2) "And they Call Him Udarnik." It transpired that in a lumber yard of Krasnoyarsk only 13 of the 179 *udarniki* had achieved the average productivity level of the branch. In the No. 2 Transport company, the title was conferred on a list of names by order of the management. The same article goes on to say that as soon as a production unit distinguishes itself to the slightest degree, it immediately receives the title of "Communist Collective." It is no surprise, then, to learn that a commission set up in 1982 by a local Party committee and the trade union discovered that in the local metallurgical industry half of the *udarniki* did not meet standards set by the commission. Why, then, is the title of *udarnik* conferred so easily? The fact is that if at least two-thirds of the workers of an enterprise earn the *udarniki* title, the factory wins the title of "Communist Labor Collective." Plant managers, therefore, try to keep the number of title-winners high, presumably because this will work in their favor when negotiating production targets and resources with higher authorities.

Here a question arises. That is: What are the attitudes of the "normal" workers toward the *udarniki*? In the Polish film, *The Man of Marble*, set in the 1950s, a young "shock worker" in one scene is laying an incredible quantity of bricks in record time when malicious fellow workers arrange for him to pick up a scorching-hot brick. Is the present situation any different? Yes, in the sense that the formalistic approach to "shock labor" has in some way defused the tensions in the workplace; no, in the sense that nowadays, as in the past, the *udarniki* seem not to be much loved or respected by their fellow workers, as the following cases demonstrate.

A Soviet economic journal reports on a steelworks where a champion labor brigade was employed. Headed by the foundryman Fomin, the brigade had won a national "socialist competition." The results of a survey carried out in the factory showed that 70 percent of the respondents thought that the brigade was mediocre, did not deserve its official reputation, and received privileged treatment from the administration. The author of the article goes on to say that such fame provokes hostility because, independently of his qualities as a person, the model worker represents a threat to his workmates in the sense that they fear a tightening of production norms for the near future (Tselms 1977). To support this observation, we can quote the results from one of the rare "participant observations" carried out by Soviet sociologists. The research, conducted in the Vladimir Ilyich factory of Moscow, focused on the ethical norms governing the interactions in the work groups and the sanctions adopted by the group to induce its members to conform to these norms.

In that factory was a brigade that distinguished itself from others by its slightly higher productivity. The administration exaggerated the brigade's results, praised its members on the radio and in the company newspaper, and so forth. However:

> The workers' shop collective reacted very negatively to this brigade and called its members "boot-lickers" (*podkhalimov*), "braggarts" (*khvastunov*), and "exhibitionists" (*vyskochek*). (Selyukov 1971:14)

Another aspect of the so-called productive self-government of the workers is "socialist competition." In discussions of the 1950s this has been called *paradnoi shumiki* ("the ballyhoo"). Today's version of socialist competition can be characterized by some letters to the press written by "heroes of labor" and people involved in the handling of this movement. The letters describe how socialist competition works in its various phases: involvement of the working people, definition of output commitments, and the final account of results.

The first letter comes from the Dzerzhinski tractor factory in Volgograd. Written by a fitter honored with the title "Knight of the Order of Lenin and the October Revolution," it is entitled "After the Thunder ... Silence." The letter begins by describing the start of the working day. The first thing the worker does when entering the shop is called "chasing the deficit"—that is, checking what material is lacking at the various work stations and then trying to obtain the needed materials from the next shop. In this way—according to the author—the section foremen have to become *tolkachi* ("expediters") (*Sovetskie Profsoyuzi*, 1:1980:9–10).

The supply problem must be severe if production stoppages last sometimes for more than half a shift, obliging workers to do overtime and work on rest-days to compensate. But "storming" on Saturday and Sunday causes, in turn, imbalances in the production cycle from batch preparation to assembly. How does "socialist competition" function under these conditions?

> Well, let's say that master Rumyantsev is top worker in his shift for a week. Everyone congratulates him and his photograph is stuck up with a lot of ballyhoo. But after the ballyhoo—silence once again.

The following week, the same scene repeats itself with another collective, and when the monthly accounts are made, top place will go to the shift that has done the most overtime and worked the most rest-days:

> And this is what they call "competition!" It's no surprise that we regard these production competitions as sheer formalism (*splashnoi formalnost*) and that nobody takes the results seriously. (*Sovetskie Profsoyuzi*, 1:1980:9)

The author concludes that these deficiencies are so deeply rooted that, by now, people have grown accustomed to them and no longer pay them any attention. Thus, each section of the factory is concerned only with its own interests and treats the overall result with indifference. All this is detrimental to the quality and regularity of the production sequence because the staff responsible for organizing "socialist competition" limits itself to merely toting up the results. Moreover, this "staff" sometimes exists only on paper—it is the administration that compiles the final results table, without the participation of the social organizations (*Sovetskie Profsoyuzi*, 1:1980:9).

When this letter appeared in print, a debate ensued, sometimes with the editor's comment that not all of the opinions expressed were shared by the editorial board of *Sovetskie Profsoyuzi*. Among the most interesting letters on this subject was one from an engineer in charge of organizing socialist competition at the Kirov Tool Works in Tbilisi.

The letter begins by pointing out that once the republic's trade union council has decided to embark on a certain project, it must be adhered to by every factory. The technological and organizational features of an individual factory are of no importance—neither is the fact that this new project may clash with one already in progress:

> Usually, everyone is given a certain length of time to carry out the project. On the closing-date the collective has to report how many people have taken part, the economic effect, and so forth. But everyone in the factory knows: the greater the support reported for the project, the better. (*Sovetskie Profsoyuzi*, 2:1980:8)

After providing various examples of how these "projects" only exist on paper, the writer concludes by describing how the "socialist competition" results are arrived at:

You start every morning with solicitous telephone calls to the Factory Committee. When all the deadlines have passed, there's nothing else to do but go and get information on the results of socialist competition yourself. You enter the office of the president of the FZMK and you catch him "red-handed" faking the report of the assembly where the results are supposed to have been compiled. Formalism? Certainly. But this is imposed formalism, and neither I nor the other members of the Factory Committee have the right to punish him for it. (*Sovetskie Profsoyuzi*, 2:1980:9)

A third letter continues the theme of formalism, listing its three most common aspects. First, disparities among the results achieved by various participants in the competition are not taken into consideration:

Of course, there's the "coefficient of participation" which is set monthly by the brigade soviet. But how? On the basis of the number of shifts, the level of discipline, and the quality of work. However, only the first two indices and the skill grade count when the results are announced and the prizes awarded. Quality and the other factors in an individual's contribution are only estimated roughly, not properly calculated. So it becomes impossible to make comparisons among the results obtained by the individual competitors. (*Sovetskie Profsoyuzi*, 17:1980:8–9)

The fact that disparities in individual results are not taken into account is explained by the lack of criteria for assessing the individual performances. And this is the second aspect of formalism. The third is reminiscent of the procedures adopted sometimes by certain Italian political parties in order to increase membership, for example: "So-and-so has been called upon to take part in the competition ... but how? They write down his name without his having the faintest idea that he has been entered" (*Sovetskie Profsoyuzi*, 17: 1980:8).

The debate concludes with an article written by a senior trade union officer. The article, for obvious reasons, gives a generally positive assessment of socialist competition, but all the points made by the previous letter are confirmed. Among reasons for formalism the senior union officer cites the following: The organizational model is the same everywhere—whether or not the same economic and organizational conditions apply. Says the writer: "The conditions are badly thought out, and then issued in carbon copy" (*Sovetskie Profsoyuzi*, 24: 1980:9).

The importance of this last letter is clear: The writer's position gives her an overview of the entire problem. The fact that she confirms the criticism made in the preceding letters demonstrates how far they reflected a general unsatisfactory state of affairs.

Further confirmation of the widespread nature of the formalistic approach is provided by research conducted by Soviet sociologists. According to Melnikov, the main deficiencies of socialist competition are the following: badly organized work that makes it difficult to fulfill the output commitments, which, in turn, are often vague and badly formulated; the management's over-hasty awarding of honorary titles to collectives who still have not fulfilled their quotas—sometimes with the sole intention to give people incentive to fulfill the plan targets (Melnikov et al. 1973:153–154).

Another study conducted on a sample of 4145 workers from various factories in the district of Sverdlovsk, reports that the majority of respondents thought that "socialist competition" still had not realized its true potential in the achievement of those objectives for which it was designed: the instilling of a "sense of ownership of the factory" (*chuvstvo khoziaina*), improving technology, the rational use of work time, improved quality of output, reduced waste, the bringing of new reserves to the fore, and so forth (Volkov & Cherviakov 1977:110).

The participation of workers in the leadership of production has a third aspect: the movement of "rationalizers" of production processes and "inventors." Here, too, of particular relevance is a letter written by a lathe operator in a Moscow factory and published by the trade union journal. The writer—a known "rationalizer"—begins by observing that many of the widely publicized suggestions for rationalization amount often to merely pointing out simple errors in design and construction that have been noticed by the workers while using the machinery. Nevertheless, it is "rationalization" that gets much of the publicity in the mass media, while far less attention is devoted to "invention" (*izobretatelstvo*). Why is this so? Technical innovation is the most effective way of increasing productivity and improving the quality of output, says the "rationalizer," but the fact is that

every manager is aware that innovation will bring economic advantages not only to his own factory, but to many others. However, this will happen at some time in the future. In the meantime, the innovation could easily become a nuisance and put the plan fulfillment at risk—with a consequent loss of premiums and other benefits. (*Sovetskie Profsoyuzi* 23: 1980:8)

So, nobody in the factory mentions technological innovation. Its introduction will depend entirely on "the energy and insistence of the person proposing it" (*Sovetskie Profsoyuzi* 23: 1980:9).

Neither is the cause of innovation furthered by those who are supposedly in charge of it. The central council of the Soviet of Inventors and Rationalizers (VOIR) is only rarely able to accelerate the introduction of new ideas—despite the fact that the spread of technological innovation would make a significant contribution to solving a major problem of Soviet enterprises: the shortage of manpower (*Sovetskie Profsoyuzi*, 23: 1980:9).

Research conducted in several factories in Chelyabinsk on behalf of the local Party committee confirms the state of affairs described in the last letter. The sample comprised 438 workers and 592 technicians and engineers (ITR). Negative evaluations of the way in which "technical creativity" associations operate were given by 20 percent of respondents. The most widespread complaint was that they have a *pokaznoi kharacter*, that is, that they are a sort of window dressing. This answer was given by 9 percent of the workers and 20 percent of ITR. Among the ITR no less than 38 percent gave negative evaluations (Nesterov 1969:107).

Another problem concerns the amount of effective notice an enterprise will take of suggestions for rationalization. The testimonies gathered by Berliner have already indicated that management does not usually set much store by these suggestions, and contemporary Soviet research confirms this impression. In the *Elektrosila* factory of Leningrad, for example, 61 out of 107 "rationalizers" pointed to the "bureaucratic mentality" of the management as the major obstacle to the introduction of new ideas, and only 24 were of the opinion that they encountered no obstacles (Nesterov 1969:148). And *Elektrosila* is frequently praised in the Soviet press. Here, however, one has to be aware that the so-called bureaucratic mentality is a definition taken from the official sloganeering that hides managerial behaviors that are not bureaucratic but oriented toward the research of a "safety factor" against planning uncertainties (as indicated in the preceding chapter).

TRADE UNIONS, BARGAINING, AND LABOR DISPUTES

There is a difference in meaning between the use of the terms *trade unions, bargaining,* and *labor disputes* in the USSR and in the West—both in theory and in practice.

The Soviet trade unions have a dual function: to stimulate working people to improve their performance and, at the same time, to protect their rights. These two functions are described here beginning with the various ways in which trade unions seek to improve production.

To illustrate this function, let us describe a case where a meeting is convened by the FZMK (Factory Committee of trade union) to examine the production accounts for the preceding months. The meeting has been going on at the paper *kombinat* of Volzhk. A senior engineer from the plan section makes the report and announces that the plan targets for the main indices have not been fulfilled. He lists the reasons: nondelivery of raw materials, machinery lying idle, waste, uneconomic use of resources.

> You expect these remarks to be followed by a detailed analysis of the errors and failures in the handling of "socialist competition" for the best use of productive resources.... Not a bit of it. No useful, effective discussion follows, and a few minutes later the assembly passes the bland resolution: "The information has been duly noted." (*Sovetskie Profsoyuzi,* 1:1981:24)

But, asks the correspondent, what point is there in giving this information to the FZMK if they are not capable of drawing any conclusion from it, and if there is no debate at the meeting?

After a description of another, very similar, meeting of the production conference, the correspondent of the union's journal concludes that once again there has been a mere recording of the information followed by a pro forma resolution. But the *kombinat* is a member of the national movement of "social control" on the efficient use of materials and energy. To this purpose a commission has been set up and issues high-sounding resolutions. Thus, the journal correspondent comments: "But where is any attempt at a thorough analysis of things as they really stand? Where is the careful reasoning? Where, finally, is the truth? (*Gde nakonets istina?*)" And the correspondent's report concludes thus:

TABLE 7.2   *The Practice of Workers' Meetings (n = 6,700)*

Issue Debated	Number of questions	Total number of speeches	Number of speeches by workers	Total number of suggestions	Number of suggestions adopted
Figures regarding work by the collective in the preceding month or year	1135	2141	1527	751	571
State of machinery and equipment	175	406	316	255	191
Technological innovation	115	247	174	131	110
Product quality	265	530	289	305	256
Measures to reduce stoppages and delays in production	211	373	360	94	40
Supplies	93	295	112	80	54
Possible increases in productivity	283	489	270	494	273
Reduction in production costs	76	193	127	93	72
Improving the economic calculation	32	75	49	50	36
Scientific organization of work, improving the environment and culture of production	177	276	147	369	333
Improving wage levels	45	145	111	36	29
Labor standards	56	150	129	53	45
Technical training and retraining	72	169	94	58	47
Raising the cultural level of the workers	44	125	71	49	50
Discipline on the job	224	698	526	146	124
Others	146	102	226	71	34

SOURCE: Iovchuck and Kogan (1972:201).

As the saying goes, "on paper everything runs smoothly." ... The conditions are good, they say. Appeals are drafted. Finely worded reports are typed. The minutes are printed. But what's the use of all this if nothing in the *kombinat* has changed to the benefit of the people? (*Sovetskie Profsoyuzi*, 1: 1981:25)

TABLE 7.3 Levels of Interest Shown by Workers in Production Progress

| | Enterprises | | | | | | | | |
	NTMK	TMZ	UVZ	UETM	KRZ	URAL KABEL	SZP	SKK	Average %
Are you aware of the progress of the "production programmes"									
In your department?									
Yes	88.1[a]	75.7	63.1	63.7	88.8	63.0	72.6	73.6	76.0
Not always	7.6	16.5	15.1	21.2	8.4	16.9	22.8	12.5	15.0
No	4.3	7.8	1.8	15.1	2.8	20.1	4.6	13.9	9.0
In the factory?									
Yes	59.9	34.7	66.3	32.4	66.6	26.9	30.0	39.4	44.5
Not always	23.2	25.9	20.8	27.2	21.2	11.1	36.7	21.2	23.3
No	16.9	39.7	12.9	40.4	12.2	62.0	33.3	39.4	32.2
Do you know if the enterprise is operating at a profit or a loss									
In your Department?									
Yes	60.9	67.3	72.4	64.5	68.3	51.9	78.0	63.8	65.8
Not always	23.6	18.0	15.4	12.1	12.1	18.2	10.1	15.4	15.6
No	15.5	14.7	12.2	23.4	19.6	29.9	11.9	20.7	18.6
In the factory?									
Yes	44.7	65.5	74.9	52.3	49.1	26.2	53.5	55.1	52.6
Not always	27.9	11.8	9.3	16.9	18.5	6.5	12.7	14.8	14.8
No	27.4	22.7	15.8	30.8	32.4	67.3	33.8	30.1	32.5

[a] Percentage of those giving a particular answer.
SOURCE: Iovchuck and Kogan (1972: 202).

121

Actually, the trade union meetings, and the workers assemblies convened to deal with production problems, very often consist of a formulaic "monthly, three-monthly, or yearly balance sheet; production quotas for the following period." Significant confirmation of this is provided by the responses given by the 6700 workers surveyed in the sample of Iovchuk and Kogan (Table 7.2).

Soviet sociological literature lays great emphasis on the issue of stimulating workers' interest in the leadership of production and encouraging them to greater participation. Nevertheless, this interest seems not to be very high—as Table 7.3 indicates.

In order to increase workers' interest in management, two courses of action are proposed: improving education and "economic propaganda" on the one hand, and improving the system of incentives on the other. Regarding the first course of action, Iovchuk and Kogan (1972) report that workers' interest in management, however, cannot be aroused merely by giving economic and political training to as many people as possible. The problem, for them consists mainly in improving the quality of such training. The findings of these authors suggest that little progress is being made in this direction, and that, in any case, there are great differences among the kinds of training provided in different production units.

A study on the effectiveness of economic training was carried out in a sample of 965 workers in two factories in the Urals. In the first factory, out of 180 respondents 124 (69 percent) answered that they did not get any benefit from attending economic courses, and many added: "Better-trained managers are needed." In the other factory the picture was more favorable: 74 percent regarded economic training as good or satisfactory; almost 17 percent did not reply; and only 9.2 percent judged it unsatisfactory. Other authors think that these different assessments of the training programs are related to the practical consequences gained from the attendance of the courses (upgrading, for example) (Volkov & Cherviakov 1977:96–97).

The other major question is production incentive schemes. Table 7.4 shows that only 56–60 percent of respondents saw a correlation between wage levels and plant output. As for workers' assessment of the incentive effect of premiums and other material rewards, Table 7.5 gives some significant data. First, more than three-fourths of the informants thought that incentives led to increased productivity. However, the underlying concept of productivity here seems

TABLE 7.4 Worker Assessment of the Interdependence of Wage Levels and Collective Work Performance

				Enterprises						Average %
	NTMK	TMZ	UVZ	UETM	KRZ	URAL KABEL	SZP	SKK		
Does your pay depend on the overall work performance										
Of the brigade?										
Yes	69.5[a]	53.2	53.4	44.9	58.7	33.3	74.3	62.9		56.2
No	13.8	31.9	18.3	38.8	12.8	20.8	5.3	22.2		20.4
Don't know	16.7	14.9	28.3	16.3	28.5	45.9	20.4	14.9		23.1
Of the department?										
Yes	55.1	61.3	63.4	44.3	72.8	67.3	68.8	42.7		59.4
No	15.7	22.2	16.1	45.5	11.1	10.9	9.2	32.1		20.3
Don't know	29.2	16.5	20.5	10.2	16.1	21.8	22.0	25.2		20.3
Of the workshop?										
Yes	67.9	52.6	67.7	59.4	38.2	58.6	38.2	58.6		56.5
No	8.0	24.9	15.8	36.2	9.4	10.8	2.6	20.7		16.0
Don't know	24.1	22.3	26.6	12.0	22.9	29.8	59.2	20.7		27.5
Of the Factory?										
Yes	52.1	45.8	46.5	39.1	47.9	17.6	38.2	58.6		43.2
No	13.5	21.3	18.3	37.7	8.7	29.4	2.6	19.1		18.8
Don't know	34.4	32.9	35.2	23.2	43.4	53.0	59.2	22.3		38.0

[a] Percentage of answers given for each question.
SOURCE: Iovchuk and Kogan (1972: 211).

123

TABLE 7.5 *Worker Assessment of Pay and Incentive Schemes*

				Enterprises						Average %
	NTMK	TMZ	UVZ	UETM	KRZ	URAL KABEL	SZP	SKK		
Does the pay system encourage you to *Increase productivity?*										
Yes	78.3	73.3	89.9	74.8	71.2	63.2	81.9	68.4		76.4
Not enough	13.9	14.7	6.4	6.9	10.7	16.4	9.1	13.7		11.5
No	7.8	12.0	3.7	18.3	18.1	20.4	9.0	17.9		12.1
Fight against waste?										
Yes	71.1	71.5	52.7	58.3	77.5	41.7	67.5	54.4		65.6
Not enough	9.5	17.6	5.7	18.5	12.1	13.4	17.3	8.3		12.7
No	19.4	10.9	41.6	23.2	10.4	44.9	15.2	7.3		21.7
Take a more active part in discussion of production problems at assemblies?										
Yes	56.5	54.7	67.0	58.3	68.4	27.8	60.1	70.9		58.0
Not enough	19.7	27.0	20.7	18.5	19.1	32.7	18.9	13.9		21.3
No	23.8	18.3	12.3	23.2	12.5	39.5	21.0	15.2		20.7
Take a more active part in the work of the social organizations involved in management?										
Yes	56.5	34.4	46.9	43.2	49.3	7.0	38.8	45.7		40.3
Not enough	19.7	32.2	24.4	28.4	28.5	24.5	31.3	25.6		26.8
No	23.8	33.4	28.7	28.4	22.2	68.5	29.9	27.5		32.9
Achieve a greater volume of work with fewer people?										
Yes	30.6	44.4	47.7	51.6	46.3	44.4	26.9	31.4		40.4
Not enough	19.7	21.2	17.2	11.6	22.8	12.7	19.6	19.2		18.0
No	49.7	34.4	35.1	36.9	30.9	42.9	53.5	49.4		41.6

[a] Percentage of answers given for each question.
SOURCE: Iovchuk and Kogan (1972: 214).

to be one that is typically Soviet: Produce more, but do not worry too much about waste or production costs. In fact, the incentive values diminish by 11 percent when considered in terms of reduction of waste and are almost halved in terms of true efficiency and productivity that is, increased input using reduced manpower (40 percent of affirmative answers). Second, it turns out that more than two-thirds of respondents did not feel sufficiently motivated by incentives to increase their active participation in the various bodies concerned with managing production.

It should also be borne in mind that, in the present phase of "developed socialism," the management of social welfare plays an increasingly important role in encouraging greater productivity and increasing the intake of workers into the labor market (Boccella, 1980:131–47). A question here arises: How many people actually enjoy the social services managed jointly by factory administration and trade union? A rough picture of the situation can be derived from the following data.

At the Sixteenth Trade Union Congress of 1977, it was reported that there were 113.5 million union members in the USSR. The Congress Report stated that the total number of workers was 74 million and that the trade union holiday centers and rest homes could accommodate 735,000 persons at a time (Shibaev, *CDSP* 1977:8–9). President Shelepin declared that in the period 1964–1967 an average of 5.7 million people per year passed through the holiday centers and rest homes. By 1971 this figure had risen to 7.6 million, and by 1975 to 8.3 million. From these figures it is clear that less than 10 percent of the working population enjoyed this kind of social service. The situation is better for Soviet children in the sense that half of them passed through the Pioneer camps (Madison 1979:93).

The management of social services is not immune, of course, to the disorganization so widespread in other areas. A major reason for this is that construction of holiday centers and rest homes fails to keep pace with the rising working population—even if worker increase is very slow. As a result, amenities are overcrowded and provide substandard services, and many people who should go to rest homes are sent to holiday centers and vice versa (Madison 1979:104). There are also severe bureaucratic problems in deciding a worker's eligibility for a certain service. Administrative inefficiency is a major problem, and radical solutions do not seem to be in sight. The Soviet welfare system lacks access to information on incomes of benefit claimees because these remain in the files of the workplace. And even if the latter were to supply information to a centralized institution, the technical means available could not process it. As a result, many errors are committed, which, in turn give rise to a multitude of complaints. This is understandable: One would hardly expect trade union delegates—who are largely indifferent to these issues—to rouse themselves sufficiently to provide an efficient welfare service (Madison 1979:108).

A further consideration of the Soviet social welfare system concerns its meritocratic nature. On the one hand, the government has long pursued a policy of standardizing basic salaries—a policy which only now is going to change; on the other it has made use of pensions, sickness pay, maternity benefits, rent subsidies, and so forth to obtain increases in productivity of labor and to reduce worker turnover rates. The essence of the Soviet welfare state has been brilliantly captured by A. McAuley:

> In his *Pygmalion*, George Bernard Shaw has the dustman Doolittle make a distinction between the deserving and undeserving poor. The former are those who adopt the attitudes of the dominant class in society and attempt to live by their precepts; the undeserving poor are the rest. Adapting these concepts, it is possible to conclude that the Soviet welfare state has been designed to cope with the needs of deserving families. It offers little help, or even understanding, to the undeserving. There is little overt sympathy expressed for the inadequate or the incompetent, for those who one might call social deviants, and few attempts made to explain their behaviour in terms of the social and economic pressures to which they are subject. (McAuley 1981:228)

Since the "deserving" are so few and the "undeserving" so many, the motivating power of social welfare is considerably reduced.

The difficulties of the trade union in its role as "School of Communism and Management" do not stem only from the reasons quoted in the preceding paragraphs. The most fundamental difficulties stem from the way in which Soviet factories are actually managed. As Gusakov has pointed out:

> It quite often happens that collectives worked successfully for technical improvements or to reorganize ... only to find themselves at a disadvantage with respect to those enterprises that continue to work in the old way (Gusakov 1972:47)

The economic reform of 1965 should have radically changed this state of affairs, and the same reformist intention is expressed now by the new Soviet leadership. It seems, however, that observations such as the following are still valid:

> Unfortunately, it still happens in many enterprises that the workers receive premiums for indices that add nothing to effective output. Also the premiums for these indices are paid as much out of the wages fund as out of the funds provided for the incentive scheme. Under these conditions, the premiums are simply transformed into ordinary pay bonuses and have nothing to do with any real extra contribution to output by the workers. (Gusakov, 1972:160)

Here one enters the field of wage cheating: a long-standing and deep-rooted practice in Soviet factories. The testimonies gathered by Berliner list the following as the most common strategems: (1) the making out of orders (*nariadi*) for work that has not been carried out (especially the movement of materials); (2) the making out of orders where the amount done is overestimated; (3) the programming of work on the basis of official norms, but in fact applying easier norms (Berliner 1957:174–175).

Wage cheating is widespread mainly because of the manpower shortage. But there are also an array of minor causes: inaccuracy in the planning of wage levels; availability of extra payments for those who temporarily perform tasks inferior to their qualifications; payments for work time lost during stoppages for organizational malfunctions; and, finally, the pressure brought by workers on their brigade leaders and foremen to find ways to increase their wage packets (Berliner 1957:174–175). And the foremen quite often comply with workers' unofficial pressures. Thus, it is not rare to find references in newspapers to the "leveling-down of the collective," "indiscriminate awarding of premiums," "premiums to everyone: good or bad" (Di Leo 1973:179–187).

As discussed at the beginning of this chapter, the other basic function of the trade union is to safeguard workers' rights. Studying how this function is performed in practice can start with an example from an important and technologically advanced factory.

A trade union journal printed a letter from a group of crane-loaders, entitled "And the Workers Weren't Asked," denouncing the bad working conditions in the heavy machine-building *kombinat* at Zhdanov. The complaint centered on: (1) the arrogant treatment of the workers by the workshop managers; (2) difficult and hazardous working conditions; (3) reductions of piecework rates by the office of work organization—to the indifference of the FZMK.

That these complaints were justified was confirmed by the correspondent of the trade union journal. He reported, for instance, that during a two-year period nineteen accidents had occurred while heavy frames and beams were being transported, and that one of these accidents had been serious. He also reported that: (1) working conditions in various departments were definitely dangerous; (2) the general tendency was to make improvements in production, but not in auxiliary activities; (3) the cause of these hazardous working conditions was the fact that orders were not carried out immediately—contrary to what was believed by the management. The complaints about labor norms and the trade union's behavior were justified, too.

According to labor law and the company's contract, any modification of production norms must be discussed by workers' meetings. But when asked why this had not happened, the chairman of the FZMK answered: "*Esli po takomu voprosi sobrania sozyvat, to i rabotat budet nekogda*" ("If we had to call an assembly for this sort of thing, the work would never get done") (*Sovetskie Profsoyuzi*, 15:1980:10). A trade union meeting was held instead of the workers' assembly, where the new quotas were swiftly "rubberstamped" (*prosto-naprosto prostampovali*). Under the terms of the contract, the department head was obliged to inform workers of new labor norms by displaying them on the notice board two weeks prior to their introduction:

> As for information ... well, we were informed. But how? First V. Likhoded and sometimes S. Ivankin would come into the department and say, "We're going to cut your rates soon." (*Sovetskie Profsoyuzi*, 15:1980:10)

When the correspondent told the chairman of the FZMK that in Department 15 the quotas had been raised and the rates cut without consultation, the chairman answered:

> "I have nothing to say on the matter. I must check. Have they been raised by much?"
> "On average by 2 percent."

"Well, that's easy to bear. It would have been different if they'd raised them by 12 percent."

"But are you aware of the working conditions in the department?"

"I can't possibly concern myself with everything. There are thousands of departments in the Association with tens of thousands of workers." (*Sovetskie Profsoyuzi*, 15:1980:10)

The correspondent concludes, admitting that the crane-loaders' letter is thought-provoking:

How could all this have happened at the *Zhdanovtiashmash*? The enterprise is well known; it is one of the best plants in the sector. Here they hold every possible kind of seminar and conference, with metal-workers coming from the entire country to study the vanguard methods. (*Sovetskie Profsoyuzi*, 15:1980:10)

But what about enterprises that are not so advanced? What happens there? Let us take, for example, the question of accidents at work.

One particular report published in a trade union newspaper is most informative in two respects: first, it shows how various attempts are made to cover up factory accidents; second, it illustrates the complicity of management, FZMK, and labor inspectors that can occur in such coverups.

The accident in question happened at the *Frunze* plant in the Odessa region. After one month's employment at the factory, a female worker received severe burns as the result of an explosion. A few days later, the section head visited the injured woman in the hospital and informed her that if she stayed in the hospital longer than a month, the accident would have to be classified as serious. Would she, therefore, please report back to work the next day? The woman agreed and arrived at the factory swathed in bandages. Thus—even though she then immediately returned to the hospital—her appearance in the factory was sufficient to count her as having officially returned to work. This scene was repeated several times.

The management then asked the woman to sign a declaration of her own responsibility for the accident. The woman refused at first, but finally gave in and signed "under duress." But the subterfuge had not finished yet. The section head wrote a declaration that

sought to play down the seriousness of the accident in the name of
the woman's brigade. And he made the workers sign it. Then the
management stepped in and arranged for the hospital to send a
statement to the plant declaring that the worker had been under
treatment for less than a month, and only for slight injuries, even
though the hospital register reported burns severe enough to incapa-
citate the woman.

These events—arousing considerable unrest among the
workers—finally came to the notice of the Regional Trade Union
Council. An inquiry was conducted by a union inspector and a
representative of the ministry. It concluded that nothing irregular
had occurred (the news article points out that the union's inspector
had a history as a "coverup specialist"). However, the situation did
not quiet down, and a newspaper correspondent arrived at the
factory. At first the injured woman assumed all the responsibility
for the accident, but later, on meeting the journalist at the factory
gates, said, "Don't believe anything I told you in there" (Kroncher
1979:1–2).

Cases such as this are far from infrequent, judging from other
letters in trade union journals on the subject. One such letter
describes how an *udarnik* in the joinery department at the ZDK
Factory in Gorky had to quit "out of desperation." The worker—
described as "one who searched out the truth at any cost and on
every occasion"—clashed with the department head because the
Inspector of Safety at Work had not been called to investigate the
causes of an accident. Once again the injured worker had been sent
home and the absence from work covered up (Di Leo 1973:200).
The same happened in Gorky, in 1973, for one-third of the accidents that occurred in the town's factories (Madison 1979:102).

Another letter describes "the anti-accident campaign, which has
by now become standard procedure." The "campaign" was conducted in the manner described in the preceding examples: No
report was written, and the injured workers were considered to be
at work.

Two additional letters provide a general survey of the problem.
The first comes from the president of the Supreme Court of
Armenia, who described a long series of violations of the law by
plant managers. The second, from the director of the trade union's
Technical Inspection Division, analyzes the situation in detail and
sees "the race to fulfil the plan and win the bonuses" as being the

fundamental cause of labor-laws violations, "storming," the subordinate role of the FZMK, and the obstruction of inspectors by
management (Di Leo 1973:208). A worker's letter offers a synthesis
of the situation: "Here they only follow one rule: Get moving and
finish the plan." It is worth noting that the same worker once
proposed a modification in the manufacture of a certain plant
product that would have significantly lightened the workload. In
reply, the foreman asked the worker if he thought of himself as
being cleverer than the engineers (Di Leo 1973:128).

In its "hunt for the plan," it is evident that management must
often breach a number of clauses in the collective contract. For
example, investigation of to what extent the terms of various labor
contracts had been fulfilled was carried out in a generator factory in
Khabarovsk during the first half of the 1970s. The study revealed
that: (1) very little had been done to meet the health and safety
requirements of the contracts, especially those regarding the factory
health service; (2) only relatively few people took part in checking
to ensure that such requirements were honored—and many of them
had several other responsibilities as well; (3) these reviews
were carried out haphazardly, and only twice a year, just before
meetings about contractual issues on the agenda; (4) at these
meetings the FZMK accused the management of not observing the
contract, and the management, in turn, accused the FZMK of not
checking on the contract properly; and (5) the unfulfilled clauses of
the old contract were reproduced word-for-word in the new one
(*Sovetskie Profsoyuzi*, 21:1980:30–31).

If this is representative of general practice, workers must hold
their collective contracts in low esteem. Quite significant verifi-
cation of this is provided by Yovchuk and Kogan's study involving
6700 informants (Table 7.6).

Generally speaking, data and testimonies reveal a tendency by
both workers and management to set little store by the company
contract. And when the new contract is presented to the workers'
assembly, it is almost always approved *en masse*. As an ex-plant
lawyer (*iuriskonsult*) has explained, the reason for this can be seen
in the fact that workers and shop stewards do not usually have
sufficient legal expertise to be able to discuss the many clauses of a
detailed document such as a contract (Shelley 1984:101).

As far as nonobservation of contracutal clauses is concerned, the
most important cause is undoubtedly the lack of funds necessary to

TABLE 7.6 Worker Assessment of the Collective Contract

	Enterprises					Average %
	TMZ	UETM	URAL KABEL	SZP	SKK	
Are the interests and needs of production sufficiently reflected in your enterprise's collective contract?						
Yes	48.8[a]	53.1	43.2	54.7	38.4	47.6
Not fully	34.2	26.3	16.2	18.7	25.4	24.2
No	8.2	2.3	7.6	0.6	9.3	5.6
Don't know	8.8	18.3	33.0	26.0	26.9	22.6
Are the interests and needs of the workers sufficiently reflected in your enterprise's collective contract?						
Yes	44.6	40.8	20.9	45.8	19.0	34.2
Not fully	37.3	24.0	51.6	19.7	36.9	33.9
No	11.4	8.0	16.1	11.5	10.8	11.6
Don't know	6.7	27.2	11.4	23.0	33.3	20.3
Does the management respect the collective contract?						
Yes	33.2	22.4	14.3	36.6	19.0	25.5
Not fully	37.1	28.0	42.3	29.8	36.9	34.8
No	14.4	11.2	14.3	8.6	10.8	11.9
Don't know	15.3	38.4	29.1	25.0	33.3	27.8

[a] Percentage of answers given for each question.
SOURCE: Iovchuck and Kogan (1972: 205).

132

carry them out. And this inability to carry out the contract is the key to understanding the scant regard both management and work force show for the contract.

Three separate decision-making processes supply the guidelines for drawing up the company contract. The first is Party and government labor policy, in the form of laws, decrees, and resolutions, drafted with the participation of the Central Council of Trade Unions. The second is the negotiation process between the industrial ministry and the trade union council at the republic level. The third process is "planning by negotiation"—that is, the bargaining process between the economic plan agencies and the plant managements over output targets and the resources necessary to fulfil them. As strong impressions indicate, it is the third process that has the most direct bearing on workplace industrial relations.

Berliner used the term "planning by negotiation" in his analysis of the extremely important role played by personal factors in the relationship between management and higher authorities. As he pointed out, "more than most modern states, the Soviet state evokes among outsiders an image which stresses the formal, the logical, the homogeneous. Soviet society is often thought of as more 'rational' than others, in the technical sense that large segments of it have been consciously and deliberately legislated into existence" (Berliner 1957:224). The resulting image of a perfect organizational structure is in part the consequence of the enforced reliance on official sources: a fact that dulls the sensitivity of the researcher to the role of the people in the system. The testimonies gathered by Berliner and other scholars in recent times show instead a pervasiveness of the personal factor in the allocation and utilization of resources:

> While it is impossible to offer a quantitative estimate, it is clear from the interviews that the output plan depends in large measure upon what the enterprise has been able to bargain out of Moscow. (Berliner 1957:224)

Naturally, plant administrators can only exercise their negotiating skills within certain limits. In other words, an enterprise can obtain concessions only up to a certain limit, otherwise the ministry, which has its own plan to fulfill, will have to shift the more onerous work onto other enterprises in the sector. But the results of negotiation can be significantly improved if the plant director enjoys a personal rapport with officials at various levels of the Party appartus and the planning organs. Hence, as one informant has said, "The authority lies in the man and not in the position he holds," adding that a skillful and persuasive director can be extremely useful to his enterprise:

> If the plant is asked to do the impossible and the director is not a good one, he will not be able to defend his plant. But the man we have just been talking about will gather his staff, will go with them to the highest organs, and insist on the interests of his plant. If he does not get satisfaction in the chief administration, he will go to the ministry. It is in the interests of the engineers that the director is powerful in the Party circles, that he is not a man who can be chased around. We look to the director to promote our interests, to push through for us at the ministry and to defend the interests of the plant. (Berliner 1957:230)

The fact that personal influence has become a decisive factor in the management of the planned economy has been demonstrated by studies carried out in Poland and Hungary. In one of these studies a director states:

> Because circumstances are very uncertain and changeable, personal and subjective judgment [has] by all means, a great importance in decision [making.] Therefore, we try, even instinctively, to develop good personal relations with those of superior authority, and to give a favorable picture of the enterprise, since this might increase the chances of the enterprise in getting its share from the various sources and grants. (Laky 1979:235)

The real bargaining seems actually the one between management and planning authorities, while the collective contract is of secondary importance even today—despite the new legal power granted to the Factory Committee of Trade Unions (FZMK) in the last twenty years or so. Looking into the many functions of the FZMK reveals the persistence of its subordinate role. The functioning of the Commission of Labor Disputes can serve as a good example of this.

The truth of the observation that—in Soviet factories—the real arbiter of the law is not the judicial system but the plant management seems assured judging from a series of conversations with 25 former *iuriskonsult* conducted by Shelley. The findings are summarized as follows:

The *iuriskonsult* usually has a consultative role, and also acts as a mediator in the handling of labor disputes in the plant. The FZMK appears almost always subordinate to the management. It will support a worker only if its members believe that he can win an appeal, in case the matter goes to a court. Procurators in such cases usually ensure that labor legislation is enforced, so management will take every step, legal or illegal, to make sure that disputes do not go that far. A decision by the court in favor of a worker will almost never result in the condemnation of those guilty of an illegal act. The regional trade union may act as an appeal court for the worker, but there is no guarantee that it will not condone illegal acts by management. When a manager deliberately infringes on the labor laws because he knows he can afford to, there is little hope that the worker will have his rights protected. The members of the FZMK are very rarely fully cognizant of labor legislation and seek help from the enterprise *iuriskonsult*—as do the individual workers (Shelley 1985).

Dismissal is one of the most frequent causes of labor disputes. This is rarely connected with the laying off of manpower due to organizational redesign, even if this should become the case more frequently in the near future. Today the most common reason for firing a worker is lack of discipline. There is no longer any doubt that indiscipline is a major problem in Soviet industry. The press and the mass media have always talked of layabouts, habitual absentees, drunkards, "waste-producers," hooligans, and so forth. The number of these trouble makers is by no means insignificant—as will be shown in the next chapter—and the damage they cause to production is considerable. Suffice it to say here, for example, that estimates, by a Soviet author, of the working days lost through absenteeism in 1972–1973 range from 52 to 59 million working days. The same author estimated that if alcohol was removed from the workplace, productivity could increase by 10 percent (Sonin, 1978).

The general problem of alcoholism combines with other causes of labor indiscipline, such as administrative disorganization and the purely formalistic and vacuous roles of educational activities and social programs in most of the factories. An interesting picture of how management copes with labor indiscipline is offered by a letter to the editor in *Literaturnaia Gazeta* (April 5, 1978:10).

The author of the letter gives the example of a newly appointed director who was concerned about the effects of alcohol abuse on his plant's output and decided to clamp down on drunken and indisciplined behavior. A year later, however, he decided it was better to recommend to the workshop supervisor these guidelines for action: "If someone can't stand up, he's drunk. If he can, leave him alone." What caused this dramatic change of attitude?

It turned out that the factory buildings were decrepit, the machinery continually out of order, the production plan in danger, and wages shrinking. Under these conditions it was considered a success merely to keep workers and technical personnel from leaving the factory, let alone to impose some sort of discipline.

This state of affairs is quite widespread. As a trade union official stated:

> It is no secret that you meet masters, workshop heads, and even factory directors who, because of the shortage of manpower (especially skilled workers), turn a blind eye to infringements of discipline—when they are not trying to hide them. On the other hand, there exist also instances of the hurried sacking of anyone guilty of a breach of discipline, without any attempt at discovering the cause. This is violation of labor law. (*Sovetskie Profsoyuzi*, 13:1980:15).

Thus management's decision whether to adopt a tough line in these cases depends not so much on legal considerations or on a fear of possible clashes with trade unions, as on the availability of manpower in the labor market. Generally, however, the soft approach seems to prevail because the workers may move elsewhere—unless they happen to work in a military or high-priority factory where stricter disciplinary rules are compensated for by better working conditions and higher wages (Zaslavsky 1979:15–17).

It is the duty of the trade union and Party organs—within the plant and outside—to ensure that workers' rights and "socialist legality" are respected. If the practices described in the preceding discussion correspond to reality, however, we need to know more about the behavior of Party and trade union officials in their dealings with plant managers.

The higher organs of Party and trade union (and of government) issue a constant stream of decrees and resolutions, whose practical implementation is left to the local functionaries. These official directives are very often mismanaged, as several letters published in the press demonstrate. It is interesting, for example, to see how the Party Committee of the Perm region announces its decisions, but takes no steps to ensure that they are carried out. Thus, if its first pronouncement has no effect, they issue another, identical one. The Committee then "forgets about" its resolutions until the eve of the annual review assembly.

Naturally, the Regional Trade Union Council behaves in the same way. Year after year it passes practically identical resolutions calling for stricter discipline in the collectives and improved safety standards, but it never investigates whether or not directives have been followed. The author of one letter in the press—a chief of the Organization Section of the Central Council of Metal-Workers—draws on his knowledge of the problems and declares that this behavior is typical of the regional trade union councils of Armenia and Tadzikistan, and of the territories of Khabarovsk, Dzhezkazgansk, Karaganda, Murmansk, and Kustanaysk (*Sovetskie Profsoyuzi*, 19:1980:16–17).

To clarify the underlying reasons for this state of affairs, one must identify those unwritten laws that govern the relations among the three separate entities that run Soviet enterprise. Once again, the evidence gathered by Berliner can serve as a good starting point.

The function of the Party inside the factory is to ensure "socialist legality"—that is, to ensure that the interests of the enterprise are not pursued to the detriment of the state and the workers. In practice, however, the Party secretary is assessed by his superior mainly in terms of his plant's performance:

We had a Party secretary who was appointed by the Central Committee. He was usually between the hammer and the anvil. He was responsible for the fulfillment of our production program, and he was always eager to send a good telegram to Moscow.... It was of great advantage to the Party secretary to be able to send a good telegram, and therefore he did everything possible to help us to fulfill the plan. Sometimes he "would look the other way" at some manipulation of ours so that we could carry it out in order to fulfil the plan." (Berliner 1957:264)

Certainly, a Party secretary can refuse to ignore these irregularities, but generally it is not in his interest to do so:

If he discloses one of the unlawful operations some time and creates a big scandal, then he may be raised in his job. But everybody in the Soviet Union will know that he had informed on his director. Then the whole body of producers will look upon him as an informer. If he gets a new job in a new factory, everybody will be afraid of him. Then he will not be able to find out what is going on in the plant. Nobody will have any confidence in him, and they will all just say that everything is going fine, and someday there will be a check and his head will fall together with the director's. Therefore the Party secretary, like the resident ministry representative, tries not to have trouble with the director. (Berliner 1957:265)

The management personnel of an enterprise have a whole series of material rewards at their disposal, which they can exploit surreptitiously to persuade the Party secretary to keep to the *modus vivendi*, to identify with the firm, and to think of it as "we." The local organs too, take this sort of behavior for granted, as long as it leads to the fulfilment of the plan. They also are judged on the basis of the plan performance in the enterprises under their jurisdiction. Divergences between the interests of the individual enterprise and those of the regional and district Party committee will arise only when the unlawful practices of one enterprise are detrimental to other enterprises in the area. To sum up, it is quite easy to see a shift from plant patriotism to the "family circle" or *krugovaia poruka*. Here it is worth adding that in the family circle there is also room for the chairman of the FZMK, even if in a subordinate position, because his cooperation can prove useful in avoiding adverse outside publicity.

PLANS FOR THE SOCIAL DEVELOPMENT OF THE COLLECTIVE: SOME UNRESOLVED QUESTIONS

The various social-development plans of the work collectives are rarely anything more than mere declarations of intent. The reasons are to be found in the practical constraints that govern plant management and, second, in the "system of external bureaucratization" in which the enterprise is embedded.

In their analysis of the deficiencies of social planning, Kerimov and Pashkov (1975) examine its political roots, beginning with the principle of "democratic centralism." This principle is meant to unite the centralized management of social processes with the problem-solving procedures applied at the local level. These procedures are to be as democratic as possible and rely on the initiative of the production collectives. Actually, things proceed in quite a different way.

The principal features of social progress are defined by Party and government resolutions and then written into the plan directives. However,

> the absence of a well-developed legal framework means that sociocultural, political, and spiritual planning remains at the abstract level of broad orientations and generalized procedures, devoid of the specific social criteria needed for their realization. Concrete indices and detailed analysis of the social mobility of the various components of the population are almost never fully worked out. State control of these features of social life usually limits itself to defining the material preconditions necessary for the development of the educational, cultural, scientific, and sanitary institutions. (Kerimov & Pashkov 1975:28)

Central planners, therefore, even if they are becoming increasingly aware of the social consequences of economic development, still operate only indirectly at the level of *preconditions* for social change. This fact in itself would not be a negative one if there existed a sufficient measure of local autonomy to make decisions and act independently. But the scope of this local autonomy is extremely limited.

At enterprise and regional levels, the Party usually entrusts the social-development plans to special commissions or soviets for their execution. Little is known of the role played by the Party itself on the subject. The local Party organs seem to concentrate their efforts on the political, ideological, and educational objectives of the plans but draw no practical distinction between plans for the socialist education of the workers—the responsibility of the collective as a whole—and the planning of ideological activity, which is to be carried out by the Party organization (Podmarkov 1969:26). As for the activities of the commissions and soviets, apart from individual efforts there seems to be a marked lack of theoretical and practical training required for the plans' fulfillment. This results, among other things, in a widespread economic determinism and leads to planning "by rule of thumb" (*naglazok*) that is, without preliminary research, without analysis of the basic data, and without specialized help—a practice that "only serves to discredit the idea of social planning and damages the cause of the building of communism"

(Kerimov & Pashkov 1975:28). This practice also falls short of the second principle of social planning, that is, "scientific method and objectivity."

The third principle, that of "complexity of approach" is deemed necessary insofar as the material and cultural needs of the work-force cannot be wholly satisfied by social-development planning conducted solely at the enterprise level. The official objective is nowadays a harmonious combination of planning activities at both the industrial and the territorial level. There exist, however, two major difficulties. First, the city constitutes a geographical entity but its development is largely determined by the specific social programs of the various industries that have factories in its territory. Second, although there exist many schemes for economic planning for the territories, there is not a single, all-embracing plan that will handle all the various aspects of urban development and provide a unified program of town and city planning (Mezhevich CDSP 1978:13).

Each city draws up a five-year plan for the construction of its city services which can be coordinated with the plan for various enter-prises in two ways. If all goes well, the enterprises and the urban soviet consult reciprocally over the general policy to adopt regarding the construction of various types of infrastructures and social services. Otherwise, the city's soviet has to trim its programs to suit the interests of local industry, as laid down by the republic or the union. And these bodies are primarily concerned with their own labor force, not with the citizenry as a whole. This is the principal weakness of social planning at the territorial level: The urban-planning authorities have only very limited means at their disposal to tackle the problems of living conditions and economic develop-ment in their areas. The consequences of this sectorial approach to urban planning are as follows:

> The cities ... grew more rapidly than was foreseen. This uncontrolled growth of the cities in terms of population and area has exacerbated the shortage of manpower, has aggravated the problem of commuterism, and has created acute environmental problems and difficulties in the building programs. (Mezhevich CDSP 1978:13)

The final principle, that of "concreteness," requires that two factors be borne in mind. The first is the specific nature of the Marxist–Leninist principles in concrete situations, and the second is the actual availability of human and material resources (Kerimov &

Pashkov 1975:29). As for resources, a plant is often hampered by shortages of resources and a high level of uncertainty as to whether these resources will become available within the timespan allotted by the plan. So it comes as no surprise that

> Various managers, rather than dedicate themselves to a detailed, scientific realization of the plan for social development, merely compile lists of indices taken from the plan for the introduction of new techniques, the collective contract, and the plan for organizational redesign. (Khokhlyuk 1976:130)

In these cases it can easily happen that "the recommended measures are not economically justified," or that the social objectives (educational activities, participation in production management, and so forth) are vague and ill-defined and that workers are misinformed or kept ignorant. If sociological research is conducted, it is based solely on questionnaires; excluded are other methods such as statistical analysis, the study of documents pertaining to social organizations, direct observation, and so on. The consequence is that "Not infrequently the plan for social development includes hastily thought-out measures and proclamations. These make a lot of promises, but never keep them" (Khokhlyuk 1976:130).

V. G. Podmarkov identified the cause of this as, above all, the conservatism of many plant managers, among whom *perestrakhovka* is rife—that is, the tendency to protect oneself against plan uncertainties by shifting the blame for possible failure onto others.

In short, the phenomenon of *perestrakhovka* provides sufficient reason to maintain that the Soviet art of "window-dressing" also applies—with few exceptions—to social planning.

An exception could be considered the case of Leningrad, where, as early as 1966, joint efforts by social scientists, managers, and politicians had led to the drafting and implementation of a grandiose plan for territorial development (subsequently abandoned, however, because of its impracticability).

As a result of the favorable climate stemming from the economic reform of 1965, a series of experiments in social planning at the enterprise level were launched in the second half of the 1960s. The first, and best known, was conducted in the Svetlana industrial association, which manufactures electronic instruments. Its aim was to apply drastic remedies to the problems of indiscipline, spontaneous turnover, and time-wasting. These measures—subsequently introduced elsewhere—consisted of the regrading of workers and managers, and of various forms of technical and organizational redesign accompanied by improvement in the work environment (Ruble 1982:167).

It should be remembered that innovative plans such as these have been speedily enacted because the projects drafted by the experts were backed up by the local political authorities—who also ensured that they were implemented. Nevertheless, as Ruble reports, the events in Leningrad revealed a fundamental ambiguity. On the one hand, social scientists and managers regarded social-development plans as a new form of social contract, which would have led to increased productivity among the labor force. On the other hand, the politicians saw social-territorial planning as an opportunity to increase their power over the local economy at the expense of the industrial ministries. In other words, the attempt to shift power away from the ministry into the hands of local authorities met with only limited success in Leningrad, because of the peculiar situation of that city. Leningrad, in fact, as the former capital, has a history of relative isolation from Moscow. The local political leaders have always sought to reverse this tendency—especially under the leadership of Romanov (Ruble 1982:172).

Thus, even in advanced Leningrad, this basic ambiguity, has imposed severe limitations on the impact and efficacy of the new forms of planning. In this case, too:

> Even if it is clear that socioeconomic planning has become a useful instrument for discussing complex and urgent issues such as the allocation of the workforce, social services, and the distribution of income, there is very little evidence that the plans have brought developments that would not have occurred without them. (Ruble 1982:174)

Unless the modification now in progress in the whole political power structure produces a profound change in the relations between local authorities and the industrial ministries, social planning is destined to wield little influence over the traditional patterns of economic planning. As for the social-development plans of production collectives, one may suppose that they will have some effect in a certain number of enterprises. But in the majority of cases, the practice of social planning will be similar to the one currently criticized in the Soviet press.

CHAPTER 8

Improving Material Conditions: The Individual's Choices

In the preceding chapter an attempt was made to provide an idea of the "rules of the game" that characterize labor relations within Soviet enterprises—rules that have both advantages and disadvantages for employees. When the disadvantages are prevalent, and this is a frequent occurrence, there exist bodies and procedures designed to safeguard the workers' rights and interests. Collective, organized defense by the working people of their rights, however, unless they are willing to incur great risks, is not a viable proposition. What is then the outcome when the working people realize that labor relations in their factory are more constricting than gratifying?

The means at employees' disposal—to extricate themselves from an unsatisfactory work situation, or to improve their working and living conditions—may be grouped under three headings: (1) searching for a better job, (2) actively participating in various forms of "social self-government of production," and (3) taking shelter in the "shadow economy" (*tenevaia ekonomika*).

This chapter examines these three individual strategies in an attempt to provide quantitative data and evidence for each, along with a socioprofessional description of the people who choose to change jobs, participate in the "leadership of production," and deal in the "shadow economy."

First we will discuss the issue of labor turnover, which involves mainly young people under age thirty. As the cycle of labor and life moves onwards, a number of these young people will become more oriented toward the second alternative; others toward the third. A further group will seek to combine the advantages to be gained by one or the other alternative whenever objective circumstances permit it. Some will also find themselves involved in strikes and industrial unrests—but of these something will be said in the next chapter.

CHANGING JOBS

The phenomenon of labor turnover has always had significant impact in the Soviet Union. During the first half of the 1970s the "fluctuation of personnel" (*tekuchest kadrov*) in the industrial system as a whole was approximately 20 percent (Porket 1985:21). This means that more than 20 million people annually move from one enterprise to another. These fluctuations cause heavy losses to the economic system. The average interim between jobs is 28 days; and job turnover gives rise to a series of problems involving retraining and adaptation to the new work situation (Pravda 1979).

Most Soviet research into the subject was carried out during the 1960s and early 1970s. It demonstrates significant variations among turnover rates according to the industry, geographical area, the size of the enterprise, and the socioprofessional characteristics of the workforce.

On the basis of statistics published in 1971, the turnover rate in the coal mines was 47.1 percent, in the building material industry 34.4 percent, in the food industry 35.5 percent, in light industry 28.8 percent, in the metalworking industry 18.1 percent, and in the chemical industry 18.1 percent. The highest rate was in the textiles industry with 65.4 percent (Teckemberg 1978:201).

Regional differences are just as apparent. In 1967 the turnover rate in Tadzikistan reached almost 40 percent. At the opposite extreme came the central area of RFSSR with 15.7 percent. Turnover is also particularly high in Siberia and the Far East (Teckemberg 1978:195).

Regarding these variations in turnover rates, it is important to point out that in the Soviet Union just as in Russia of the past, it is the differences between the enterprises that represent the decisive factors in determining the working and living standards of working people. It is the enterprise, in fact, that supplies the apartments, the nurseries, the cafeterias, holiday accommodations, and so forth.

At first glance, the Soviet worker's situation seems rather favorable. Large firms with more than 1000 employees accounted for approximately 61 percent of the workforce in 1973—a percentage that has not changed significantly since—and large firms theoretically offer more benefits to workers. On the other hand, the 55 percent of enterprises with fewer than 200 employees account for only 9 percent of the workforce (Yanowitch 1982:66). However, not all large firms enjoy a favorable situation in terms of the financial resources they obtain from planning authorities if they have difficulties with plan fulfilment with the consequence that services such as apartments and holidays are provided in a largely insufficient manner. Moreover, not all employees of large enterprises have equal access to social services. Those who find themselves at the "back of the line" are usually unskilled auxiliary workers—of which there are many, given the relative organizational backwardness of many large enterprises. This gives rise to a further difference among turnover rates, one which depends on skill level.

For the more highly skilled workers, changing jobs does not involve changing job rank. This is not the case for semiskilled or nonskilled workers, who often seek to move from heavy, hazardous work to lighter auxiliary work, even if it may be less well paid. Data gathered by the sociologist Shkaratan during the latter part of the 1960s show the following turnover rates for various occupational groups: mechanics 26.8 percent, electromechanics 48.6 percent, machinists 48.6 percent, nonskilled workers 62.7 percent (Aitov 1975:188–219).

A portrait of those who leave their jobs, and why, may be derived from a comparison of various Soviet research programs on the subject, carried out over two decades. We comment here on three of the most important studies, conducted during the second half of the 1960s in Ufa (Republic of Bashkiria), Leningrad, and the Autonomous Republic of Udmurt.

The first project (see No. 1, in Table 8.1) carried out by Aitov (1975) was organized into two stages: the first took place January through March, 1965, in fourteen factories of Ufa (four mechanical, four chemical, two automobile, and four light industry). The total workforce was 25,000; the sample was composed of 857 newly hired workers and 846 who left the factories. The second stage (B)

TABLE 8.1   *Relative Weights of Various Reasons for Leaving Employment (in percentages)*

Causes	Numbers 1 & 2	Number 3	Number 4	Leningrad Study	Izhevsk Study
Transfer to another city	19.5	14.4	42.6	–	27.4
Breach of labor disciplinary code	3.0	1.7	5.0	–	5.1
Family reasons (lack of daycare)	14.7	10.7	10.1	–	5.9
Low wages	19.4	26.4	10.9	21.5	16.0
Uninteresting work	4.9	6.6	2.2	–	5.5
Excessive distance between house and work	10.2	9.5	6.5	8.8	–
Bad relations in production collective	1.2	0.8	1.6	2.5	2.3
Job rank lower than qualifications	0.3	1.9	0.9	–	–
Little hope of finding an apartment	5.9	7.1	9.8	2.0	13.3
Bad working conditions	9.3	13.8	4.6	19.6	18.7
Content of work not corresponding to personal qualification	–	6.2	3.4	–	–
Lack of opportunities for upgrading	–	0.8	1.6	9.8	5.0
Other	10.8	–	–	15.4	–

NOTE: In this and the following tables, unless stated otherwise, the percentages refer to the total number of job-leavers and newly hired workers.

SOURCE: Osipov and Szczepanski (1975: 220); Iovchuk and Kogan (1972: 255).

of the research was carried out from October to December of 1966. Here, a second type of questionnaire was administered to 2397 people dismissed at their own request and to 2201 newly hired workers in a petrochemical plant.

The second research program (see No. 3 in Table 8.1) was conducted by L. A. Blyakhman, A. G. Zdravomyslov, and O. I. Shkaratan on a sample of 10,720 workers who had left various enterprises in the Leningrad area during 1963. The third project (No. 4) was conducted by M. T. Iovchuk and L. K. Kogan during the period 1968–1969 in a group of factories in the city of Izhevsk, on a sample of 1920 individuals. Thus, altogether, 14,343 workers in various sectors and geographical areas of the country were interviewed (Iovchuk & Kogan 1972:250–270).

As Table 8.1 shows, the most common reason for leaving employment was dissatisfaction over wages, together with desire to transfer to another city (mainly because of housing problems). Factors that would probably lead to labor disputes in the West (headings 5, 8, 9, 11, 12, 13) accounted for 30 percent of the replies in Nos. 1 and 2, 50 percent in No. 3, 23 percent in No. 4, 53.3 percent in the Leningrad research, and 42.8 percent in Izhevsk.

These results have been substantially confirmed by other research carried out in recent years in Moscow, Novosibirsk, Tallin, and other Soviet cities; therefore, we can assume they sufficiently indicate the general situation.

Transfer from one city to another is determined by several factors: the mismatch between the geographical distribution of industries and their corresponding professional and technical institutes; the existence of many small and medium-sized cities, where industry is still relatively underdeveloped and where many employees are obliged to migrate; the fact that a certain number of employees leave their job for family reasons (which often means difficulties in using social services). The latter reason—indicated mainly by female workers—accounts for 55.5 percent of the total working hours lost because of turnover (34.3 percent on average). Among women the average time period of unemployment was 406 days. In the first survey the average period of unemployment (for men and women) was 28 days, but for those who quit for "family reasons" the average was 406 days (Aitov 1975:199).

Dissatisfaction over wages is one of the most common reasons for leaving the factory, especially among young people in unskilled auxiliary jobs. These jobs still exist in great numbers but, with the raising of educational levels, there are fewer young people willing to fill them (Grancelli 1974).

Housing has traditionally been a serious problem, and even today various enterprises compete in the labor market by offering better housing facilities rather than improved wage conditions (*Pravda*, January 1, 1983:2).

From the studies quoted earlier, it appears that the workers who frequently change jobs are predominantly under thirty, highly educated, but with low professional qualifications, and who are low paid as a consequence (see Table 8.2). Dissatisfaction among young workers over factory life in general is a growing problem. According to researchers, this is due to the widening gap between the

TABLE 8.2   *Details of Job-Leavers and Newly Hired Workers in the First Part of the Study*

Characteristics	Percentage in the organization of the 14 factories	Percentage among job-leavers and newly hired workers
Workers of less than 30 years of age	55.7	73.0
Workers with more than 7 years of schooling	39.5	51.0
Workers on the lowest pay scale	–	60.1
Average salary	59.8	73.5

SOURCE: See Table 8.1.

worker's general education received at school—aimed at developing personality and the quality of individual needs—and the worker's satisfaction within the existing employment organization.

The research of Iovchuk and Kogan substantially confirms the findings of other researchers and furnishes some interesting correlations between leaving employment and level of social and political activity. It turns out, for instance, that almost three-fourths of those who left their jobs were not involved in sociopolitical activity, either permanently or temporarily. This confirms previous findings that show members of the Party and trade union *aktiv* are seldom people under thirty years of age, because in this younger age range, the major preoccupation is still finding the best socio-professional conditions possible—by moving from one enterprise to another, and often by taking courses at night school (see Table 8.3).

Subsequently to this research, changes took place in the turnover rates of the various sectors; these changes were due to the revising of pay levels in the sectors with the most unfavorable salary conditions. So, for example, in light industry the average wage in 1966 was 67 percent of the overall industrial average and 77 percent in 1975. In the food industry the percentage in 1966 was 87 percent and in 1975 90 percent. Wages that dropped toward the average were in metallurgy (from 121 to 116 percent), electrical energy (from 106 to 103 percent), and chemicals (from 103 to 102 percent). Moreover, a study carried out by the Institute of Research into Work in 1973 showed that dissatisfaction over wages, which had been the principal cause of turnover in the 1960s, had passed to

TABLE 8.3 *Reasons for Leaving Employment (by age group)*

Reasons (grouped)	Workers of less than 30 years of age [a]	Workers of more than 30 years of age
Breach of labor disciplinary code	3.7	8.0
Hazardous character of the production	6.0	16.0
Uninteresting work, or, at a low grade, below the worker's qualifications, bad work conditions in general	13.1	8.0
Low wages	31.0	25.0
Bad relations with management and/or little hope of obtaining an apartment	15.0	13.4
Transfer to another city, excessive distance between home and work	14.2	7.1
Family reasons	17.2	22.5

[a] As percentage.
SOURCE: See Table 8.1.

third and fourth place after the reforms of 1965–1970 (Chapman 1979: 171–176).

Research carried out in the city of Borisov, in 1974, on a sample of 1631 people who had changed their jobs, showed that 25 percent of the men had quit because of low wages, while only 8.7 percent of women reported the same reason. Among women, dissatisfaction over working conditions and family circumstances predominated: 19.2 percent and 20.3 percent respectively. This research also shows that, despite the wage reforms of 1965–1970, there still persisted differences in earnings for the same job ranks in different sectors of the economy or in different enterprises within the same sector (Skarupo 1978:118–125).

This research also sheds further light on the correlation between educational level and the propensity for changing jobs. In this case, too, turnover is most pronounced among young workers under thirty years old (53.3 percent of the total), but those who changed their jobs most often had lower levels of education: 67.6 percent among those who had not completed general secondary school, and only 3.8 percent of those who had received higher or specialized education. It is important, then, to distinguish between general education and specialized education.

Other research in the early 1970s confirms the finding that young workers under thirty years of age represented easily the most mobile section of the labor force. They changed jobs approximately four times more frequently than did workers in the age range 30–39, and ten times more frequently than those over 50. Neither did young people change jobs solely to improve their career chances. In fact 42 percent of the age range 20–24 were married, as were 85 percent of the age range 25–29. Thus, these young workers were also concerned with the problems of housing, day care, and other social services (Kotlyar & Talalai 1977:1–3).

To sum up: The results of this latter research show widespread dissatisfaction among young people with their working and living conditions. Policies of personnel management have proved insufficient to satisfy their needs, above all as far as the combination of work and study is concerned. Besides, the situation seems to vary greatly among different enterprises, with turnover rates oscillating between 3 percent and 114 percent. Differences of 10 to 20 percentage points also exist among enterprises in the same economic sector and located in the same region. Nor is the situation always better in large enterprises as compared to medium and small ones. For example, of the 9000 employees in a car factory in Zavolzhye (province of Gorky), almost 4000 were leaving annually—the main reason being the housing shortage in that small center. Social services were also very unsatisfactory. Besides, only half of the necessary shopping facilities were available, and only a fifth of the necessary goods and services (*Pravda*, April 15, 1977:2).

Among small enterprises, generally under the jurisdiction of local authorities, the situation was worse. As a consequence turnover was even higher. An example is provided by light industry, where turnover was 40 percent in enterprises with fewer than 250 employees, 20.9 percent in enterprises in the 1000–2000 range, and only 7.9 percent in enterprises with more than 10,000 employees. Apart from the wider range of services available in large firms, the main reason is that such firms also provide opportunities for mobility within their factories (Teckemberg 1978:197).

A final point needs to be made. Those workers who repeatedly change their jobs are not only young people, or those who carry out heavy and hazardous jobs, or are employed in small enterprises. In the car factory of Zavolzhye, up to 2800 seasonal workers, originating from the rural regions of Ukraine, Moldavia, Mordvinia, and Chuvasha, were recruited annually. These workers, who represented almost a third of the factory manpower, were employed for one to two months, although it was not reported in which capacity. Given that the annual turnover rate was 50 percent, it is fair to suppose that these workers were taken on in order to plug gaps in the manpower levels. In closed cities, like Moscow and Leningrad, for example, the people who fill the gap in the manpower levels are the so-called *limitchiki*, young people without permanent certificates of residence (Zaslavsky 1981; Belyavsky 1986).

Another growing phenomenon is that of *shabashnichestvo* (dropping out)—or *otkhodnichestvo* (roving)—which seems particularly widespread in the republics of the Caucasus (Murphy 1985). The total number of these freelance workers is not known. At any rate, Soviet sources report that in 1977, 30,000 workers were officially registered as "migrant" (and many of them were Party members) in twelve regions of the RSFSR and in three other regions in Kazakhstan, Belorussia, and the Ukraine. In 1979, remittances made by these workers to the families were equal to the wage funds of two construction ministries in Armenia. The same situation seems to apply in Georgia (Tenson 1980:1–3). The number of the *shabashniki* has certainly increased since a decree issued by the Council of Ministers in 1973 that authorized managements to stipulate contracts with nonstaff workers. These contracts contain clauses governing the volume and nature of work, rates of pay, and output. Given the scarcity of labor, these contracts are more advantageous to the work squad than was foreseen, and, in some cases, the plant director also "takes his cut" (Tenson, 1980:3).

Why does a worker decide to become a *shabashnik*? Some ideas may be provided by the following conversation with one of these workers who had been earning 1000 rubles a month freelance but who, for family reasons, decided to become a full-time, permanent worker in a building enterprise where he earned less money—his reason being that the permanent job seemed to offer him an income sufficient to cover his family requirements. Here are the reasons why he decided to become a shabashnik once again:

> True, during this time there was hardly enough work for a month. And this time could barely be called working in the full sense of the word, said

my companion. Rushing about, nervous strain, no organization, long cigarette breaks. Literally on the second day it was already clear that you would not earn the cherished 300 rubles at that rate. You would not even earn 150. I would have stayed if the 300 rubles had been hard and fast, if they had been there winter and summer, spring and fall. But, after all, what happens? It is difficult to find work in Armenia in winter. And even if you find it, you are not able to earn the minimum you need for your family. None of us would go off anywhere if there were not these ups and downs in the pay of a construction workers. Now you are earning, now you are not. (Tenson 1980:1)

In conclusion, there is a final observation to be made concerning the practically negligible role played by the employment offices in regulating the allocation of the labor force. Personal initiative is not exclusive to the enterprising *shabashniki*: in 1974, for example, 80 percent of those who had left their jobs had found new employment on their own initiative (*Pravda*, April 15, 1977:2), probably, in many instances, through "labor recruiters" sent out by enterprises when the need for manpower becomes particularly pressing (Di Leo 1973: 106–108).

PRODUCTION PARTICIPATION AND SOCIAL ACTIVISM

To understand the phenomena of production participation and social activism, let us allow a concept commonly used in the official definition of production relationships to serve as a frame of reference. The concept is "the feeling of being the master" of the factory (*chuvstvo khoziaina*). In a speech delivered to the Conference of European Communist Parties, Brezhnev declared:

Under the conditions of socialism, a truly precious quality has developed in the Soviet man: the feeling of being the master of the country; a master who fully understands the ties that bind his work to the needs of society, who understands and respects the interests of everyone. And this is not something platonic, but the real commitment of millions. (Volkov & Chervyakov 1977:20)

Here some questions arise: How many are these millions? How much is real and how much "platonic" (in other words, formalist) in this commitment? What are the socioprofessional characteristics of those who possess this *chuvstvo khoziaina*? What are the motives behind the desire to show production participation and social activism?

The Soviet publicity machine churns out a constant stream of declamatory rhetoric concerning the "feeling of being the master." Sometimes, however, there emerges from the ballyhoo a striking phrase that captures our attention. For instance, a worker, on being asked whether he felt this *chuvstvo khoziaina*, replied: "*Ya sebya khoziainom chuvstvuiu, a menya khoziainom ne chuvstvuiut*" ("Personally, I regard myself as a master: it's the others who don't see me as such"). And from the rest of the conversation, it turns out that "the others" are those who, really manage the means of production (Olshansky 1966:185).

At this point, to provide a rough idea of the real situation, the most productive approach would seem to be a close examination of various Soviet sociological studies on the issue of participation "in the leadership of production."

At the present time, the party is placing the maximum emphasis on the process of democratization of production relationships, and sociologists have been called on to provide analysis of and suggestions on the possible ways to implement this process. In particular, empirical research must draw up a set of indicators designed to display the objective and subjective characteristics of the *chuvstvo khoziaina*, that is, the degree of production activism characteristic of the various types of working people, their attitudes, and motivations.

Much Soviet sociological research is, for obvious reasons, profoundly impregnated with official rhetoric. To demonstrate this, one example should be sufficient: In one survey the interviewees were asked, among other superficial questions, if they were willing "to work to the utmost" (*s polnoi otdachei sil*). Obviously, there was a chorus of "Yes, we are!" (90 percent of the respondents) (Volkov & Cherviakov 1977:25). Fortunately, though, there also exist valid studies that provide data of considerable interest.

The first aspect of worker participation to be examined is the objective one. As early as the 1960s, several studies that should have highlighted the productivity activism of young workers revealed instead, under careful scrutiny, that activism was rather scarce—in

TABLE 8.4 *Worker Participation in the Campaign for the Protection of Socialist Property, for Cost Reduction, and Against Mismanagement*

| | | Workers (grouped) (%) | | | | | | | | |
| | | By sex | | By age | | By level of qualification | | | Seniority | | |
Level of activism	Behavior at various levels	M	F	Below 30	Over 30	1st–2nd	3rd–4th	5th and above	Up to3 years	4–10 years	More than 11 years
High	Strictly observes the economy norms, intransigent toward bad management	27.1	34.6	21.1	35.6	24.8	25.2	35.2	21.5	31.3	35.5
Average	Is not to be criticized for the organization of his work. He could participate more actively in the camp—for cost reduction	62.1	58.4	67.0	56.0	62.6	65.7	55.0	68.2	59.3	55.9
Low	Tolerates episodes of bad management, is not economical with materials	10.8	7.0	11.9	8.4	12.6	9.1	9.8	10.3	9.4	8.6

SOURCE Smirnov (1979: 77–78).

both its objective and subjective aspects (Yadov & Zdravomyslov 1975:51–68).

More recent research has revealed a significant gap between officially expressed requirements on the one hand and the quality and extent of activism on the other. Today the emphasis is on economic accountability, on the quality of work, and on productivity. However, even if official requirements have generally been brought up to date, managerial practices in various enterprises are founded on firmly established lines, and participation from below cannot have changed its features to any great extent (see Table 8.4).

The degree of activism shown by the table has been tabulated on the basis of interviews with 2255 workers in four factories and one mine, analyzed by V. A. Smirnov. Each worker in the sample was also questioned concerning the *chuvstvo khoziaina*. Fifty-eight percent of the interviewees replied that they felt, wholly or partially, "master of the factory," while 20 to 25 percent replied that they did not feel themselves such. The remaining 17 to 22 percent did not give a definite answer. Moreover, fully 20 to 25 percent wholly felt themselves to be "masters," the same percentage as those who definitely did not feel themselves to be "master." In fact Smirnov states:

> The research has shown that, for the moment, only a minority of workers (23.7%) display a high level of awareness of the essence and of the principal properties of that quality of the vanguard Soviet worker which is constituted by feeling himself master of socialist enterprises and of the whole country; 40.2% display a low level of awareness of this quality, and the rest an average level. (Smirnov 1979:86)

A very significant step toward understanding the quantitative and qualitative aspects of workers' participation in management has been provided by the research of A. K. Orlov (1978). This author divides the workers in his sample according to four patterns of behavior: those who display continuous activism, who show it occasionally, who rarely show it, and who do not show it at all.

This research is of great importance because it is the only study, to our knowledge, that has sought to quantify *actual* participation as well as the differences between it and the *pro forma* activism. Orlov does this by carrying out a detailed analysis of the situation in the Construction Association of Agricultural Machinery of Chelya-

TABLE 8.5 Participants in the Management of Production and Members of the Trade Union and Party "Aktiv" at the CTO

Social forms of management	Number of participants	Politico-social organizations	Number of participants
Production Conferences	468	Party aktiv	330
Popular Control	932	Trade-union aktiv	1.691
"Komsomolskii Prozhektor" ("The Komsomol's Designer")	110	Komsomol aktiv	237
Soviet for the Scientific Organization of Work (NTO)	116	TOTAL	2.258
Soviet of Rationalizers and Inventors (VDIR)	270	Total number of workers:	3.570
NTTM Soviet	95	a) participating in the social forms of management	2.567
Social Bureau of Economic Analysis (OBEA)	30	b) belonging to the politico-social organizations	1.003
Social Bureau of NOT	14	Total number of ITR:	2.333
OBNT	28	c) participating in the social forms of management	1.078
Social Bureau for Design (OKB)	19	d) belonging to the politico-social organizations	1.255
OOK (OBK)	101	TOTAL (a + b + c + d)	5.903
OPB	10		
Soviet of the "master" workers	146		
Soviet of the young specialists	50		
Creative brigades	151		
Commissions of the management of departments	123		
Comrades' Court	133		
Active participation in workers' assemblies	823		
Other organizations	26		
TOTAL	3.645		

SOURCE: Orlov (1978: 133).

NOTE: 24 sections, 1975, total manpower = 15,161. Statistics supplied by the administration.

binsk (CTO), the most significant results of which are summarized as follows.

Orlov starts with the official data provided by the CTO administration concerning the participants in various forms of "social management of production" plus the official statistics concerning activists in the trade union and the Party *aktiv* (see Table 8.5). The total manpower of the Association in 1975 was 15,161 employees, of which 12,129 were workers. Mention should immediately be made of the extreme differences in coefficient of participation (Kp) among the various sections of the Association. In fact, the Kp varies between 13 percent and 15 percent in three sections, and reaches 73 percent in another where the members of the *aktiv* were also numerous (43 percent). In the other four sections, however, the number of activists was very low (less than 8 percent). Overall, the Kp is 24 percent in terms of participation in management and 15 percent in terms of participation in the *aktiv*. For the workers in particular, the two coefficients were 21 percent and 9 percent. For the engineers and technicians (ITR) the coefficient was far higher—that is, 35 percent and 77 percent respectively.

A first point to note here concerns the striking disproportion between the respective rates of activism for technical personnel and workers. It should also be pointed out that participation by women, who make up 48 percent of the manpower, was 16 percent less than that by men. A third point can be made concerning the high rate of activism in sections where technical staff are concentrated, matched by an extremely low rate in auxiliary departments. Also to be noted is that the correlation between the size of the enterprise and the coefficient level is not as important as one could expect: in the three largest factories participation rates were lower than in one workshop with 684 employees (20 percent compared with 32 percent). Finally, the lower degree of involvement in Party and union activity was found in the two mining sections of the Association, the coefficients being 11 percent and 8 percent. In short, the ratio of participation depends mainly on the composition of the labor force.

Compared with similar studies, the really new aspect of Orlov's research lies in its use of the coefficient of *real participation* (Krp), which takes into account the number of people who participate in more than one of the innumerable social organs. The number of these people amounted to 1207; this figure is then subtracted from 5903, the total number of participants as supplied by the admin-

istration of the Association. The real number of participants is then
4696 (5903 minus 1207), that is 70 percent of the official figure.
This is an average. The so-called polymorphism in management
participation is actually a typical phenomenon among the ITR.
Here, of 1207 individuals who participated in more than one
organization, 1071 were ITR. And this is how the "formalism" of
workers' participation is explained:

> If one considers that a number of workers in this category are appointed
> to these positions against their will and that the carrying out of a number
> of social duties damages the quality of work, then this "polymorphism"
> proves to a certain extent to be a negative phenomenon, one which leads
> to formal participation in the leadership of production. (Orlov
> 1978:139)

To determine the degree of real participation, the identification of
the number of people who have been counted two or more times is a
necessary step, but not a sufficient one. It is also necessary to verify
which and how many people are actually involved, and the *concrete
results* of their involvement. This has been done by Orlov by using
the *coefficient of practical participation* (Kpp), which is expressed
by the ratio between the number of participants who produce
concrete results and the number of real participants.

The working people producing concrete results have been identified by a combination of methods such as organizational analysis,
socioeconomic experiments, interviews, and evaluations by a panel
of experts. In this way, Orlov found that the real participants in the
CTO were 4696, but that 1951 individuals are to be subtracted
from this number because they produced almost no results in the
participation movement. In conclusion, only 3125 of the 5903 listed
by the administration were the authentic "participants in the leadership of production." In percents the participants were not 39
percent of the total manpower, but 20 percent. For the workers the
percentage was 17 percent, and for the ITR 34 percent. This process
of successive elimination reduced the percentage of activism and
participation reported by the administration to practically half. As
Orlov notes, the higher the official figures are, the more drastic must
be the refinement, of these figures (Orlov 1978:144).

Orlov's research deals with participation in all forms. For "socialist competition" in particular, significant data are offered by
another study carried out in 1977 on a sample of construction

TABLE 8.6 Objective Indicators of the Performance of Workers at the Three Levels of Activism[a] (statistics relative to the new type of brigade; n = 420)

	Objective indicators of performance										
Carrying out work duties		Quality of work		Improvement of qualifications		Participation in "rationalization"		Discipline at work		Participation in the campaign for cost reduction	
High	Low	High	Low	High	Low	High	Low	High	Low	High	Low
79.1	0	68.7	1.5	50.7	0.7	6.7	47.7	46.3	0.7	53.0	0
41.2	1.8	36.6	3.3	27.5	4.3	2.5	63.3	21.4	8.3	28.3	4
11.1	9.1	0	9.1	9.1	36.4	0	61.1	0	27.3	9.1	8

[a] For the purposes of simplification the percentages referring to average level of performance have been omitted. These may be obtained by subtracting the percentages of high and low levels from 100.
SOURCE: Smirnov (1979): 124

159

workers in Murmansk. Given its socioprofessional features, this is certainly not a representative sample. However, the findings of this research deserve consideration. The building industry is one of the sectors, in which attempts are being made to introduce as widely as possible the concept of "brigade economic accountability" (*brigadni khozraschet*). The sample was divided between 420 workers who worked by this method and 363 who continued to work in the traditional way.

The active participants in "socialist competition"—including those who made personal pledges for a given quota—represented 31.8 percent of the new-type brigades, and 17.4 percent of the old-type work squads (V. A. Smirnov 1979:123). The main results of this research are summarized in Table 8.6. Another study quoted by Smirnov (1979), conducted by Tukumstev in a Kuybishev auto factory, shows that 38.5 percent of the workers were active and very active participants in socialist competition. In these studies, however, there is no distinction between participation on paper and participation yielding results.

Smirnov (1979) has also measured the degree of activism in the "rationalization" movement using a sample of young workers under age thirty. The main data (see Tables 8.7 and 8.8) are similar to those obtained in other studies in the country and may therefore be regarded as representative of the general situation. What actually emerges is a very low level of participation. In practical terms, "rationalization" is nothing more than the process of workers detecting defects in design and construction of machines through use and reporting them. More interesting is the author's examination of various typologies drawn up by Soviet sociologists that jointly consider the objective and subjective aspects of activism and participation (Smirnov 1979).

The first typology was drawn up by E. G. Komarov, based on a study carried out in 1966 in two enterprises in Krasnoyarsk and repeated in 1971. It was based on five indicators of participation in "socialist competition": technical creativity, scientific creativity, artistic creativity, and sociopolitical activity. The fifth indicator was the combining of work with study. According to these indicators, the percentage of the workers judged most active in one enterprise rose from 7.9 percent in 1966 to 20.5 percent in 1971. In the other enterprise the percentages were 12.1 percent and 28.5 percent, respectively.

TABLE 8.7 *Participation by Young Workers in "Rationalization"*

| Level of activism | Metalworking sector | | | Pulp and paper, Moscow region (1971–1973) | Building indus-try, Murmansk region (1977) | Five enterprises in Smirnov's sample (1977) |
	Mogilev (1971–1973)	Moscow region (1971–1973)	Murmansk (1975)			
High (constant participation)	2.1	2.8	1.3	3.1	2.5	5.9
Average (occasional participation)	14.7	18.1	13.7	11.9	21.9	37.6
Low (nonparticipation)	83.2	79.1	85.0	85.0	75.6	56.5

SOURCE: Smirnov (1979: 104–5).

TABLE 8.8 Indicators of Productive Activism in Relation to Age and Seniority

Sociodemographic characteristics	Do you participate in activities connected with the management of production (drafting the plan, revising the norms)?			During the last year have you criticized—verbally or in writing—examples of disorganization or waste?	
	Yes	Sometimes	No	Yes	No
Age					
0–18	7.7	27.2	65.1	–	100.0
18–25	12.3	26.0	61.7	7.3	92.7
26–28	21.7	32.6	45.7	15.6	84.4
29–35	22.0	44.2	33.8	26.4	73.6
36–40	28.2	34.0	37.8	15.0	85.0
50 or older	25.0	33.5	41.7	22.7	77.3
Length of service					
less than 1 year	4.0	22.0	74.0	4.3	95.7
1– 3 years	14.0	24.7	61.3	10.1	89.9
3– 5 years	24.6	30.8	44.6	7.6	92.4
5–10 years	15.0	49.2	35.8	21.4	78.6
10–15 years	31.9	35.4	32.7	21.0	79.0
more than 15 years	19.5	31.7	48.8	17.5	82.5

SOURCE: Volkov and Cerviakov (1977: 137).

Smirnov criticizes this typology because participation is not evaluated in terms of various levels of activism, and the number of those judged most active probably also included those who had participated in a *pro forma* fashion. Besides, as Smirnov (1979:135) notes, activism does not depend only on individual motivation, but also on the quality of organizational work.

M. A. Nugaev's typology, like Komarov's, is based on the objective indicators of production activism: productivity, improving qualifications, participation in rationalization, participation in "socialist competition," and the scientific organization of work (NOT). The general index resulting from the combination of these indicators, as they apply to a sample of 3000 workers in the Republic of Tataria, gave the following picture: 11.1 percent of the workers displayed high activism, 52.2 percent average activism, and 36.7 percent low activism (Smirnov 1979).

Smirnov's criticism of Nugaev's typology centers on its "objectivist" character, and on the fact that the five indicators have different degrees of representativeness. He argues that workers' participation is not so much a question of their "technical-scientific creativity" as, for example, is the quality of their work and the avoidance of waste in the use of materials (Smirnov 1979:137).

The typology set up by Smirnov in cooperation with B. F. Usmanov actually reveals a more sound basis. It is the product of a kind of action research aimed not only at investigating participation, but at promoting it, too. This action research—and the organizational redesign resulting from it—brought in one year an increase in activism among young workers participating in the "Leninist Test" (*Leninski zachiot*). The percentage of the most active workers increased from 17.1 percent in 1972 to 24.9 percent in 1973. But this action research also displays serious methodological limitations—as the authors themselves admit. Many of the criticisms leveled at previous typologies also apply to theirs, including the point that it neglects a factor that is currently heavily emphasized: the protection of "socialist property" and the drive to economize resources (V. A. Smirnov 1975). Smirnov, this time in cooperation with V. E. Boykov, attempted to remedy these defects in two subsequent studies: one carried out in 1976 on a sample of 700 metalworkers, and the other on 783 construction workers in the Murmansk area. The following indicators were used: (1) participation in the enforcement of discipline; (2) carrying out of work

duties; (3) improving skills; (4) improving the quality of work; and
(5) caring about issues concerning the production collective (*kho-
ziaiskaia zabota*).

On the basis of evidence provided by experts, the 700 metalworkers were classified at five levels of decreasing activism. The relative
percentages were: 13.5 percent, 29 percent, 27.2 percent, 15.3
percent, 15 percent. The top level comprised workers judged to be
highly active on the basis of all five indicators. In the following
groups, the degree of activism appeared as average or low in one or
more of the applied indicators. Thus, workers judged as corresponding to the "ideal type" represented 13.5 percent of the total.
Those judged as lacking discipline and being the "producers of
rejects" represented 15 percent. In Smirnov's opinion, only the first
and second groups were worthy of the title "vanguards of production" (*peredoviki proizvodstva*), or 42.5 percent of the total.

A typology based on the subjective components of participation
was subsequently drawn up. Here, indicators taken into account
included the job's place in the subject's personal life, the subject's
evaluation of its social significance and creative potential, the
importance attached to wage level, and the attitude toward poor
discipline at work. Three attitudinal variants were considered for
each indicator.

In decreasing order of activism, the results were as follows: 14.7
percent, 32 percent, 16.3 percent, 15 percent, and 22 percent. So,
the "ideal workers" here number 14.7 percent. These are the
workers who, according to the authors, display the highest productivity level, but do not necessarily attribute "communist intentiona-
lity" to their work behavior. It is no coincidence that only 55
percent and 48.7 percent of the workers showing the highest degree
of productivity (1st and 2nd group) turned out to be "vanguard
workers from the ideal point of view."

Here it is worth noting that 4 percent of the "ideal workers" did
not take part in sociopolitical activities, while among "backward
workers" this percentage was 46 percent (Smirnov 1979:152). But
this means that the majority of the latter supposedly participate in
social activities: a clear demonstration of the *pro forma* character of
these activities. Indeed, 12.5 percent of "ideal workers" are placed
in the bottom group from the subjective point of view. This means
that they place little importance on the social value of their work
and are completely indifferent to the state of discipline in the

workplace. On the other hand, there exist a certain number of workers who come close to the ideal model of "communist attitude to work" without obtaining good objective indicators of performance: They amount to 20 percent in the first group and 30 to 50 percent in the second. The Party members among the workers of the sample amounted to 9.2 percent (Smirnov 1979:152).

The various possible combinations of the subjective and objective indicators of workers' behavior were finally arranged on three levels. At the top level stand the "front rank workers" (*peredoviki proizvodstva*), who comprise 21.7 percent of the total; then come the "individualists" (*seredniaki*), who comprise 45.9 percent; and then, at the bottom, the "backward" (*otstaiushchie*), who comprise a good 32.4 percent. Within each of the three basic types there are various subtypes. Thus, those in the vanguard who scored maximum points for both the objective and subjective indicators amount to only 13.1 percent of the total. The great majority of "individualists" (33.1 percent of the sample) scored maximum points for one of the ten indicators, as did a third of the "backward." The ones who one might call "the absolute backward"— that is, those that scored minimum points in all ten indicators— make up 4.7 percent of the total (Smirnov 1979:147).

Similar studies were conducted in the late 1960s in several metalworking factories of Kharkov. The aim was to measure the level of personal responsibility and consciousness in correlation with variables such as age, seniority at work, educational level, job rank, and social duties carried out. The following indicators were used to measure the individual sense of moral responsibility and sociopolitical awareness: (1) conscientious work, probity, and dedication to the common cause; (2) intransigent attitude toward any violation of "social interests"; (3) active participation in the correction of inadequacies; and (4) the demonstration of "masterly solicitude" for everything that concerns not only the collective but society as a whole.

On the basis of the gathered data, the workers of the sample were classified in the following groups (various authors 1968:213–217).

First Group: highly conscientious workers. They display a notable sense of moral responsibility. These are workers who obtained maximum scores for all four indicators. They represent 5 to 10 percent of the total in all sections of the factories. The authors call these workers "the gold stock" (*zolotoi fond*) of the production collective.

Second Group: workers with characteristics similar to those in the first group, except that their interests do not extend beyond the perimeter of the factory. In other words, they put the interests of the enterprise before the interests of the society as a whole. These represent 5 to 8 percent of the total.

Third Group: workers who rate positively for the four indices but who—although not tolerant toward mismanagement—take no active part in attempts to correct defects and inadequacies. These represent 8 to 10 percent of the total.

Fourth Group: workers who display the positive quality of Groups 1–3, but who show indifference to organizational inadequacies. These workers, like those of Group 3, play a passive role in campaigns aimed at improving production efficiency. They amount to 25 to 30 percent of the total.

   The last two groups comprise workers who, according to the authors, show low levels of moral responsibility or none at all. These are workers who are "still not free of the psychology and the morality of the private property-owner" (1968:216):

Fifth Group: good workmen who often overfulfill production targets. However, they display individualistic motives for their productive efforts. They refuse social responsibilities. They might make critical speeches at workers' meetings, but these derive from purely personal considerations. These, too, amount to 25 to 30 percent of the total.

Sixth Group: also generally good workmen. But they almost never take an active part in the social life of the collective:

Many of them live outside the city, they have their own houses, a plot of land and manage their household economy carefully. They work in the factory so that ready cash (*svezhaia kopeika*) is not lacking at home and so that they have a right to a pension when old. This is as far as their thinking goes. (1968:215)

Soviet research provides some data concerning the sociodemographic variables influencing the level and quality of production activism and social activism. Enrollment in the Party is a decisive variable. In Smirnov's sample, 9.2 percent of the total but 43.2 percent of the "vanguard workers" were enrolled in the CPSU. Many "individualists" were also members of the Party, although none of the "backward" were. It is worth noting, though, that 12 percent of the "backward" were members of the *Komsomol*. The percentage of young workers not enrolled in the *Komsomol* was 34.6 percent (Smirnov 1979:152). The other discriminating variables were age and seniority (see Table 8.8).

Thus, the typical worker in the *aktiv* is between 30 to 50 years of age with at least ten years of seniority. He has professional qualifications, is a member of the Party, and engages in social activism. It should be borne in mind, however, that the percentage of the *aktiv's* members is significantly higher among the technical personnel.

The Soviet mass media frequently report mass participation under headlines such as "Politics: The Inspiration of Millions," "Millions of Enthusiasts," "The Creative Activity of Millions." But one may ask: How big a percentage are these millions in terms of the total workforce?

The investigations on workers' participation quoted in the preceding pages may be regarded as sufficiently representative of the state of affairs in large enterprises in heavy industry, at least for the most part. The samples, in fact, amount to some tens of thousands of people and are representative of the various professional groups. The studies have been carried out in different industrial centers. The last two typologies seem to adequately reflect the range of attitudes and behavior to be found among the employees of the larger industrial establishments.

With the help of these data one can try to imagine the pattern of participation from below, both in routine situations and during the periodic campaigns of mobilization launched under a variety of slogans. In the normal routine of Soviet factories there should be 15 to 20 percent of the workers involved, more or less deeply, in their role as "vanguards of production." At the other extreme are the 5 to 7 percent of indisciplined workers and drunkards. Between the vanguards and the drunkards stand the great majority—the normal workers who have been labeled "individualist" or "backward" by Soviet sociologists.

Now let us picture what must happen in the periodic "campaigns." In these times of general mobilization, the 15 to 20 percent who compose the "vanguards" manage somehow to involve the rest of the workforce. It is fair to suppose that some kind of reaction comes from a quota of workers in the third and fourth groups. In the best of cases, the mobilization campaigns should have some effect, albeit temporary, on approximately half of the working people. But these "best cases" appear to be very infrequent. The writer Shatunovsky (1970:14), who demonstrates a good knowledge of factory life, describes an apparently typical campaign in these terms: "They shout in the meetings, they write on the wall-newspapers, they condemn the parasites, and they calm down until the next campaign."

The majority of workers, the "individualists" and the "backwards," keep their heads down until the storm has passed. And then they go back to their old ways.

To gain a clearer idea of the behavior and motives of the different groups of Soviet working people, it is necessary not only to report on the situation in the big enterprises and in large cities; we must also take into account the situation in small and middle-sized enterprises located in outlying areas. This is done in the next section.

DEALING IN THE "SHADOW ECONOMY"

Soviet sociologists have found that the percentage of workers dissatisfied with working conditions is far from negligible. And when wages, family incomes, and purchasing power are examined more closely, the reasons for dissatisfaction become clearer. Official sources, however, do not give detailed data on the strategies working people adopt to improve their living standards. Thus, to do this, we must integrate Soviet data with data gathered by Western scholars.

An interesting example of one such survey was done by Rallis (1981), who gathered the opinions on wages and purchasing power expressed by a sample of 500 Soviet workers on holiday in the West. These workers were extracted from an overall sample of 5000 Soviet citizens who visited several Western countries on package tours in the period between February 1975 and August 1978. The questions were posed by interviewers—who obviously did not identify themselves as such—in the course of informal conversations. The information gathered was of particular interest because, among other things, it was provided by people living in areas closed to foreigners.

In this investigation the dissatisfaction with wages appeared to be relatively common. A certain number of workers (from Ivanovo, Kirov, Togliattigrad, for example) reported that their premiums had been cut because of difficulties in fulfilling the plan, which in turn had been caused by problems with supplies. But this was not their main problem. Their greater difficulty was in obtaining consumer goods, a difficulty summed up in the comment of a skilled worker from Sinferopoli: "Our material life is much more difficult than you imagine." Other comments give a more detailed picture and are worth quoting:

> Queues outside the shops haven't disappeared, nor are they likely to do so in the future [skilled worker, fifty years old, Vladivostock, one of the cities closed to foreigners].
> Since the shops are virtually empty, the black market flourishes [factory foreman, fifty, Murmansk].
> We lack basic items like cotton, rice, and foodstuffs [thirty-year-old worker from Berdyansk].
> We lack everything [electrician from Engels].
> I think that if things don't get better, we'll soon be out of noodles, rice, and bread [twenty-four-year-old worker, Moscow].
> Groceries and vegetables are very scarce and expensive [worker from Ivanovo].
> Items like coffee and chocolate are so rare that you only buy them on special occasions like weddings and christenings [worker, thirty years old, Oremburg]. (Rallis, 1981:231–236)

Testimony gathered by journalist Feifer (1976) confirms this and also conveys the feeling—widespread among Soviet citizens—

that things are far from getting better, that the shortage of goods can no longer be regarded as the temporary difficulty of a developing economy:

> Everyone I met had gone into a kind of underground business. They were buying and selling, bribing, arranging favors, and concocting deals to obtain scarce items.... Anything of commercial value is immediately siphoned off to this "second economy." ... It's hard to imagine the extent to which theft and corruption have become expected.... The assumption that everybody steals is erasing the whole nation's sense of right and wrong. (Feifer 1976:212–213)

One might suspect that these reports are exaggerated or, at least, that they cannot be applied to the country as a whole. But a comparison with Soviet sources—on the subject of "theft of socialist property"—gives the impression that there is much truth in the foregoing quotation. Let us take, for example, the description of the unofficial economy in the city of Odessa made by the trade unions' newspaper, *Trud*, and reported by Kaser (1976). The article begins with the description of private shoemakers who manufactured high-quality footwear out of leather stolen from a shoe factory. None of these shoemakers remotely considered the possibility of going to work in a factory:

> Because there you have to work in a small, cold doghouse, whereas at home you can create good working conditions for yourself and make a lot of money. (Kaser 1976:371)

The article also described the activity of a private shop where wreaths were made for funerals, and the "Jacks of all trades" who could be hired at the farmers' market for any sort of job. People with something needing repair must hire such freelance, "fix-it men" privately—and pay three times the official price. The *Trud* correspondent acknowledged that the unofficial economy is a consequence of the fact that the state enterprises "do not do their duty." But Odessa is a special case as far as the unofficial economy is concerned. What happens elsewhere? In a "vanguard" factory, for instance?

The case of the Voronezh tire factory provides interesting evidence. A female worker from this plant sent a letter to *Pravda*. In it she recounted how her husband had started to drink to excess without any official body at the plant paying the slightest attention—even though, the newspaper commented, out of a total staff of 11,502, there were more than 6000 "front-rank workers," 2000 Party members, and 2000 members of the Komsomol. The factory detachment of the voluntary militia (*druzhinniki*) was deemed one of the best in the region; 3000 people "creatively" used their leisure time, and there was also a club for young working people. However, an investigation carried out in 1980 revealed 320 cases of lawbreaking tried by the "comrades' courts." In the same year, losses to the tire factory from pilfering amounted to an equivalent of 2480 man-days. As far as plan fulfillment is concerned, in the previous two years, the plan had been fulfilled with difficulty and only because management resorted to the usual practices of "storming," side payments, and so on. If this is the state of "socialist legality" in a "vanguard" factory, it is easy to imagine that elsewhere the pilferers–labelled as "predators of socialist property"—are much more active.

Soviet sociologists claim that the overwhelming majority of working people regard the creation of an uncompromising attitude toward "predators" as important or very important. But a question concerning the concrete attitude of the collective toward the "predators" was given the following replies: 46.7 percent thought that the majority of the collective strongly disapproved of the behavior of "predators"; 20 percent thought that "predators" are disapproved of by a significant part of the collective; 11.6 percent thought they are blamed only by some members of the collective; and 5 percent thought that the blame comes from nobody at all. In addition, 12.6 percent replied that they had never thought about this issue, and 4 percent declined to answer (Smirnov 1979: 82). These data speak for themselves. It only remains to point out that they confirm the existence of a dividing line between "production vanguards" and the great majority of "individualists" and "backwards."

But why does pilfering not disappear? ask Soviet sociologists. The workers provide them with eloquent answers (see Table 8.9). The most common reply is "*Ne vsyo mozhna kupit v magazine*" ("Not everything is available in the shop") (29.1 percent). Another interesting reply—*Iz za khishchenie gosudarstvo ne obedneet*" ("The state won't fall into poverty because of larceny") (15.1 percent)—confirms the impression that "the fight to defend socialist

TABLE 8.9   *"Why, according to you, have cases of theft of socialist property still not disappeared?"*

Response	Percentage
You cannot find everything in the shops.	29.1
The inventory and surveillance are badly organized in the enterprise.	20.9
Many think that the State will certainly not fall into poverty because of larceny.	15.1
The "predators" go unpunished.	12.5
The laws for the protection of socialist property are not made known or not applied to the collective.	10.4
These facts are not condemned with sufficient severity in the collective.	9.2
No answer	2.8

SOURCE: Smirnov (1979: 84).

property" is much more a question of word than deed, (even if one may suppose that the state of "socialist legality" has improved somewhat under the new leadership). On the subject of the responses elicited in this study, V. A. Smirnov comments:

> Comparison between the distribution of the replies collected in different factories has shown that, despite the slight extent to which the individual percentages differ among themselves, in general they follow the order given. This demonstrates that the distribution is not random; that it does not merely reflect local conditions, but is common to diverse regions. (Smirnov 1979: 84).

Zeitlin (1971) wrote that "a little larceny can do a lot to improve employee morale." Perhaps Soviet sociologists suspect this is the point, but they do not (or cannot) analyze the reasons—for example, focusing on the relations between the widespread theft or misappropriation of "socialist property" and the variety of unofficial markets existing in the Soviet Union.

In a previous chapter we described the functioning of "georgian" and "gogolian" management. Here, it is worth adding that in low-priority industrial sectors, management is often pushed toward illegal behavior not only from above—that is, from the combination of a taut plan and uncertainty in material supply—but also to keep the needed workforce, who tend to quit if pay and bonuses are insufficient. In such circumstances it can easily happen that factory management tacitly agrees that material which, according to plan figures, should have been used in production, in reality remains unused, since part of the work was carried out on paper alone. These materials are removed illegally by workers for their own use (a second job perhaps) or are sold to individual consumers (Kroncher 1982: 5).

Despite the fact that people usually speak of only a "black market," in the USSR many markets exist outside the official one. Aaron Katsenelinboigen (1978) proposes a classification of these markets according to their degree of legality and their source of supply. These classifications are *legal*, *semilegal*, and *illegal*, each with subdivisions reflecting the degree to which they are condoned by the authorities. The various market types are also subdivided into three groups according to generative factors. The first group comprises the *immanent markets*, which exist in every economic system because of the passions and desires of human nature itself. The second group comprises the *socialist markets*, those generated not by theoretical but by practical functions of the economic system, on the basis of central planning and state ownership of the means of production. Finally, there is the third group: the *rudimentary markets*, that is, those that have grown up in the Soviet Union as a result of the specific conditions of development of a peasant population with a low living standard and a low cultural level.

Each market is classified with a color that symbolizes the amount of official approval or disapproval it incurs—from the *red* of the official market to the *black* of the most illegal market. Other markets lie between these two extremes. These include the *pink*, the secondhand goods markets, also directly controlled by the state; and the *white*, the designation of the flea market and the *kolkhoz* (farmer's) market. The latter comes under less direct state control: Here the state merely fixes the maximum level of prices. The red, pink, and white markets are officially sanctioned. The red and pink (and the black) are markets that also belong to the *immanent* category.

At the semilegal level is the *grey* market. This market offers goods and services that are also available through official channels. Here, illegality lies in the fact that these transactions are not registered and, consequently, not taxed. There also exists a grey market for industrial production, resorted to by firms in search of supplies needed to fulfill plan targets. Katsenelinboigen rightly stresses the corrupting influence of this market, inasmuch as it accustoms people to use illegal means to obtain legal ends. Once the first step has been taken, it is a short distance to the black market (Katsenelinboigen 1978:185–186). The grey market belongs to the category of true *socialist markets* alongside that part of the black market in which theft and sale of "socialist property" is involved.

Two markets function at the level of complete illegality: the *brown* market and the *black* market. Both markets deal in both production and consumer goods. As far as the type of goods is concerned, the difference lies in the fact that in the *brown* market illegal transactions are resorted to for the legitimate end of fulfilling the plan, whereas in the black market individuals benefit. As for consumer goods, *brown market* implies, for example, under-the-counter sales in state-run shops on an individual basis. The brown market turns into black when under-the-counter sales are organized on a large scale by shop personnel and intermediaries who set up a network of collusion. The brown market, together with the white and grey markets, belongs to the category of *rudimentary markets*.

Thus, from the state monopoly of the economy stems a paradox: What in theory is the most advanced form of ownership and management, has produced in fact an allocation of resources largely based on an informal system of barter between enterprises—in which certain goods (cement, bricks, pipes) have come to play the role of money (Zaslavskaya 1981: 39).

At this point two further considerations remain (before addressing the questions of workers' wages, family income, and living standards). Soviet sources usually stress that the average worker's family enjoys two separate incomes and a "social wage," the latter of which represents a significant proportion of the family income (see Table 8.10).

The available data demonstrate that enterprises finance health, rest, and holiday centers for approximately 10 percent of their employees, that is, for those that authorities regard as "deserving." The other, being less "deserving" insofar as they are "individualists" or "backward" workers, have largely to look after themselves. Of course, there do exist services and amenities that are open to all; but in the case of these services there is the problem of quality. For example, those desiring satisfactory standards of medical care have to pay privately for a doctor's treatment. Patients in hospitals have to pass cash to the nurses if they wish to be given special care

TABLE 8.10   *Income Structure for the Families of Industrial Workers*

Income Source	1965	1977
Salaries	73.1	74.3
Cash transfers	9.0	9.2
Income from personal plots of land	1.7	0.8
Other sources of income	2.4	2.3
Family income	86.2	86.6
Social wage[a]	13.8	13.4

[a] State benefit for education, health, and so on.
SOURCE: McAuley (1980: 206).

(Katsenelinboigen 1978:182). The same system applies to other social services that are supposedly gratis.

Specific data are also available on the issue of the double income of the family. The average worker's salary for the 1976–1980 plan was set at 150 rubles per month. Daily expenditure on food for a family of three in 1976 was calculated at 7.30 rubles, that is, 225 rubles per month, plus an additional 25 rubles for soap, toothpaste, detergent, some cosmetics for the wife, and the occasional icecream for the child. In addition, many fruits and vegetables are not available in state shops—or are more or less rotten—so they have to be bought at the farmer's market where prices are at least three times higher (an extra 50 rubles).

Altogether, the estimated minimum monthly income required by the average family amounts to 300 rubles. And then there is a further series of expenses to be taken into account—such as rent, telephone (if the family has one), entertainment, shoes and clothing, transport, and so on. Thus, the total necessary monthly income rises to 450 rubles. Assuming that the two incomes entering this typical family average 150 rubles each, they total only 300 rubles, a monthly shortfall of 150. More realistically, we might assume the wife earns rather less than her husband (suppose, 100 rubles); thus the monthly shortfall becomes 200 rubles (Turovsky 1981:160).

Soviet research into family budgets confirms these estimates, taking as its standard a worker's family of four members. During the period 1965–1970, the minimum subsistence level was 205.6 rubles per month, that is, 51.4 rubles per person. The Soviet researchers then established the "rational family budget"; this, for the period 1971–1975, was set at 613.2 rubles, that is, 153.3 rubles

TABLE 8.11 *Weekly Basket (for four persons) of Consumer Goods at Soviet Level of Consumption in March 1982 (expressed as work-time units)*

Item	Kilograms	Washington	Moscow	Munich	Paris	London
Flour	1.0[a]	5	28	9	6	6
Bread	7.0	112	119	189	126	175
Noodles	2.0	28	68	32	22	28
Beef	1.0	69	123	150	119	115
Pork	1.5	63	176	150	108	117
Minced beef	1.0	37	123	70	80	63
Sausages	1.0	33	160	75	75	51
Cod	1.0	61	47	45	118	72
Sugar	3.3	30	191	33	30	36
Butter	0.5	28	111	26	24	25
Margarine	2.0	46	222	34	36	64
Milk (litres)	12.0	72	264	84	96	108
Cheese	2.0	200	370	130	118	130
Eggs, cheapest (units)	18.0	14	99	22	23	29
Potatoes	9.0	63	63	36	36	27
Cabbage	3.0	27	36	21	27	30
Carrots	1.0	11	19	10	7	13
Tomatoes	1.0	23	62	28	25	32
Apples	1.0	10	92	15	15	23
Tea	0.1	10	53	10	17	5
Beer (litres)	3.0	33	48	24	21	54
Gin/Vodka (litres)	1.0	87	646	106	153	187
Cigarettes (units)	120	54	90	96	48	150

	(Hours of work-time)				
Weekly basket, as above	18.6	53.5	23.3	22.2	25.7
Weekly basket for "statistically average" family of 3.5 persons	16.3	46.8	20.4	19.4	22.5
Rent, monthly	51	12	24	39	28
Color TV	65	701	143	106	132
	(Months of work-time)				
Small car	5	53	6	8	11
Medium car	8	88	9	12	18

[a] Minutes of work-time.
SOURCE: *The Soviet Worker*, Second Edition, edited by Leonard Schapiro and Joseph Godson. © Leonard Schapiro and Joseph Godson, 1981, 1982, 1984. Reprinted by permission of St. Martin Press, Inc.

TABLE 8.12 *Average Gross and Take-Home Pay in December 1981*

	(a) US (dollars)	(b) USSR (rubles)	(c) FRG (marks)	(d) France (francs)	(e) UK (pounds)
1 Average gross monthly earnings	1,426.45	177.30	2,772.50	5,023.06	483.20
2 *minus* Income, state and church tax	190.90	18.25	331.74	nil	80.69
3 *minus* Social security contributions	95.57	nil	249.53		
4 *minus* Medical insurance premiums	156.00	nil	155.26	637.32	38.66
5 *minus* Unemployment insurance payment	nil	nil	55.45		
6 *plus* Family allowance	nil	12.00	150.00	389.72	41.17
7 Average monthly take-home pay	983.98	171.05	2,130.52	4,784.46	405.02
8 Monthly take-home pay converted to US $	983.98	402.47	959.69	822.63	741.79
9 Take-home pay ($) per work-hour	5.69	2.28	5.37	4.87	4.15
10 Take-home pay (c) per work-minute	9.48	2.26	8.33	7.76	6.89

SOURCE: *The Soviet Worker*, Second Edition, edited by Leonard Schapiro and Joseph Godson. © Leonard Schapiro and Joseph Godson, 1981, 1982, 1984. Reprinted by permission of St. Martin Press, Inc.

per person—an estimate that more or less coincides with Turovsky's for 1976.

A clearer picture of the Soviet worker's family income can be derived by integrating the aforementioned estimates with the findings of a comparative study of living standards in the Soviet Union and the West conducted by Keith Bush (1981). This study records the retail prices of a typical basket of consumer goods and services in Moscow, Munich, Paris, Washington D.C., and London in March 1982. The working time equivalent to these prices was calculated on the basis of the estimated average net salary of industrial workers. The net salary is arrived at by deducting the income tax and national insurance of a worker with three dependents. In the Soviet Union there are no payments for health coverage. In the United States, payments for voluntary health insurance are deducted. In Germany, Great Britain, and France, family benefits and unemployment insurance contributions are deducted (in the United States, unemployment is paid by the employer). In the USSR, family benefits of 12 rubles per child are paid to families with a per-capita income of less than 50 rubles. A comparison was also made between the average gross salaries of Soviet workers and those of their American, German, English, and French counterparts (see Tables 8.11 and 8.12).

The statistics given by Bush's tables prompt the following remarks. The average Soviet salary, converted into dollars, is less than half of the average salary in the United States and West Germany; it is about half of the average salary in France and Great Britain. It should also be remembered that the conversion into dollars has been made at the official rate, where the ruble is overevaluated by at least a third. There is no doubt that Soviet workers have to work much more than their Western counterparts to obtain the same kinds of goods. The problem is to determine how much of their earnings come from their official job and how much is classified under the heading of "nonlabor income" (Orland 1986).

Assessing how much Soviet workers supplement their incomes with moonlighting and other dealings in the shadow economy is by no means an easy task. Soviet statistics are far from complete and sufficiently broken down. Several Western scholars, however, have developed refined techniques of interpolation and extrapolation using Soviet statistics. The works of Gur Ofer and Aaron Vinokur (1979) are a case in point. Offering interesting data on family incomes of Soviet workers, they draw both on official sources and on surveys of ex-Soviet citizens (see Tables 8.13 and 8.14). From these findings emerges the conclusion that Soviet supplementary incomes are around 30 percent of the total.

Important data on how Soviet working people try to improve their living standards is offered by the Soviet Interview Project (SIP), in particular in a paper by Gregory (1986). Among SIP's 2900 informants there was the widespread perception (in the second half of the 1970s) that real wages were falling: 61 percent reported that living standards were declining. Informants also categorized one-third of the people in their community as living in conditions of poverty.

The feature of Soviet life that evoked the strongest dissatisfaction was the general unavailability of goods in the state shops (95 percent). For meat and dairy products in particular, 81 percent reported that usually these were in short supply (Gregory 1986: Table 3).

Asked about the effect of trade unions on wage matters, 25.4 percent said that unions make things better, 2.7 percent that they make things worse, and 72 percent that they had no effect. It is well known that Soviet trade unions are not of the wage-demanding type, as are their Western counterparts: Soviet trade unions main activities are in the sphere of social welfare. But here, too, their actions seem not to have a great influence if 37.3 percent thought that they made things better and 61.7 percent thought that they had no effect (Gregory 1986: Table 1). In short, respondents generally agreed that the planned economy offered low rates of return on efforts and that this fact is the prime reason for the Soviet economy's poor performance and negative impact on standards of living. Consequently, many people try to get out of the vicious circle, transferring energy, time, and workmanship from the official to the unofficial economy.

In recent years the Soviet press has frequently accused managers of doing everything possible to attract workers into the enterprise, promising high earnings, soft output norms, slack work discipline, and *opportunities for moonlighting*. This informal culture of the factory seems to be condoned by union and Party functionaries too (Porket 1985: 24). The data gathered in the SIP study allow us to make a quantitative assessment of the opportunities for moon-lighting.

TABLE 8.13   *Available Monthly Income in Families of Industrial Workers*

		1973		1975	
		rubles	percentage	rubles	percentage
1	Available family income comprising:	307.2	100	341.2	100
	Total wage	260.2	84.7	289.0	84.7
	Funds of social consumption	32.9	10.7	38.2	11.2
	Private plots	5.2	1.7	4.1	1.2
	Other incomes	8.9	2.9	10.2	3.0
2	Per capita income	(83.5)		(93.2)	
3	Net per capita wage	131.2		144.5	
	No. of employed persons per family	(1.98)		(2)	
	Members of the family	(3.68)		(3.66)	

NOTE: The figures in parenthesis are extrapolations based mainly on the General Censuses of 1959 and 1970.
SOURCE: Vinokur and Ofer (1979: 185, 190).

TABLE 8.14   *Comparison Between Official Soviet Data and Data Gathered in Research on Emigrés for the Year 1973*

	Emigré Data	Official Data
Total income	329.3	
Comparative income comprising:	299.3	307.2
total wage	283.0	260.0
funds for social consumption	6.3 ⎤	32.9 ⎤
private plots	1.8 ⎬ 16.3	5.2 ⎬ 47.0
other incomes	8.2 ⎦	8.9 ⎦
Noncomparable income comprising:		
additions to official salary	15.5 ⎤	
supplementary public work	6.5 ⎬ 29.9	
supplementary private work	7.9 ⎦	
Per capita income	93.0	83.5
Comparable per capita income	89.6	83.5
Number of persons employed per family	2.123	1.98
Members of the family	3.339	3.68

SOURCE: Vinokur and Ofer (1979: 190).

Fifty-nine percent of SIP respondents reported engaging in time theft, that is, they used work time for personal business and second jobs. Gregory attempted to spell out how enterprises' working arrangements—such as firing patterns, use of merit criteria in advancement, and so on—affect behavior in the workplace and time theft. Gregory's results may be summarized as follows: Time theft is systematically lower when management rewarded according to merit and fired poor workers. Workers who felt that they were working in poorly run enterprises were more likely to steal time. There was no strong evidence of systematic time-theft differences among sectors. However, among those who did steal time, the amount of time theft was greater in material-technical supply and other production services, in municipal services, and in housing. Some 13 percent of the respondents reported having private work other than a private farming plot. A second job in the state sector was held by 6 percent of the respondents. Enterprises' work arrangements appear to have less influence on second jobs than personal characteristics, such as being young or being male (Gregory 1986:30–32).

Moonlighting in the Soviet Union is often carried out during the slack period of the first half of the work month. The moonlighting work performed is manifold and generally at a high level of skill. Katsenelinboigen (1978:191) noted, for example, the production of spare parts for agricultural machinery. Moonlighting can also be carried out during leisure time (Grossman 1979, 1981; Kaser 1976). Also, Shatunovsky described some interesting cases. Here is one of them:

> Whenever five mechanics of the "Ordzhonikidze" factory in Muromsk left work for the day, they would take some parts with them. In their free time they would try to put these stolen parts together.
>
> —Hey! It works!
>
> Yes ... it worked. The result was a perfect copy of the "OKD-3" refrigerator manufactured by the factory. After the first, they assembled the second, then a third, a fourth, a fifth. ... (Shatunovsky 1970: 70)

To pile up the components for five refrigerators means you have reached a good level of organization, says Shatunovsky (1970: 70). He adds: "Besides this, there is the well-known case of a car built entirely out of parts stolen from the assembly lines in an automobile factory."

Nowadays central authorities seem resolute in fighting against various illegal activities. To this aim they are now using administrative law mainly, as the decrees on "nonlabor incomes" demonstrate (Orland 1986). But there is no unanimity of intention, especially at the local level. Here it seems, the observations of Gregory Grossman remain largely valid:

> True to their reputation, the Soviet authorities see everything and know everything, but they are particularly sharp-eyed in the spotting of opportunities for taking bribes. Moreover, the causal link is often inverted. The local authorities begin to demand tribute, and the enterprise managers embark on penally punishable activities in order to collect the money required to pay them off. (Grossman 1981: 14–15)

CHAPTER 9

Collective Tensions and Conflicts

The deception by which officially granted liberties are evaded in practice has inevitably become a source of repeated conflicts and fierce hatreds, more bitter than those provoked by the old, explicitly repressive system
—Max Weber, *Sulla Russia 1905–6/1917*

The largest strike in the post-Stalin period of the Soviet Union occurred in Novocherkassk in 1962. It was terribly repressed, with many casualties, arrests, and deportations (Haines & Semyonova 1979:76–81). The Party adopted the same repressive policy in other cases of disturbances that took place in 1959 through 1964 in Temir Tau (Kazakhstan), Kemerovo (Kuzbas), Krasnodar, Donetsk, Yaroslaw, Zhdanov, and Gorky. In all these cases, at least one of the following factors led to the strike: (1) rise of output norms with cuts in wages; (2) shortages of food and consumer goods; and (3) substandard or inadequate housing. The reaction of central authorities to these outbreaks of protest was a combination of selective · repression and the granting of concessions on wage levels and the supplies of state shops (Haines & Semyonova 1979).

In the period 1964–1969, the only significant strike was reported at the Gorky tractor factory in 1967. Strikes increased in frequency during the 1970s, the most important being reported in Dnepropetrovsk and Dneproderzhinsk in 1972. In the former incident, thousands of workers took part in a strike calling for wage increases and a general improvement of living standards. This strike is significant because it marked the appearance of a new demand by the workers: the right to choose their work, rather than have it imposed on them. Their lack of choice was probably one of the consequences of the economic reform of 1965: the displacement of redundant labor through organizational redesign.

At Dneproderzhinsk (Brezhnev's home town) the protest led to ten casualties. Here, the rioting was sparked by a case of police brutality. The mob attacked the police station and then the Party headquarters. Eight rioters and two policemen died (Krawchenko 1977:166). Other strikes occurred during this period at the Kiev hydroelectric station and at the machine factory in the same city, in 1969 and 1972 (Haines & Semyonova 1979:81–86).

The most important strike of 1973 took place in Vytebsk, in the largest factory of the town, triggered by a 20 percent cut in wages imposed by new output standards for skilled workers. The industrial action lasted two days before the KGB intervened; it ordered the director to reinstate previous wage norms and tried (apparently without success) to arrest strike organizers. Work stoppages were also reported in the same period at building sites in Moscow and Leningrad. A strike involving thousands of workers closed the metal works in Kiev. This large number of strikers provoked a swift reaction by the Party. At eleven o'clock in the morning the strikers presented their demand for wage increases. The director immediately phoned the Central Committee of the Party, and a member of the Politburo arrived in the early afternoon. He met a delegation of workers and promised that their demands would be satisfied. At three o'clock in the afternoon the workers were informed that their pay would be increased and that the top administrators of the factory would be fired (Krawchenko & Desolre 1978:40).

In the 1970s a new pattern seemed to emerge: an overall reduction in the level of violence in collective conflicts. On the one hand, the workers no longer rushed headlong into violent rebellion; on the other, the authorities tended to grant concessions more easily and to use more flexible and selective strike-breaking methods. The strikes in Krasnodarsk and Gorky, for example, were due to the usual motive of shortage of goods. But the workers' action was innovative. In the first case, the workers refused to report for work; in the second, the female workers walked out, declaring that they had to go to buy meat and would not return until they had found enough (Krawchenko 1977:168).

Vadim Belotserkovsky reports other forms of industrial action. The first is called "strike Italian-style": The workers clock in but refuse to work. The second consists of a form of indirect pressure on the foremen: Machinery is sabotaged, or spare parts are made to disappear. The breakdown is repaired, or the spare part is retrieved in exchange for extra premiums. A case of the first type happened in the Kirov workshops in Leningrad. Here, approximately 400 workers used this form of industrial action to protest the treatment of prisoners who worked in the factory during the day (Belotser-kovsky 1978:6). Another case was reported by F. Turovsky, a former *iuriskonsult* in the Moscow building industry. In a cement works in Moscow, the director decided to introduce new work schedules without prior consultation with the union committee. When the workers opened their pay packets, they found they had only earned 20 rubles in two weeks. They decided on a strike which lasted two days:

> The workers sat about in the shop, doing nothing. The conveyor belt moved along empty. The shop foreman begged his men to get to work, threatening them with legal action, but they demanded to see the factory director. The director, terrified by the strike, was afraid to enter the shop. At that point, one of the strikers telephoned the local Party committee and announced the strike. (Turovsky 1981:175)

The secretary of the local Party committee hurried to the factory, promised to loosen the production standards, and the strike ended. A few days later a group of workers went to Turovsky to ask if they were entitled to be paid for the two days they were on strike. The *iuriskonsult* replied that there existed a law which provided for half wages to be paid in the event of enforced work stoppages due to managerial mistakes. The workers were not satisfied and went to talk to the director. It is not known whether he acceded to their demands; what is certain is that, in one way or another, all the strikers were subsequently forced to leave the plant (Turovsky 1981:176).

Strikes in the 1980s remain uncommon, but they are not unknown. In 1982, for example, a *samizdat* reported a strike in the Zhdanov bus-building factory of Pavlovsk (district of Gorky). For some years this factory had not fulfilled the plan, although it had systematically resorted to storming and overtime. Perhaps because of these difficulties, the management had committed a series of infractions, and working conditions in the plant deteriorated badly. The first signs of worker unrest appeared in 1981, with a refusal to contribute gratuitous work on Saturdays (*subbotniki*). On October

5 of the same year, the workers were informed that they would not receive their bonuses because the plant was lagging behind its plan targets. The following day a strike broke out, involving approximately 600 workers. The reasons for the protest were: (1) bad working conditions; (2) management rudeness; (3) cancelation of the bonuses.

The management's intention to tighten work norms further increased the tension among workers. At assemblies held in the factory (and in a neighboring plant), banners appeared with the words: *Esli norma budet bolshe, to my sdelaem kak v Polshe* (If the norm increase, we'll do the same as in Poland), and *V poliakov streliat ne budem i churkam ne dodim* (We won't fire on the Poles and we won't give any more to the incompetents) (*Posev*, 9: 1983:6).

A strike was threatened in Vyborg in January 1983 because management did not have the cash available to pay wages. The cash was immediatedly found. Even the newspaper *Izvestia* reported a strike in a car-park in Narva, although it used the euphemism *buza* (scandal, disorder) (*Posev*, 4: 1983:9).

In conclusion, according to Krawchenko and Desolre, there were approximately thirty recorded strikes in the decade 1969–1978. If the period 1959–1964 is added, the total rises to about sixty. From the analysis of this small sample, the two authors make some observations. The first is that strikes and street demonstrations tend to occur most frequently in outlying areas. There are three reasons for this. In the first place, the system of priorities governing the distribution network results in big cities being much better supplied with foodstuffs and consumer goods than the other areas of the country. The second and third reasons are also connected with the system of priorities but in different ways. Basically, the authorities believe that if strategic centers are kept under political control, the outlying regions will not be able to upset the stability of the regime to any serious extent. Consequently, political and police control are much tighter in big cities and in major industrial centers.

Krawchenko and Desolre's second observation about strikes concerns the swift reaction of central authorities to industrial unrest; the speed of the reaction is in direct proportion to the economic importance and geographical location of the plant concerned. This rule, however, has its exceptions. The authorities did not bother too much with the repeated strikes of the fishermen in Murmansk. Even in the strike of a gas works not far from Kiev in 1973 they took it easy and intervened only after the strikers threatened to set the gas in the pipelines on fire (Krawchenko & Desolre 1978:417).

The third point in this 1978 report relates to the causes of strikes and riots. Most frequently the causes are to be found in internal working arrangements. Nevertheless, the rarer strikes sparked by external conditions are more violent, more protracted, and more widespread. These are strikes that most often end in rioting, where the mob attacks the police and Party headquarters. And the main reason for unrest is always the same: shortages of foodstuffs and consumer goods. These strikes represent a serious threat to the regime because they concern not only the workforce but the local population as well.

As far as industrial actions are concerned, the confrontations of the 1970s revealed a change of tactics by both workers and authorities. The former no longer rushed headlong into an assault on the seats of power but tended more to put down tools and stay in the factory—or even not to report to work at all. The latter tended to meet workers' immediate demands more easily and, not infrequently, to make scapegoats of plant administrators. It remains to be seen, however, what will happen if the economic reorganization proclaimed by the present leadership is actually applied on a large scale.

If it is difficult to gather information about strikes in the USSR, it is much more so to know who the leaders of the strikes really are. Krawchenko and Desolre (1978:41) quote a document, written by Marxist political prisoners, which provides evidence that, in some instances, leadership of strikes has been assumed by members of the Party or Komsomol. This may be the case, for the only way to gain real political and organizational experience in the USSR is by filling a position in the Party.

According to Krawchenko, there are two main reasons why Party members are to be found at the head of a strike. First, they have greater organizational experience. Second, in most cases they are skilled workers or "production vanguards," and thus enjoy greater authority and lend increased legitimacy to the workers' demands. This will bolster the courage of the mass of workers, who find themselves for the first time in direct confrontation with the authorities. Nevertheless, if the confrontation should become prolonged, more radical workers, perhaps with a history of police and bureaucratic troubles, move to the forefront. Their personal histories become, in the eyes of their workmates, a guarantee of their courage and resolve in the bargaining with plant management and Party representatives.

THE CASE OF THE "FREE TRADE UNION"

As there have been strikes and protests in the USSR, so too have there been attempts to create workers' defense organizations. These organizations have been short-lived; their members have been immediately subjected to the harsh repression of the system.

Yuri Andropov expressed the reasons for this intolerance in clear terms that by and large remain valid even today. The official argument is based on the premise that Soviet law grants the widest possible freedom to its citizens. Thus, those who criticize the system are in error and must be treated as misguided. They must be induced to change their minds and mend their ways. However, some of these individuals—the "dissidents"—have acted in breach of the Soviet law. They have supplied the West with slanderous stories, spread false rumors, and attempted to organize various "antisocial attacks." They are "renegades who are not—and cannot be— tolerated in our country" (Haines & Semyonova 1979:25).

This language has been abandoned by Mikhail Gorbachev, who also freed Andrei Sakharov. In this section, however, the focus is not on dissidents but on people who have tried to oppose the arbitrary behavior of management or local authorities. Such people also have tried to set up a "free trade union," an idea that remains strictly taboo (even if, in the new climate of *democratizatsia*, almost all their criticisms can be found in the Soviet press).

Who are the approximately 200 working people who in the late 1970s realized—on the basis of their personal experience—that the effective protection of workers' rights required an independent trade union? What is the state of labor relations that emerges from their testimonies? What were their objectives?

The first thing that emerges from these workers' reports is the gap between the continuous official appeals to strictly observe the regulations and correct abuses wherever they occur and the repressive tactics of local authorities against those who actually observe the regulations and speak in the interest of the enterprise (Haines & Semyonova 1979:29; Scheez 1978:1–6; Michael 1979:1–8).

Biographical notes for founders of the "free trade union" reveal that at the beginning many of them saw the Soviet Union's system and central authorities as good. They believed it was representatives of power at the middle and lower levels who committed injustices in order to protect their own interests. But when the free trade unionists took their petitions to the Central Committee of the Party in Moscow, they were handed over to the police, who gave them "marching orders" at best and, in some cases, "insults, beatings, prison, and the psychiatric hospital" (Haines & Semyonova 1979:23).

The hardships suffered by these people are worth discussing because they shed some light on the dark side of factory life that is not revealed by sociological research. The Soviet press, and sociological literature too, report cases of *zazhima kritiki* (suffocation of criticism) not infrequently. The analysis of these cases reveals that three-quarters of the workers who write letters of protest are not satisfied with the way their complaints are dealt with (Pravda 1979). Here one enters a shadowy zone, which can only be partially explored if one relies on the help of the official press. In other words, the mass media report cases of even serious breaches of the law, but once they have been denounced publicly, the happy ending is almost mandatory. Thus, for instance, if a worker has been unjustly fired, the "story" officially ends with the reinstatement—but, in reality, the story does not end here. On the contrary, it is at this point that one can hear the worst tales, as some examples will demonstrate.

A foreman in a generator factory in the region of Rostov criticized the management. A short while later, he was demoted to the status of worker. This was only the beginning: The next step was his assignment to unskilled work on the night shift without extra pay. The foreman refused to accept this treatment. Then the management passed off his refusal to work below his skill as absenteeism and tried to have his dismissal ratified by the workers' assembly. The attempt was not successful but, some time later, the foreman was finally fired. He commented bitterly:

> I have given twenty years, the best years of my life, to the energy industry. I have fourteen incentive awards and decorations, I have the medal for "outstanding work." I have appealed to all the official organs

and I have received in return either formal rejection or from some institutions, *no reply at all.* (Haines & Semyonova 1979:49)

A female worker in a canned goods factory in Machachkala found herself in trouble for reporting the collusion of management and the FZMK in pilfering plant products. Here, too, the "troublemaker" was first transferred to a lesser-paid job in the hope that she would leave the factory of her own accord. This she refused to do; instead, she decided to take the case to court—but without success. This allowed the director to fire her for absenteeism (Haines & Semyonova 1979:53).

A bus driver in Alma Ata reports how, for five years, he had been a "shock worker" but had fallen foul of the management because of his refusal to participate in the squandering and theft of materials. In 1974, he underwent an operation that should have entitled him to a lighter work load. Instead he found himself assigned heavier, badly paid jobs. He complained to the management and to the trade unions, but with no success. Instead, he added, "The management set drunks and thugs to beat me up." A false document was then prepared by the administration, which purported to show that the driver had been found drunk on the job. On this pretext, he was dismissed, and his appeal to the court and the Party organs were useless:

> Thieves stick together, and as if that wasn't enough, one member of the Regional Party Committee said to me: "Why don't you bugger off to America?" (Haines & Semyonova 1979:56)

An administrative clerk in a holiday camp in the Crimea belonging to the Belaia Kalitva aircraft factory (in the region of Rostov) tells how she persisted until official measures were taken to deal with the perpetrators of financial malpractices in her place of work. As a result, the manager of the camp was fired, but so was the clerk; she was then reinstated four times on appeal. Perhaps because he was tired of seeing her in his courtroom, the Vice-Procurator General finally declared the clerk a "speculator" and threatened to have her arrested. The woman comments:

> ... but I'm still being held terrorized and fired without reason. How many times can they do this—after all there's a limit to what a person's nerves can stand. (Haines & Semyonova 1979:55)

Faced by such treatment at the hands of enterprise managers and local authorities, the nerves of those who seek justice may sometimes give way and provoke strange behavior. Thus, they are placed in psychiatric institutions in a dynamic of "self-fulfilling prophecy." In 1959, for example, a worker from Leningrad dared to send Khrushchev a photograph of himself posing as a beggar accompanied by a petition asking compensation for his unfair dismissal. This witticism began an odyssey for the worker that ended only after eighteen years of hospitalization and imprisonment.

Desperation also drove two women, an engineer and a worker, to enter Lenin's mausoleum and lay their petitions on his sarcophagus. Their punishment was psychiatric treatment. This treatment has been used also for people who send letters to higher Party organs criticizing domestic and foreign policy. Candidates for psychiatric treatment also include anyone who attempts to enter a Western embassy to seek political asylum or who resigns in protest from the Party (Haines & Semyonova 1979:51, 54, 57, 64). The same risk is run by anyone who is particularly stubborn in defending his legal rights, as in the case of the female worker from Makhackala described earlier, who was saved from arrest only by her relatives and neighbors.

Some similar cases are described in testimonies provided by members of the Free Interprofessional Association of Workers (*Svobodnoe Mezhprofessionalnoe Obiedinenie Trudiashikhsia* or SMOT). The best documented case of enforced psychiatric treatment of a protester is that of Klebanov, leader of the group (Haines & Semyonova 1979; Michael 1979; Scheetz 1978).

This mining engineer was first arrested in 1968 for slander against the Soviet system. The truth was—says Klebanov—that from 1958 onward he had continually denounced a great many serious violations of the labor code and the theft of material in his mine. Soon illegal attempts to dismiss him began. Attempts were also made to evict him from his apartment; these attempts were physically repulsed by his fellow workers. Meanwhile, Klebanov filed a series of petitions in court against his illegal treatment at the hands of management. The court declared itself unable to act on the matter, and Klebanov petitioned the Ukrainian Ministry of Mines and the Procurator-General of the USSR. The authorities then used psychiatric treatment in an attempt to silence him. He was examined and diagnosed as being "a litigious person and a malicious gossip"—hardly sufficient grounds for his dismissal. Thus, another psychiatrist was called from Moscow, who diagnosed "pathological development of the personality." An attempt was made to intern Klebanov in a psychiatric hospital for observation; again, this attempt was repulsed by his workmates.

The final verdict of the Makaevka Court declared that Klebanov suffered from a mental disorder similar to paranoia. Nevertheless, the regional procurator of Donetsk and the deputy director of the Department of Heavy Industry for the Ukraine upheld his case and pronounced:

> Comrade Klebanov informs us that he has appealed to the Party and the Soviet organs over a number of years, with the request that they investigate malpractices in the mine—the pilfering of coal and wood, the concealment of cases of industrial injury in the official report, the violation of the labor code, embezzlement from the funds of the enterprise—and bring the guilty to account.... The evidence contained in the letters of Comrade Klebanov has been thoroughly checked.... The former head of the mine and others have been brought strictly to account by the Party and the administration for their reported malpractices in the field of production. (Haines & Semyonova 1979:40)

Actually, Klebanov reports, no action was taken—apart from the promotion of many of those responsible.

In the meantime, Klebanov was fighting to have his psychiatric diagnosis changed. He won, but the management of the mine and local officials refused to give up. In September 1968, he was arrested and interned in a special hospital of the Ministry of Interior, to prevent him from "serving as a bad example for the others," as the local procurator announced. During his internment, Klebanov suffered ill-treatment and began a hunger strike, which was broken by force-feeding. He gave up the strike; partly because he realized that the outside world knew nothing of his protest. Later, when he asked why he was not receiving psychiatric treatment, he was told that he was there "not for real reasons, but for higher necessity, in the interest of social welfare" (Haines & Semyonova, 1979:41).

In the hospital, Klebanov continued his campaign to reobtain his sickness pension and to gain a pension for his family. He was informed that pensions could only be granted if the head of the family was found mentally ill. Finally, in 1973, the Ukraine High Court ordered his release. The previous year he had been awarded damages for his four years of enforced idleness. But his persecution still continued at the local level. The Makaevka Law Court pronounced Klebanov "not responsible for his actions" and deprived him of his civil rights—an action that provoked the protest of the vice-procurator of the Ukraine. The regional court upset the local verdict, but it took the local authorities six months to reinstate Klebanov's civil rights. The administration of the mine agreed to pay him damages, but refused to give him his old job back. This meant that Klebanov could not be taken on by another enterprise because his labor book bore the endorsement, "dismissed in connection with police arrest," and his release papers had not been forwarded.

Klebanov was arrested and interned once again in 1977 in connection with the establishment of SMOT. In the meantime he had continued to take his petitions to Moscow, and he was among dozens of petitioning workers in the lobbies of the Central Committee when the decision was made to form a free trade union. The announcement was made at a press conference in November 1977, Klebanov acting as a spokesman for the group of workers.

The origin of the movement can be traced back to 1975, when a group of workers signed an appeal in favor of Nadezhda Taidar, an engineer from Kiev, who had first been imprisoned and then interned in a psychiatric hospital. The group, as it later coalesced under Klebanov, managed to broadcast various appeals to the West. In November of the same year, thirty-three workers signed a document—also delivered to the Western press—asking Soviet authorities to create a special commission to investigate the ways in which the administrative organs of the Central Committee dealt with workers' complaints.

Naturally, the members of this group were subjected to various forms of persecution and imprisonment. Nevertheless, several press conferences were held in January and February 1978, when a group of forty-three workers announced the establishment of the Free Trade Union Association of the Soviet Working People (*Assotsiatsia Svobodnikh Profsoyuzov Trudiashchikhsia v Sovetskom Soyuze*). A list of 100 candidates for membership was announced, as well as the union's by-laws, and an appeal was made to the International Labor Organization (ILO) for recognition.

By the end of March 1978, the Free Trade Union had been almost entirely dismantled by the KGB. The constitution of a new association—SMOT—was announced in October. At the time of its inception, the new organization comprised eight autonomous groups with a hundred members. Each group was to elect its representative to the general council, and only the names of these representatives were to be made public. A request for recognition was not sent this time to ILO, which had not recognized the first association, but to the International Federation of Free Trade Unions (Scheetz 28, 1978:1–6; 1979:1–12). However, the imprisonment and exile of SMOT's founders quickly crushed this second attempt at the establishment of a free trade union.

CHAPTER 10

Conclusions

MANAGEMENT AND HIGHER AUTHORITIES: COMMAND, BARGAINING, AND DEALINGS

In his study of the influence of social and economic changes on the traditional patterns of Russian political culture, Stephen White (1979:31–34) lists a series of consequences deriving from the dominance of the autocratic principle in that country's history. Of these, consequences whose influence over labor relations have been most evident are as follows: first, the lack—or embryonic existence—of social activities outside the control of the state bureaucracy; second, the fact that even when laws were passed that legalized representative organizations, their effects were largely nullified in the process of their implementation by local authorities and, in the case of trade unions, also by the behavior of industrialists; third, the defense of those limited civil liberties that had been granted by reformer Tsars was hindered by the absence of an autonomous judicial system; and fourth, the absence of control over government by elective bodies meant that the main instruments for the defense of local autonomy were the corrupting of bureaucrats and the distortion of communications with the center.

Despite huge social and economic changes, these historical continuities make themselves felt even today. The trade unions, for instance, since the passing of the Labor Code in 1970, have acquired significant power in the defense of workers' rights, but major problems persist where their practical implementation in the workplace is concerned. The new political leaders apparently do not regard themselves as standing above the law, but the traditional problem of scant regard for law shown by a large strata of the population and many Party cadres seems far from being resolved (Joffe & Maggs 1983:9). Thus, the Soviet industrial system displays a set of contradictory phenomena. Labor legislation is in the process of being developed and perfected and greater power has been granted to trade unions. Nevertheless, the tensions within industrial life continue to rise to the surface in the form of individual actions, repeated switching of jobs, absenteeism, pilfering, sporadic outbursts of violence, and informal group reactions. Many Soviet managers are becoming increasingly aware of problems in organization and personnel management, but complaints are still frequently voiced by workers concerning the "rudeness" and unfairness of factory administrators. The percentage of skilled workers and technical personnel is rising, but the large number of unskilled, auxiliary workers has not diminished to any significant degree. Thus, alongside new lifestyles there still persist the old social problems caused by alcohol abuse. The government is trying to reorganize the economic system based on new decision-making processes—but a large part of this system has been informally or illegally "privatized," with the consequence that some factories have become a sort of "zona franca" where it is even possible to produce for personal profit under the cover of the plan.

In order to understand these contradictory phenomena we must begin with a review of the major issues that relate to any program for reorganizing the Soviet system of planning and industrial management. In the 1960s the Soviet system officially entered into the new stage of intensive development. During the so-called scientific-technical revolution radical changes were to take place in the production system, but the monopolistic power of the Party and central planning were to remain basically unchanged. Changes, however, did take place in the ways in which political leadership faced the dilemma of choosing between economic efficiency and political control of society.

In order to adjust the traditional organizational mechanism to economic and social changes, the Soviet leadership tried to rationalize the role of the Party on the one hand, and to promote economic reform on the other. However, this reorganization (*perestroika*) of the 1960s was implemented in ways quite different from those intended by the economists who had advocated it. In practice, the enterprises did not obtain any significant amount of autonomy, and in the 1970s traditional administration patterns predominated once again.

William Conyngham (1973) has analyzed in detail the role of the Party in the 1960s reorganization of the planning system. Two of his concluding remarks are of particular interest here. The first points out that the *perestroika* did not disturb "the underlying community of interests binding local Party and managerial officials together against the center." The second concerns the misperception of the degree to which spontaneous and informal changes have occurred since 1965 (Conyngham 1973:285). These two observations may be taken as the starting point of the present analysis.

According to the principle of one-man management (*odinonachalie*), the director has complete authority in the enterprise. However, he or she is subordinate to both higher administrative bodies and Party hierarchies. The latter not only exercise their authority directly, they also do so through the system of workers' participation in the leadership of production. For this purpose, they utilize the trade unions and other social organizations. Thus the Party's duty within the factory is to uncover errors of management and of unfair treatment of the workers; to ensure that the interests of the enterprise are not pursued to the detriment of state interests; and to contribute to plan fulfilment without, however, interfering in managerial functions. To be able to do all this, the Party official must give his support to the managers but, at the same time, encourage suggestions and criticisms coming from the shop-floor. By doing so, he creates favorable conditions for the trade union committee to fulfil its functions of protecting the workers' rights and organizing participation in management (Sikorsky 1977).

This breakdown of the official model reveals one of its fundamentals—that is, to ensure that the relationships among the enterprise's organizational elites constitute a declaration of loyalty to the Party. Managers, Party, and trade union representatives must be constantly on the watch for transgressions of any sort and report them to Party and planning authorities. Organizational elites must cooperate, but also must keep check on one another—in an institutional framework based on the "institutionalization of suspicion" (Fainsod 1963). This is clearly shown in the significance officially attached to the company's collective contract. This document sets out the reciprocal duties of the parties concerned in terms of their cooperation over the fulfillment of plan targets and the technical and organizational innovations to be introduced. The contract also sets out the ways in which checks are to be carried out on the work of management and trade union committee, and on execution of their duties with regard to the improvement of working conditions (Bendix 1973:352).

If the system is based on the "institutionalization of suspicion," the problem arises of identifying the variables that influence cooperation, conflict, and reciprocal controls in the factory.

In an essay on the legitimation of the Soviet system of authority, T. H. Rigby (1969) noted that the Soviet system does not fit into any of the three Weberian categories. Weber, says Rigby, was right when he wrote that socialism would require a higher degree of bureaucratization, but he did not foresee that the "rules applying" institutions would be less influential than those concerned with "task achieving," which is the case of the Soviet Union—an instance of "mono-organizational society."

Actually, the Soviet command economy may be conceived of as an enormous, all-embracing organization that assigns, through the planning system, goals and resources to all enterprises and organizations. The Soviet theory of planning appropriated, more or less implicitly, several assumptions of the classic theory of rationality (Kaminski 1979:7). Thus, for example, the planners apparently assume that it is possible to quantify all objectives of economic and social planning and to foresee all possible consequences of the different alternatives involved in a decision. They seem to underestimate the uncertainties that constantly arise in organizations and their environments. These assumptions resemble what Charles Lindblom (1977:264) has called "the model of *a priori* rationality": a model that presupposes the capacity of policymakers to control the complexity of the social world. Moreover, since the planning system expresses the interest of the whole society, any activity incompatible with it must arise from private—that is, antisocial—interests. Consequently, "all the failures of the doctrine are explained by its advocates in a moralizing language mixed with some psychological arguments ('planning is good, only the society is immature'). *This precludes a possibility of organizational learning*" (Kaminski 1979:7, emphasis added).

In reality, despite all claims to "scientific-ness," policymakers and planners are very far from controlling the complexity of Soviet society, which is a multifaceted world of conflicting interests. The implementation of directives from central authorities meets with difficulties and delays, and in many cases directives are not carried out at all. The main reasons for nonfulfillment of orders from above are conflicting social interests and the lack of human and material resources in many enterprises—a lack of stemming from the priority system decided at the central level.

In this context, production organizations tend not to compete with one another on the market, but rather over obtaining resources from the higher authorities. It is this form of competition that presents Soviet enterprises with their major problems, and which obliges managers to show their ability. The negotiating skills of managers in their dealings with the planning authorities are of prime importance even if they cannot overcome the structural obstacle raised by the rank assigned to the enterprise in the system of planning priorities. In these circumstances, "the decisions that are supposed to represent the collective interests are, in fact, the result of the competition and bargaining between institutional components, each trying to impose its own specific interests" (Kaminski 1979:9).

Thus, although officially proclaimed objectives may be inspired by "*a priori* rationality" (the "objective laws of socialism"), the operational reality of industrial management and planning may be depicted as "*a posteriori* adaptation," that is, a model wherein the political leadership relies on a series of *institutional negotiations* in order to achieve economic results that would otherwise be unobtainable (Lindblom 1977; Hough 1979). Instead of a planning process governing economic operations, one finds an ever-changing process of administrative corrections of enterprise plans. Indeed, if the description of the planning system takes into consideration the operational aspects of the Soviet economy, the conclusion can only be that the central national plan is a myth and that in the Soviet Union what exists is not a planned but an *administered* economy (Wilhelm 1985; Zaleski 1980).

In the "administered economy," the dominant figure in the enterprise is the director—both formally and in fact. It is the director, in fact, who is able to cope with planning uncertainties. The director is therefore the person most able to affect the constraints and resources that influence the behaviour of all the other members of the organization (Grancelli 1983). The other influential figure in the enterprise is the Party representative. At times these two key figures may clash, but generally they tend "to work in harness" (Granick 1961:94) simply to cope with the dilemma posed for both by the existing mechanism of control from above. In fact, although the Party requires that "socialist legality" be respected, it also requires that the Party representative in the factory should contribute to the fulfillment of the plan. And this second condition is fundamental to the career prospects of both managers and Party officials (Hough 1969). The director, for his part, knows that his authority in the enterprise is under the control of the Party representative with whom he has to deal. Thus, both the director and the Party representative see it as being in their mutual interest to find some sort of organizational compromise. They know that in the system of "institutionalized suspicion" the higher authorities may tolerate breaches of "socialist legality" if the plan is fulfilled, and will punish infringements only in case of production failure or when it is politically expedient (Bauer, Inkeles, & Kluckhohn 1957:79).

There exist, therefore, a variety of factors which dissuade a director from entering into direct confrontation with the Party representative, even if, in many cases, his relations with higher authorities would protect him if he should decide to do so. The Party official, too, has good reasons for not wishing the clash with the director. If he did so, he might be deliberately isolated from the day-to-day affairs of the enterprise. Alternatively, as a positive sanction, the director can arrange for him to be compensated in various informal ways (Berliner 1957:275).

Thus, if the director and Party official come to a settlement, favorable conditions may arise for the setting up of the *krugovaia poruka*. Evidence on the actual functioning of this web of mutual involvement confirms the relevance of Melville Dalton's (1959) analysis of cliques and their function in managing organizational resources and promoting social integration. The *krugovaia poruka*, by involving persons at different hierarchical levels inside and outside the enterprise, acts as an important unofficial decision-making body, one that copes with planning uncertainties, vitiates controls from above, promotes careers, and reduces excessive strain in workplace industrial relations.

MASS PARTICIPATION AND MASS ILLEGALITY

One basic aspect of Soviet industrial management that has so far
resisted every project of *perestroika* is the community of interests
that binds local Party and managerial officials together in their
dealings with the center. But despite this fact, during the Brezhnev
era, the Soviet system underwent a process of modernization that
was consistent with the official ethos and power necessities of the
Soviet state: Development came to the scientific, technical, and
industrial fields; through urbanization; and to social and cultural
institutions able to sustain modern values (Conyngham 1982:xxvi).
Hough (1977:14), in an examination of these processes of modernization in the Soviet social organization, reaches the conclusion that
the USSR is a variant of Western modernity.

These authors, however, seem to have overlooked the fact that
the presence of many traits of modernity in a given society by no
means implies the disappearance of certain traditional features. In
fact the latter do not disappear, they only become less visible.
Moreover, these traditional characteristics of society are not only
capable of slow modernization, they can also shape the process
itself by giving birth to new types of cultural and social
phenomena—even at the level of production mode (Gallino
1978:439–441).

A more valid approach to tradition and modernity in Soviet
society has been proposed by Ken Jowit (1983). With regard to the
works of Finley and Polanyi, Jowit points out that "the organization and ethos of formally similar processes and phenomena are
decisive in establishing their fundamental similarity or differences.
In other words, when speaking of modernization processes, the
social scientist cannot abstract from the institutions in which they
are framed if he wants to avoid 'false accounts'" (Jowit 1983:276).

The problem, then, is one of grasping all the implications of the
reemergence, during the 1970s, of the traditional role of the Party.
Conyngham (1973:271–73) has noted that the failure of economic
reforms implied that a new concept of management (*upravlenie*)
had not become predominant in Soviet industry—that is, the design
of maintaining political control of the macroeconomy while permitting greater flexibility and efficiency in coordinating the micro-
economy did not succeed. This may be true, but the concepts of

"bureaucratic resistance and inertia" are of little help in under-standing what has been taking place in Soviet enterprises during the last ten to fifteen years: those spontaneous and informal changes that Conyngham (1982–274) defined as a possible "silent revo-lution" in industrial management. Today, however, new data are available, and these may prove very useful in an attempt to clear up misconceptions of this "silent revolution"—that is, the reports of ex-Soviet citizens who worked in Soviet industry until the end of the 1970s.

The Soviet Interview Project (SIP) data show that a fundamental change took place in industrial management during the 1970s. Nowadays, the informal practices that have always pervaded Soviet economy and polity are less frequently found in most important branches of industry, and this is because the ministries and other planning authorities have increased their degree of power and expertise. This means that in high-priority sectors there has been a reduction in the gap between theory and practice in management-labor relations (Linz 1986; Gregory 1986).

In enterprises that process foodstuffs and consumer goods, however, this increase in the power and control of the external bureaucracy has brought with it an increase in plan tautness without a significant reduction in the two traditional sources of uncertainty for enterprises: the material supply and the availability of manpower (Linz 1985). Thus, inevitably, the traditional informal practices necessary to cope with planning uncertainty have tended to concentrate in these enterprises. But not only this.

Because of the economic slowdown of the 1970s, greater control by the higher authorities was not accompanied by an adequate growth of material incentives. Thus, the persistent difficulties in the availability of consumer goods and the scarce effects of official incentive schemes have induced large numbers of both working people and managers to divert part of their energy, time, and craftsmanship away from official activities and toward "shadow economy" activities. Thus, the unintended result of the "treadmill of spurious reform" has been a large, underground "privatization" of light industry, of agriculture, transport, and services to the consumer.

This dualism of the economic system is simultaneously both the cause and effect of the transformation of traditional informal prac-tices into corrupt practices in "privatized" sectors. Thus, the distinction between the official and unofficial economy is not only a functional one, in the sense that the latter takes care of needs not provided by the former. Other issues are involved, all related to the practice of Party supervision and the organization and ethos of Soviet institutions.

Ken Jowit (1983:278) sees in Soviet institutions a striking amalgam of charismatic, traditional, and modern features, which find expression, for instance, in the "heroic" and "booty" orientations of the political economy, the centrality of *blat* in social transactions, and the organization of sociopolitical life around the *kollektiv*. When seen in this cultural and institutional context, the dualism of the economic system becomes

> an ingenious, not fully conscious accidental arrangement that sustains and reflects the invidious distinction between "heroic activities" and "household-pariah activities"; between the privileged exclusivity of the cadre stratum, demesne, and style of life on the one hand, and the dependent, privatized situation of the politically excluded on the other. (Jowit 1983:279)

During the 1970s a form of *political capitalism* grew up under the cover of the planned economy; its characteristics are the sponsorship by political principals of quasi-legal and illegal economic activities, and the deference, fear, and "tribute" accorded them by those given the right to engage in such activities (Jowit 1983:286). This "capitalism"—most widespread in the Caucasus and Central Asia—differs from entrepreneurial capitalism in three respects. First, the institutional framework of (illegal or semilegal) economic activity is hierarchy not market. Second, uncertainty derives not from the (illegal or semilegal) market, but from the behavior of the cadre-patrons who operate within the institutional framework. Third, the economic agents are not companies but individuals, sometimes cooperating in small, informal organizations (Mars & Altman 1983; Staats 1972).

What are the implications of this coexistence of "command" and "shadow" economies for workplace industrial relations? The following two extreme cases may provide an illustration. Every Soviet enterprise can be located at some point on the continuum between these two extreme cases, according to the way structural variables combine with the organizational behavior of labor and management.

A *high-priority enterprise* is a large-sized firm with more than 1000 employees whose production is of strategic importance. Its director enjoys good personal relations with the higher Party and state hierarchies. Here uncertainty over supply is relatively limited and can be easily overcome by recourse to official channels. "Bargaining power" is strong because the enterprise is important, and managerial skills are generally of the highest level.

The relative abundance of material and financial resources means that the enterprise enjoys a satisfactory situation as far as social-consumption funds (housing, rest homes, holiday camps, etc.) are concerned. These funds, along with bonuses, can be used effectively to stimulate productivity and various forms of "participation in the leadership of production." The availability of funds strengthens the position of the management *vis-à-vis* the workforce—especially in view of the fact that this kind of enterprise is usually located in large industrial centers or "closed cities," and that its organization and working arrangements are at the highest level. Workers are attracted to this type of enterprise because it provides them with better salaries, prospects for advancement, working conditions, and availability of goods and services. It is in this sort of enterprise that "production vanguards" are most numerous and the functioning of trade unions most closely approaches official prescriptions.

A *low-priority enterprise* is a small or medium-sized enterprise producing consumer goods and dependent on local authorities. The director is a generation older than his counterpart in the high-priority enterprise. He has risen from the shop floor; he has not received specialized training at a management institute but instead attended evening classes in his youth. His personal relations are limited to the medium-low level of the Party and state hierarchies.

Since this is a low-priority enterprise, supplies from the official channels are far from satisfactory in terms of timing, quantity, and quality. The director has no other choice than to resort—to a certain extent—to unofficial sources of supply and to bartering with other enterprises. He can also resort to the traditional practices of storming, illegal overtime, and the like. If this is still not enough, he can try to get away with such illegal practices as the "doctoring of the production figures."

Scarcity of resources entails scarcity of social consumption funds and insufficient bonuses for the workers—in a situation where basic wages are already lower than elsewhere. Indiscipline, high turnover,

and theft of time and material by workers are the result, especially if
the enterprise is situated in a peripheral area where shortages of
consumer goods are strongly felt. The likelihood of unfair treatment
of the workforce increases—both because of the predominance of
female workers, and because the factory committee is at best of only
marginal importance (and may even be a mere appendage of management).

The management is forced to violate economic and labor legislation in order to fulfill the plan, and this leads to the creation of a
network of "mutual complicity" in the administration of the firm.
In certain cases the *krugovaia poruka* turns into an illegal organization that manages the transformation of "socialist" resources into
"crypto-private" production for the illegal, semi-legal, and legal
markets existing in the Soviet Union.

Between these two extreme cases there lies a whole range of
situations wherein "mass participation" and "mass illegality" are
both present in varying combinations. In a given period, every
enterprise will tend toward one extreme or the other, depending on
the difficulties it encounters in its plan fulfillment. If these difficulties are persistent and significant, even a high-priority enterprise
may be characterized by the prevalence of illegality in its management and labor relations. Illegal behavior of management and local
Party officials lead to the proliferation in the Soviet polity/economy
of networks of "dirty togetherness" (Podgorecki 1979:203) which
are very difficult to eradicate because their members are able to use
the institutional framework as a cover-scheme for "an enormous
amount of mutual semi-private services and reciprocal arrangements" (Podgorecki 1979:203).

The system of "dirty togetherness" has provoked a top-down
propagation of illegality, but has also aroused a sense of moral
outrage, as the attempt to set up a "free trade union" seems to
demonstrate. But the situation is such as to convince the great
majority of working people that the real chance for improving
material conditions lies not in collective action, but in finding a job
in a high–priority enterprise or in arranging deals in the "shadow
economy." And this holds true even under the Gorbachev leadership, at least up to now.

Now we turn to a pivotal question: What approach proves to be
the most fruitful in interpreting the striking amalgam of command,
bargaining, and dealings that takes place in Soviet enterprises?

What is the heuristic value of Marxist and functionalist categories that has traditionally oriented Soviet and Western studies?

MARXISM AND FUNCTIONALISM IN RECENT STUDIES OF THE SOVIET WORKING CLASS: AN ASSESSMENT

The strikes that began to appear in the USSR dating from the late 1950s have been analyzed mostly by the Western New Left—who offer interesting descriptions accompanied, however, by an amazing abstractness of interpretation. Bogdan Krawchenko (1977), for instance, claims that the abolition of the market and unemployment along with the absence of workers' democracy implies that the only mechanisms at the disposal of the ruling bureaucracy to discipline workers are administrative and repressive controls. But administrative procedures, stemming from the political monopoly of the Party, make it clear to the workers where privileges and inequalities originate. In the USSR, according to Krawchenko, the disappearance of the "invisible hand" of the market and the contradictions between official ideology and the existing social structure have caused the Soviet state to exert social control in such a way as to prevent not only every political action outside the party, but also every form of spontaneous social interactions (Krawchenko 1977). Consequently, no society has ever been so fragmented as the contemporary Soviet Union. The working class, in this context, can express its opposition only in terms of deviance (alcoholism, hooliganism, shoddy workmanship, and so on) or through outbursts of violent protest in peripheral areas where repressive control is less tight. Given the centralization of economic decision making, these strikes acquire a directly political character.

Other authors also believe that since the central political organs fix both the price of labor and goods, workers' protests inevitably tend to bypass factory administration to turn toward the state itself (Zukin 1979:197). Thus, to the extent that the process of conflict displacement from the factory to the state takes place, workers must bargain and reach compromises with the local political authorities, and this means that the state becomes vulnerable to repeated claims and protests over wages and prices.

Nevertheless, the politicization of the wage issue in socialist states does not imply the emergence of political claims. What emerges instead is a moral revolt in the sense that those workers who take their work seriously refuse to accept widespread practices such as habitual tippling, the padding of production accounts, the theft of "socialist property," the cover-up of work accidents, and other abuses. That is to say, in the Soviet Union and Eastern Europe disgust with the state's hypocrisy and an appeal to state legality is expressed in individual complaints and collective protests. Workers are crying out to the socialist state that the organization of production makes it impossible for them to function *as workers*. Sharon Zukin relates this observation to the suggestion of Barrington Moore (1978) that a sense of moral outrage lies at the base of working-class politics (Zukin 1979:198).

This is an interesting point that Zukin could have elaborated on further, possibly following the methodological suggestion of Tilly and Tilly (1975), who also referred to the work of Barrington Moore. Their study of workers' collective actions has not been applied to Eastern European countries; nonetheless, it provides useful insights. They conclude that "repression works" in the sense that it can prevent the development of collective action and class conflicts. However, they add that people can innovate with individual actions within the margin of tolerance allowed by the system. In Soviet-type societies the extent of this margin of tolerance largely depends on the internal arrangements of the factory—contrary to what Zukin and other Marxist authors think.

By contrast, Soviet sociologists of the "ideologist" type cannot help but take the opposing point of view. If Western doctrinaire theoreticians see everything in terms of exploitation, opposition, and conflict, their Soviet counterparts see work under socialism as being a matter of honor and prowess among workers devoted to communism and the Motherland. Just as the New Left uses its analysis of the social problems and conflicts of Soviet society as an empirical base, Soviet "ideologists" focus on the "mass participation in social production," which they regard as an expression of the desire to work selflessly for the benefit of society.

At first sight what seems strange here is the fact that these claims are given a certain amount of credence by Western sociologists such as David Lane and Felicity O'Dell (1978). Maybe this fact could be explained by their being "functionalists with Marxist sentiments" (Zukin 1979:192).

On the basis of data gathered from Soviet sources, these authors make some assertions that resemble those of Soviet "ideological" sociologists and that contrast sharply with those quoted from the Western Marxists. Lane and O'Dell, for instance, say that "the development of Soviet unions is following a pattern not unknown in Western Europe, where the unions are becoming intermeshed with management and government, and the locus of industrial conflicts moves downward to localized shop-floor disputes" (Lane & O'Dell 1978:37). The attempt by some Soviet workers to set up a free trade union is considered an extreme manifestation of this tendency.

As for the workers as a class, Lane and O'Dell claim that alienation in the Marxist structural sense does not exist, although they concede that alienation in the sense pointed out by Blauner (1964) may still exist. In other words, it is not property relations but the technological level and the organization of production that may provoke dissatisfaction with work, a sense of powerlessness with the work situation, and instrumental attitudes (Lane & O'Dell 1978:41).

State property has placed management, employees, and workers in essentially the same class relationships to the means of production. In the USSR, the extraction of surpluses is utilized not for the benefit of a ruling class but mainly for investments in society as a whole. Sometimes, however, forms of "unequal exchange" may favor the management group (Lane & O'Dell 1978:45).

The Soviet worker is effectively socialized and "incorporated"; the working class has not developed an alternative counterculture to the dominant values of Marxism–Leninism. Subcultural differences exist only insofar as social stratification gives rise to some differences of interest among different groups of working people (Lane & O'Dell 1978:46). The only countervalues to be found among the working population are absenteeism and drunkenness. These are residuals of the peasant mentality, exacerbated by the inadequate conditions of Soviet urban life. These forms of deviance do not imply, however, that political education in its broad sense is ineffective, since the norms of schoolchildren and those of adults are similar. Rather it is a question of the relatively lower exposure of the "violators of discipline" to the socialization process (Lane & O'Dell 1978:49).

The presence of subcultures and deviant behavior in the Soviet working population does not imply the existence of the "privatized" worker as illustrated in the Lockwood (1968) typology of the English worker. "Violators of discipline" may turn into strikers and rioters if their expectations for a higher standard of living are not met—as Novocherkassk and other strikes in Soviet factories have demonstrated (Lane & O'Dell 1978:48). But this is not usually the case: "The levels of participation in management and politics by the Soviet worker, and his high level of aspiration and mobility ... suggest that there is an integration of worker and management, but not of the traditional-deferential type. Traditionalism at the place of work does not support the dominant culture, like in the West, but undermines the system of industrial production" (Lane & O'Dell 1978:47).

This synthesis of Lane and O'Dell's main assertions shows how "false accounts" are inevitable when Soviet data are taken at face value and analyzed with an inadequate approach. These authors stand in a backward position even with respect to the evolution of the Soviet sociology. To cite an example, Soviet sociologist Irina Popova (1984:32–33) warned about the influence of dominant values on respondent reactions to questions regarding their attitudes and behavior. People employ official values and norms as a means of justifying their behavior, *even when they do not actually adhere to these values and norms* (Shlapentokh 1985:39).

From the latter half of the 1970s onward, a new "hedonistic" perspective appeared in Soviet studies of workers' attitudes and motivations. This was the result of two contradictory phenomena: a slowdown in the economy and a growing desire among Soviet citizens for an orientation toward the comfortable life (Shlapentok 1985:52–54). These developments have prompted Soviet scholars to propose new interpretations of workers' motivations and behavior. According to Aitov (1981), two categories of workers are emerging in Soviet society: on the one hand honest and conscientious workers, and on the other workers who seek to minimize their contribution and often consider other activities (in the second economy, for example) their primary source of income. Aitov sees these negative attitudes toward work as a cultural legacy passed along to new generations of workers, given the critical role of the family in frequently counteracting the socialization efforts of school and the mass media (Shlapentok 1985:63–66).

These analyses are developed further by Tatiana Zaslavskaya, who argues that immediate circumstances interact with long-term historical patterns in conditioning behavior. She refers to the "spiritual influence of older generations on the younger" and the "historical receptiveness of values and specific cultural traits of various national groups." Such historical patterns "have a great inertia and will not yield easily to the influence on the part of management organs." The result is that a large and growing number of working people are characterized by

> a low level of labor and production discipline, indifferent attitude towards the work being done, low quality of work, social inertia, low importance of the work as a means of self-realization, strongly pronounced consumer orientation, and low level of morality.... It is enough to recall the broad scale of the activities of the so-called "pilferers," the spread of all sorts of "shady" dealings at public expense, the development of illicit "enterprises" and figure-finagling, and the "worming out" of wages regardless of the results of work. (Zaslavskaya 1984:40)

Zaslavskaya's analysis can be seen as a novel attempt to broaden the scope of analysis beyond immediate social and occupational conditions, a typical feature of Soviet orthodox Marxism (Shlapentokh 1985:66). It would be interesting if she extended her analysis also to the behavior of "organizational elites" and higher authorities.

It should be added here that even excellent analyses of the Soviet working class show certain shortcomings of interpretation due to the implicit acceptance of functionalist assumptions. In his study of the relation between the working class and the Soviet regime, Viktor Zaslavsky (1981) provides a number of explanations for the lack of collective action and the lack of a labor movement. He argues that the repressive capacity of the regime cannot be considered as solely responsible: Of central importance is the fact that the Party's political and ideological monopoly has brought about the fragmentation of society—that is, a situation where any individual or group initiative in the political, economic, and cultural domains is impossible (Zaslavsky 1981:28). In this context, the only option open to workers is to seek to move from a bad job to a better one in another enterprise. Zaslavsky provides a very useful description of the divide-and-conquer policies adopted by the regime, but the concept of "atomized society" may be accepted only if the reference is to political and cultural activities. This concept is not validly applicable to economic activities. Many of these activities have been and are organized by social networks with the connivance of people in positions of authority in formal institutions. Soviet society is not democratic, but this does not mean that it is "atomized." Also open to criticism are certain aspects of Zaslavsky's analysis of Soviet official ideology. The distinction between the official Marxism–Leninism and the "operational" ideology—which transmits a different set of values to the masses—is very important. But in his observations on the functions of the "operational" ideology, Zaslavsky (1981:90–97) only deals with two stages: the "revolutionary" and the "stationary," which is the stage reached under Brezhnev. The history of Soviet economics and ideology, however, does not begin with 1917. Soviet ideology, be it official or "operational," has been and is deeply influenced by pre-Soviet history, as Bendix (1956, 1970) and Gerschenkron (1974) convincingly argued. Finally, Zaslavsky speaks of "inertia" and "resistance" to economic innovations. As already pointed out, these concepts are of little help in spelling out the organizational behavior of workers, managers, and officials.

In concluding these critical notes, a rereading of Gouldner's essay on the crisis of Marxism and the emergence of academic sociology in the USSR may prove instructive.

Gouldner (1970:456) writes that the significance of Parson's equilibrium analysis—as it applies to the Soviet bloc—is that it addresses the ways in which social systems spontaneously maintain themselves and that it focuses on the inner conditions that contribute to such spontaneous self-maintenance. In the Soviet Union the old social system has been replaced and industrial takeoff achieved. Hence, functionalism is congenial to those who are more concerned with the problem of stabilizing their society. Gouldner adds that Parsonsian equilibrium analysis may be most compatible with the more *liberal* initiatives of these cultures, since self-regulation in the Soviet context means the relaxation of the massive centralized controls: As he put it: "The irony is that Parsonsianism may have greater practical use in the very society which it was in opposition to. No Hegelian could have asked for more" (Gouldner 1970:457).

Actually, sufficient evidence is now available to support a different ironic observation: It was not Soviet economic reform based on market mechanisms that contributed to social stability and economic growth, rather it was the crypto-privatization of a large part of the low-priority sectors that produced social stability—but at the expense of the official economy.

In searching for self-governing mechanisms able to protect the country against a possible recrudescence of Stalinism, Soviet sociologists have also stressed the role of morality. One of them is quoted as saying:

> There are difficulties in getting people to exert self-control.... Our legal scholars tell us that we do not need to be given new rights; the problem is to get people to use the rights they were given twenty to thirty years ago ... in factories and elsewhere. A habit of waiting for directives from the top has emerged in the past ... and it is hard to change this habit, but we are trying. We are trying to extend democracy in our country and, with this, a greater respect for the individual person. (Gouldner 1970:457)

Another seeming paradox emerges here: Many people, in factories and elsewhere, no longer wait passively for directives from above. They display strategic behavior and adapt or elude laws and regulations. However, this is far from being a sign of a significant extension of democracy.

But the mandate to integrate Soviet society, to render the system more law abiding, will not yield great results until the so-called imbalances and distortions are addressed "as a problem of fitting square pegs into round holes." This essentially technological conception of sociology entails the implicit assumption that basic social roles and institutions *are given* and that people have to be prepared to operate in them with wage and extra-wage motives (Gouldner 1970:466). Unfortunately, the problem lies precisely in the *actual* working of Soviet institutions.

According to Gouldner (1970:471), if Soviet sociologists were to reject the "cultural lag" theory as an explanation of the deficiency of their own society, and if they were to retreat from their attitude toward a full-fledged communism, the conditions for a growing convergence between the sociologies of the West and the East could become more favorable. But if the common evolution moves toward

> methodologically empiricist standpoints, such as cybernetics, systems analysis, or operational research ... it will presage a culture dominated by spiritless technicians, useful and usable creatures, where any form of sociological humanism has been blighted. Far better functionalism, even

"static" functionalism; far better Marxism, even "vulgar" Marxism. (Gouldner 1970:474)

Yes, Gouldner was right to be concerned about the basis of the convergence of academic sociology in the West and East. But today the possibility also exists of moving forward the Scylla and Charybdis of "static" functionalism and "vulgar" Marxism.

TOWARD A NEW APPROACH

In his detailed analysis of Soviet approaches to modernizing industrial management during the 1970s, William Conyngham draws some thought-provoking conclusions. Three of his points deserve special attention.

First, there is the theoretical inadequacy of many projects bent on organizational redesign. Despite mounting evidence of the nonviability of the bureaucratic model of industrial organization, the classical paradigm of rationality has remained closely embedded in the culture of Soviet management specialists. Thus, throughout the 1970s, the normative approach—that is, the definition at the central level of determinate relationships for regulating most economic and organizational processes—continued to predominate. Moreover, the attempt at formulating new concepts of human relations in industry competed rather unsuccessfully with the Taylorist approach of the Soviet's "Scientific Organization of Work" (NOT). Further, the general model forming the various rationalization strategies was a hybrid of largely incompatible submodels: a blend of bureaucratic and market models used in the economic reform of 1965; a blend of cybernetic and economic measures used in the "System of Optimal Functioning of the Economy" of the 1970s (Conyngham 1982:257–259).

The second point is that the search for a systemic, technically effective theory of management was heavily burdened by ideological and institutional interests on the one hand, and by the complexity and nonlinearity of concrete decision-making processes on the other (Conyngham 1982:257). Thus both systems analysis and behavioral approaches had to be absorbed into the existing cultural and institutional context, and this set powerful constraints on innovative management concepts. In practical terms, this was the problem of the conservative implementation at middle and low levels of rationalization programs. But crude political pressure from above and tight administrative deadlines proved to be ineffective in the building of complex projects of organizational innovation (Conyngham, 1982:268).

The third critical point in rationalization processes is the technical feasibility of programs. Feasibility is not merely a problem of resource availability. It is also a problem linked to the capacity of programs to reduce the complexity of the system. Proposals to increase the role of market criteria and to introduce forms of industrial democracy could have contributed to the simplification of the Soviet system. The rejection of these solutions—and subsequent efforts to create extremely complex norms for profitability, prices, and bonuses—considerably reduced the coherence and intelligibility of the adopted measures. Thus, many of the provisions for imposing economic and financial levers on the management of enterprises were either nominal or not applied at all (Conyngham 1982:265).

As for the social problems of Soviet industry, the feasibility of social planning was greatly reduced by the search for normative solutions required by the dependence of social processes upon economic planning and upon an ideology that stresses direct political control on all social relations. The problem of complexity and the lack of understanding of empirical social processes was also decisive in frustrating the approach to social planning (Conyngham 1982:265).

The practical results of the substantial failure of rationalization programs are dealt with by Conyngham in two observations that deserve further elaboration. First,

none of the strategies which have emerged is fully persuasive as a solution to the problems of industrial management, and none has been without a large number of *unknown and potentially adverse latent consequences* for political and ideological control [emphasis added]. (Conyngham 1982:261)

Second, changes have undoubtedly occurred, but this appears to be primarily in "informal organization," which cannot be easily measured or observed. In such conditions, the forecast for the near future is the maintenance of the traditional system with continuous and incremental attempts at reforms:

A slow and limited adaptation of the formal organization of industrial management, however, is not without its costs in terms of reduced economic efficiency. It may, on the other hand, stimulate further diffusion of authority and loss of functions to informal organization, which is a clear sign of entropy. The evidence gathered ... suggests that a "second economy" has developed. (Conyngham 1982:274)

The emergence of informal markets, illegal practices, and corruption of the official system suggest—Conyngham adds—that a "silent revolution" could be under way in Soviet management. This has been the research hypothesis of the present writer. The problem now is one of identifying analytical categories that may help us move toward an interpretation of this "silent revolution."

Soviet sociology is mainly a blend of Marxism and functionalism; nonetheless, some scholars have sometimes made interesting remarks. Irina Popova (1973:9), for example, points out that "the principal practical problem lies in the existing gap between the official norms and the diverse, informal norms that are not influenced by formal sanctions." Iuri Cherniak (1975:118–122), a social psychologist, stresses that Soviet managers are not abstractions; they are human beings who are very diverse and who have personal goals and interests. Consequently, money and petty administrative controls nowadays are tools too primitive to regulate their behavior. True, but the approach to management issues proposed by Soviet scholars is of little use in understanding and modifying the behavior of workers, managers, and officials in the Soviet context.

A point of departure in interpreting labor relations in Soviet enterprises might be the classic distinction between the "rational system" and the "natural system" (Gouldner 1959). In contemporary organizational studies there is wide agreement that the "natural system" is not only the domain of sentiments, it is also a complex of cultural, sociopsychological, and political relationships that develop around the artificial subsystem that both supports and modifies it. What is needed, then, is an *open-system strategy* for studying organizations (Thompson 1967:6–12).

To understand the natural system we need to look at the theoretical models that devote special attention to the sociologically relevant aspects of the subject. Functionalism is one of these models. However, in practice, in analyzing relations between social actor and system, it is the needs of the latter that are privileged. For example, the works of David Lane quoted earlier clearly show the persistence of the "Over-Socialized Conception of Man" (Wrong 1961). However, in no society—least of all the Soviet—is there conformity between role prescriptions on the one hand, actual behavior and motivation of the role incumbent on the other, even in the case of subordinate roles. The seeming paradox of the Soviet society is that it is a society deeply penetrated by state intervention, but despite this fact the degree of institutionalization of many social interactions is in practice very low. Many economic and social relationships, formally regulated by administrative criteria, in fact enjoy significant autonomy and are informally regulated by the market or by traditional criteria.

A classic example of highly institutionalized social interaction is collective bargaining between employers and trade unions. This kind of bargaining does not exist in the Soviet Union. What exists is institutional bargaining between enterprises and planning bodies, and a myriad of informal exchanges among individuals who fix their own conditions of reciprocity. This is not to say that government social policy and the activity of Soviet trade unions have no effect, but for the great majority of working people they are of secondary importance in comparison with the two kinds of bargaining mentioned here. Despite this, it is the functioning of trade unions and their management of social policy that have been privileged in the literature. The problem addressed here is instead the analysis of the rational but not institutionalized exchanges between workers, managers, and officials that take place in the organizational framework of the enterprise.

If the question is put in these terms, the classic approaches to industrial relations used in the West are inapplicable because the fundamental conditions are lacking—that is, the possibility of industrial action, collective bargaining, and a "claimant" union. Of heuristic value, however, could be reliance on studies that examine organizational behavior and the governance of contractual relations by market, hierarchies, and other forms of bilateral exchange.

In the Soviet case the fact that the "visible hand" of the hierarchy substitutes for the "invisible hand" of the market in the pursuit of efficiency cannot be explained in the terms used by Chandler (1977) for American industry. The peculiarity of industrial development in the USSR may perhaps be explained by referring to the distinction between the concepts of efficiency and effectiveness. Richard Butler

(1985) explains the differences between these two concepts using an approach wherein the basic unit of collective action is the *transaction*—that is, an exchange of values between two subjects (Ouchi 1980). *Effectiveness* refers to the capacity of the parties to achieve their aims without worrying about transactional costs. *Efficiency*, on the other hand, exists when the problems of social actors' bounded rationality and opportunism are addressed in order to reduce transactional costs.

In light of these two concepts, analyzing the Soviet case reveals that there has been much effective promotion of industrial development using the hierarchical-governance mode, starting from extra-economic purposes. But the "visible hand" of hierarchy has increasingly produced effects that put at risk exactly those extra-economic purposes that are fundamental to the system. The attempt at rationalizing the system by employing efficiency criteria has been based on the limited introduction of market transactions, but always with the constant aim of subordinating them to improved control from the hierarchy.

If one considers the volume of feedback—the quantity of information and adjustments needed in a given transaction—as an approximate measure of the transaction cost (Butler 1985:320), one may say that the costs of preserving the dominance of the hierarchy are high in the Soviet context. In fact, here, too, one may note the importance of two issues in the behavior of managers, workers, and officials: The first is the bounded rationality (March & Simon 1958; Simon 1972), and the second is the seeking of self-interest with guile, that is, the question of opportunism (Williamson 1975; Williamson & Ouchi 1981; Butler 1985). *Bounded rationality* relates to the inability of parties to foresee all possible events that could influence transactions. *Opportunism* means that the partners in the transaction may resort to lying or cheating in order to better defend their interests. Opportunism increases transaction costs insofar as it requires a greater quantity of information to oversee and to apply sanctions if necessary. But transaction costs are also linked to a situation's complexity, that is, to the multitude of contingencies that arise during the transaction (Butler 1985:322).

Williamson, Ouchi, and Butler carried out comparative analysis in terms of efficiency between market, hierarchy, and "other forms of bilateral exchange." They conducted their examination by (1) framing the dimension of transactions (degree of uncertainty, frequency, costs); and (2) joining these dimensions with alternative governance modes such as market, administrative coordination, or bilateral exchanges where the equivalence of the exchange is not implied as it is in the market. Each of these governance modes has strengths and weaknesses to be matched to transactions in a discriminating way. Each of them may present attractive features at a given stage of industrial development, but these may be offset by later disadvantages from the point of view of efficiency (Williamson & Ouchi 1981:389).

Many criteria used by these authors may be usefully applied to the Soviet case. This is particularly true with regard to the concept of complexity and the way it is treated by Butler. The complexity of transactions has three components. The first is uncertainty: the unpredictability of all the events involved in the transaction, whether the transaction is among peers or whether it is an "assignment transaction" (Butler 1985:336). Unpredictability requires continuous adaptations to unexpected events. In Soviet industrial management this is particularly true in cases of material supplies and manpower availability.

Complexity's second component concerns the multiplication effect produced by combining uncertainty with the interdependence of activities. In the Soviet case, this is apparent in the relations among organizational subunits and among different organizations.

Finally complexity's third component is "vagueness," that is, the difficulty to prepare plans and procedures in advance for a series of activities. In Soviet enterprise, vagueness appears to contribute to increasing complexity insofar as formal structures have to cooperate in performing a multiplicity of economic, social, and educational functions. Consequently, they establish diverse and ambiguous functional relationships in order to cope with tasks set up by the political leadership.

Butler (1985:343) applies the concept of complexity in his assessment of conditions for efficiency of the market and hierarchy. He also assesses the situation of the *collective*—conceived as a governance mode based on mutual adaptation, trust, barter, and exchange of favors at different times. The interest of his analysis lies in the fact that he takes a possible complication of the picture into consideration—one that arises when social actors do not adhere to the rules of the dominant governance mode.

Assuming an institutional interest in efficiency, any failure in one of the three governance modes should prompt corrective measures. Generally, these attempts prove to be unsuccessful when social actors adhere only formally to the official rules of one governance mode, but in fact behave diversely and cover up their real activities (Butler 1985:344; Hood 1976:150–165). This is precisely the case in Soviet enterprises when the collective is characterized by an informal network producing working arrangements quite different from official ones, even if formally they seem to comply with official programs and procedures. The terms used to refer to these situations are "dirty togetherness" (Podgorecki 1979), "fraternities" (Pomorski 1986), "family circles" (Conyngham 1982), *blat* and *krugovaia poruka* in the Russian parlance.

The Soviet version of administrative coordination produces a great deal of uncertainty for production units. Higher authorities, in fact, require that production targets be fulfilled without ensuring the full availability of corresponding resources (high-priority organizations excluded). This fact is decisive in shaping the organizational behavior of managers, officials, and employees. Butler (1985:337) maintains that uncertainty creates room for opportunism among organization members, and opportunism implies the search for power resources to control the sources of uncertainty. Here, he adds, Crozier's political paradigm of organization comes into play. In fact, the paradigm proposed by Michel Crozier and Emile Friedberg (1978) offers a number of methodological insights which could be profitably applied to analyzing transactions between "organizational elites" and "lower participants" in Soviet enterprises.

Crozier and Freidberg, starting from a critique of functionalism and its "systemic reasoning," propose a "strategic reasoning" that takes as its starting point the social actor, his "strategic behavior," and his "degrees of freedom." These authors address the fundamental problem of cooperation in organizations and try to answer this question: How do relatively autonomous actors, with their available resources and capacities, solve the problem of collective action (that is, cooperation in the organization) despite their divergent orientations? According to Crozier and Friedberg (1978:7–8), the solutions social actors arrive at presuppose and create at the same time "fields of social action," which may become formalized or "naturalized" by the historical process.

Before criticizing these solutions, it is necessary to spell out their logic and rationality and the problems they solve. This can be done by clarifying all the *unintended consequences* at the collective level of a multitude of individual choices that at their own level, are to be considered rational. If individual action has unintended consequences, the dilemma cannot be solved by discussing personal intentions and motivation; neither can the relation of collective action with the "objective law of history" prevent the emergence of perverse effects. If cooperation within organizations produces results contrary to the intention of the social actors, the reasons for it are to be found in the structuring of the "fields of action." Consequently, analysis should focus on these "fields" (Crozier & Friedberg 1978:9).

The main applications of this paradigm to organizational behavior and transactions in Soviet enterprises may be summarized as follows (Crozier & Friedberg 1978:25–85).

Every bureaucratic system, with its centralization and its minute prescription of duties and behavior, constantly creates areas of uncertainty in problem solving. This uncertainty requires that an organization provide its members with varying margins of freedom—and therefore of power—which they seek to exploit in their negotiations over the fulfillment of organizational aims. In other words, every hierarchical structure creates differences in power, inequality, and social control but also creates "unanticipated consequences of social action" (Boudon 1977), namely, compartmentalization; distortion and breakdown in communications; deviations from official directives; and so on. Consequently, it also allows individuals in subordinate roles to exercise margins of choice in setting up "strategies of independence" (Bendix 1956; 1970).

In this context, the problem becomes finding out how cooperation and conflict manifest themselves in organizations. Thus, we need to identify the role played by forms of manipulation and constriction on the one hand, and of "implicit and explicit bargaining" on the other. This problem should be dealt with not from the system's point of view but from the social actor's (strategic reasoning). On this basis, attention should focus on the "strategic options" available to members of an organization in relation to their resources (professional and relational skills, for example) and the constraints the organization imposes on them. Here it is important to bear in mind the difference between formal rules and the "rules of the game."

Within "strategic reasoning," the concept of "role" acquires a different meaning from that usually assigned to it—in the sense that, here, it is considered a set of possible behavioral strategies to be selected from by individuals according to their resources and the characteristics of the "field of action" in which they operate. In a given role, irregularities and deviations become important subjects for analysis, in that they demonstrate the possibility of choosing among different options, even in a situation in which constraints are strong. Hence, irregularities and deviations from role prescriptions are not to be conceived in terms of deviance as they are in the functionalist model.

The strategic behavior of social actors reflects their relational skill, which is a product of their culture. It is important, then, to study not only the "field of action" that underlies formal organization, but also the institutional and cultural environment in which organizations operate.

The last important point in Crozier and Friedberg's paradigm is organizational change. Every structure of collective action founded on the uncertainties of problem solving turns into a system of power. On the question of power, these authors reject both the neo-Marxist and technocratic conceptions. They do not see every form of authority as mere domination based on strength and imposed on social actors; neither do they regard technological regulation of the social system possible because social actors always enjoy certain degrees of freedom. Power, then, is not the product of a structure of authority, nor is it an attribute to be appropriated—as, for example, the appropriation of the means of production by the working class.

Organizational structures and the constructs of collective action within them are a human product; their creation and evolution are not based on any universal law or historical tendency. If one recognizes the "constructed" character of collective action, of cooperation and conflict in organizations, this also demands recognizing that the agents of organizational change are not "enlightened technocrats," nor are they the "vanguards of the proletariat." Change can be conceived of as a process of collective creation and the learning of new modes of cooperation and conflict—that is, the learning of new cognitive, relational, and organizational capabilities. The alternative to technocratic or authoritarian conceptions of change may only be the extension of experimentation, conceived of as a process of "collective and institutional learning at all levels." Within this framework, the results of innovative action are not decided by the formal coherence and consistency of projects and programs: They are decided by the impact of innovation measures on the existent "constructs of collective action." Thus, it becomes of prime importance to identify these "constructs" in order to measure their resistance to change and their potential for innovation.

This paradigm provides a series of analytical tools useful in interpreting the "silent revolution" under way in the Soviet industrial system and the behavior of the social actors who are carrying it out—although it requires integration with a number of insights offered by studies on the "hidden economy." Thus, for example, the "informal" or "hidden" institutions (Henry 1981; Mars 1982) operating in Soviet enterprises may be seen from the point of view of the people who create and sustain them. In fact, these institutions constitute, as in Western enterprises, a logistical infrastructure for informal activities that are not only of a "destructive" (such as damaging machinery) or "redistributive" (such as pilfering or embezzlement of enterprise property) character, but which also possesses "regenerative" economic functions (for example, when moonlighting leads to the formation of new business) (Mars 1984:202–203). It is also possible to take as a hypothesis for further research some of the conclusions reached concerning the social consequences of the "hidden economy." The second job, for example, has been conceived of as "an instrument—even if distorted, hidden, ungoverned—of a modernization process which individuals and families manage *in advance* of available institutional opportunities" (Gallino 1982:288).

A last point on the political paradigm of organization must be made: The issue of organizational change and new modes of governing transactions between officials, managers, and working people is not only one of learning new cognitive and relational capabilities. The Soviet case indicates that several preconditions are necessary. Here one should pay attention also to the question of political power.

Analyses of organizational change in terms of power—such as the one conducted by Charles Perrow (1981)—explain why in many cases organizational efficiency is sacrificed to the power interests of organizational elites. Debating Perrow, Williamson and Ouchi (1981:355) pointed out that neglected opportunities of achieving greater efficiency are always an incentive to reorganize, "except when there are perversities associated with the funding process, or when strategically situated members of an organization are unable to participate in the prospective gains." This is indeed the case of the Soviet Union today. But if this is so, the new political leadership's attempt at bringing about a *perestroika* will only succeed if it is accompanied by a real *democratizatsia*. In practical terms, this implies giving new "transactional guarantees" to both managers and workers. The former should manage in actual fact and not "administrate" on behalf of higher bureaucratic authorities; the latter should be permitted to create trade unions quite different from present ones (Grancelli 1987). Should significant steps in this direction be made, real possibilities for the modernization of management and labor relations in Soviet enterprises could materialize. At present some encouraging tendencies are emerging, but their consolidation is by no means an easy matter.

Bibliography

AFANASIEV V. G. [ed.] (1970) *Nauchnoe upravlenie obshchestvom*. Moskva: Mysl.

AITOV, N. A. (1975) "I problemi sociali dell'avvicendamento del personale," in B. Grancelli (ed.) *Operai e tecnici in URSS e Polonia*. Milano: F. Angeli.

AITOV, N. A. (1981) "O dalneishem sovershenstvovanii sotsialnogo planirovania i upravlenia." *Sotsiologicheskie Issledovania* 1:43–48.

AJANI, G. (1986) "Social organizations and administrative law: The hypothesis of socialization of the Soviet state." Paper presented to the *International Conference on Soviet Law and Administration*, University of Trento, December 1986.

ANDREENKOVA, N. V. (1980) "Aktualnie problemi upravlenia sotsialnimi protsessami na promyshlennom predpriatii." *Sotsiologicheskie Issledovania* 1:13–20.

ANONYMOUS (1983) "Popytka Zabastovki v vyborge." *Posev* 4:9.

ARKHIPOV, V. C., KONYAEV, N. I., and P. S. KHOREV (1976) *Kommentarii k polozheniu o poriadke rasmotrenia trudovykh sporov*. Moskva: Iuridicheskaia Literatura.

ARMSTRONG, J. A. (1969) "Sources of administrative behavior: Some Soviet and Western European comparison," in F. Fleron, Jr. (ed.) *Communist Studies and the Social Sciences*. Chicago: Rand McNally.

AVAKOV, M. M. and V. A. GLOZMAN (1971) *Trudovoe zakonodatelstvo*. Minsk: B.G.U.

BAIBAKOV, I. K. (1983) "Rights and duties." CDSP, Vol. XXXV, 33:5–6. [*Izvestia*, Aug. 18:3.]

BARTOCCI, E. (1980) *Sindacato e potere nella Russia Sovietica*. Milano: F. Angeli.

BARU, M. I. (1971) "Unificatsia i differentsiatsia norm trudovogo prava," *Sovetskoe gosudarstvo i pravo* 10:45–50.

BAUER, R. A., INKELES, A., and C. KLUCKHOHN (1957) *How the Soviet System Works*. Cambridge, MA: Harvard Univ. Press.

BELOTSERKOVSKY, V. (1977) *Svoboda, vlast i sobsvennost*. München: Achberg.

BELOTSERKOVKY, V. (1978) "Workers and employees in defence of human rights." *Labour Focus on Eastern Europe* (March).

BELYAVSKY, Y. (1986) "Obshchezhitie. Istorii iz 'limitnoi' zhizni." *Iunost* 8:85–90.

BENDIX, R. (1956) *Work and Authority in Industry*. New York: John Wiley.

BENDIX, R. (1970) *Embattled Reason: Essays on Social Knowledge*. New York: Oxford Univ. Press.

BENDIX, R. (1978) *Kings or People: Power and the Mandate to Rule*. Berkeley: University of California Press.

BETTELHEIM, C. (1978) *Le lotte di classe in USSR. 1923–1930*. Milano: Etas Libri. [*Les luttes de classes en USSR. Deuxieme periode, 1923–1930*. Paris: Editions du Seuil].

BERLINER, J. (1957) *Factory and Manager in the USSR*. Cambridge, MA: Harvard Univ. Press.

BIALER, S. (1980) *Stalin's Successors: Leadership, Stability and Change in the Soviet Union*. Cambridge: Cambridge Univ. Press.

BIRMAN, I. (1978) "From the achieved level." *Soviet Studies* 2:153–172.

BLACKWELL, W. L. (1982) *The Industrialization of Russia: An Historical Perspective*. Arlington Heights, IL: Harlan Davidson.

BLAUNER, R. (1964) *Alienation and Freedom: The Factory Worker and His Industry*. Chicago: University of Chicago Press.

BLYAKMAN, L., and O. SHKARATAN (1977) *Man at Work*. Moscow: Progress.

BOCCELLA, N. (1980) "Il salario sociale," in R. Di Leo (ed.) *Occupazione e salari in URSS: 1950–1977*. Milano: Etas Libri.

BONNELL, V. E. (1979) "Radical politics and organized labor in pre-revolutionary Moscow, 1905–1914." *Journal of Social History* 2:282–300.

BONNELL, V. E. [ed.] (1983) *The Russian Worker: Life and Labor under the Tsarist Regime*. Berkeley: University of California Press.

BORNSTEIN, M. (1985) "Improving the Soviet economic mechanism." *Soviet Studies* 1:1–30.

BOUDON, R. (1977) *Effect pervers et ordre social*. Paris: Presses Universitaires de France.

BRODERSEN, A. (1966) *The Soviet Worker*. New York: Random House.

BROWER, D. R. (1982) "Labor violence in Russia in the late nineteenth century." *Slavic Review* 3:417–435.

BROWN, A., and J. GRAY [eds.] (1979) *Political Culture and Political Change in Communist States*. London: Macmillan.

BROWN, E. C. (1966) *Soviet Trade Unions and Labor Relations*. Cambridge MA: Harvard Univ. Press.

BUSH, K. (1981) "Retail prices in Moscow and four Western cities in March 1979," in L. Schapiro and J. Godson (eds.) *The Soviet Worker: Illusion and Realities*. New York: St. Martins.

BUTLER, R. (1985) "L'efficienza organizzativa nei mercati, nelle gerarchie e nei collettivi" in R. C. D. Nacamulli and A. Rugiadini (eds.) *Organizzazione e mercato*. Bologna: Il Mulino. ["A transactional approach to organizing efficiency: Perspectives from market, hierarchies and collectives." *Administration and Society* 10, 1982.]

CARLINI, R. (1975) *Il comitato sindacale di fabbrica (FZMK) nella legislazione sovietica*. Pisa: Colombi.

CARR, E. H. (1978) *Le origini della pianificazione sovietica. Il partito e lo stato 1926–1929*. Torino: Einaudi. [*A History of Soviet Russia. Foundations of a Planned Economy 1926–1929*, Vol. I. London: Macmillan, 1972.]

CARR, E. H., and R. W. DAVIES (1974) *Le origini della pianificazione sovietica. Lavoro, Commercio, Finanza. 1926–1929*. Torino: Einaudi.

CHANDLER, A. D. (1981) *La mano visibile. La rivoluzione manageriale nell'economia americana*. Milano: F. Angeli. [*The Visible Hand*. Cambridge, MA: Harvard Univ. Press, 1977.]

CHAPMAN, J. (1979) "Recent trends in the Soviet industrial wage structure," in A. Kahan and B. A. Ruble (eds.) *Industrial Labor in the USSR*. New York: Pergamon.

CHERNIAK, I. (1975) *Prostota slozhnogo*. Moskva: Znanie.

CONQUEST, R. (1967) *Industrial Workers in the USSR*. London: Bodley Head.

CONYNGHAM, W. J. (1973) *Industrial Management in the Soviet Union: The Role of the CPSU in Industrial Decision Making.* Stanford, CA: Hoover Institution Press.
CONYNGHAM, W. J. (1982) *The Modernization of Soviet Industrial Management.* Cambridge: Cambridge University Press.
CRISP, O. (1979) "Lavoro e industrializzazione in Russia," in *Storia Economica Cambridge*, Vol. 7. Torino: Einaudi.
CROZIER, M., (1964) *Le phenomene bureaucratique.* Paris: Editions du Seuil.
CROZIER, M. and E. FRIEDBERG (1978) *Attore sociale e sistema.* Milano: Etas Libri. [*L'acteur et le système: Les constraints de l'action collective.* Paris: Editions du Seuil, 1977.]
DALTON, M. (1959) *Men Who Manage.* New York: John Wiley.
DELAMOTTE, J. (1975) *Shchekino: entreprise soviétique pilote.* Paris: Les Editions Ouvrieres.
DEUTSCHER, I. (1968) *I sindacati sovietici.* Bari: Laterza. [*Soviet Trade Unions.* New York: Oxford Univ. Press, 1950.]
DI LEO, R. (1973) *Operai e fabbrica in Unione Sovietica.* Bari: De Donato.
DI LEO, R. (1980) *Occupazione e sallari in URSS. 1950–1977.* Milano: Etas Libri.
DITTON, J. (1977) "Perks, pilferage and the fiddle: The historical structure of invisible wages." *Theory and Society* 4:39–71.
DMITRIK, M. A. (1972) *Sotsialnaia aktivnost proizvodstvennogo kollektiva v uslovyakh ekonomicheskogo reforma.* Minsk: B.G.U.
DROBNYS, A. (1978) "The science and practice of management: The town is small." CDSP, Vol. XXX, 20:13. [*Pravda*, May 21:2.]
DYKER, D. A. (1981) "Planning and the worker," in L. Schapiro and G. Godson (eds.) *The Soviet Worker: Illusions and Realities.* New York: St. Martins.
DYKER, D. A. (1985) *The Future of Soviet Economic Planning.* London: Croom Helm.
ELDMAN, D. (1977) *Trade Unions and Labor Relations in the USSR.* Washington: Council on American Affairs.
ENGELSTEIN, L. (1982) *Moscow 1905: Working Class Organization and Political Conflict.* Stanford, CA: Stanford Univ. Press.
ESPER, T. (1978) "The conditions of serf-workers in Russia's metallurgical industry, 1800–1861." *Journal of Modern History*, 4:660–679.
FAINSOD, M. (1963) *How Russia is Ruled.* Cambridge, MA: Harvard Univ. Press.
FELDBRUGGE, F. J. M. (1984) "Government and shadow economy in the Soviet Union." *Soviet Studies* 4:528–543.
FEDOSOV, I. A. [ed.] (1981) *Istoria SSSR (XIX-nachalo XX v.).* Moskva: Vishaia Shkola.
FEIFER, G. (1976) "Russian scenes, Russian voices." *Reader's Digest* (August): 207–214.
FLERON, F. [ed.] (1969) *Communist Studies and the Social Sciences.* Chicago: Rand McNally.
GAERTNER, W., and A. WENIG [eds.] (1985) *The Economics of the Shadow Economy.* Berlin: Springer Verlag.
GALLINO, L. (1978) *Dizionario di sociologia.* Torino: UTET.
GALLINO, L. (1982) *Il lavoro e il suo doppio.* Bologna: Il Mulino.
GELARD, P. (1965) *Les organizations de masse en Union Sovietique.* Paris: Cujas.
GELMAN, A. (1977) "The heights: The chariot of success, its motors and its brakes." CDSP, Vol. XXIX, no. 1:10–11. [*Literaturnaia Gazeta*, March 16, 11.]

GERSCHENKRON, A. (1974a) *Il problema storico dell'arretratezza economica*. Torino: Einaudi. [*Economic Backwardness in Historical Perspective*. Cambridge, MA: Harvard Univ. Press, 1962.]

GERSCHENKRON, A. (1974b) "Politica agraria e industrializzazione in Russia, 1861–1917," in V. Castronovo (ed.) *Storia Economica Cambridge*, Vol. 6. Torino: Einaudi. [H. I. Habakkuk and M. Postan (eds.) *The Cambridge Economic History of Europe, Vol. VI: The Industrial Revolution and After*. Cambridge: Cambridge Univ. Press.]

GERSCHENKRON, A. (1978) "Recent Soviet novels: Some impressions." *Soviet Studies* 4:443–465.

GIDWITZ, B. (1982) "Labor unrest in the Soviet Union." *Problems of Communism* 6:25–42.

GOLDMAN, M. I. (1983) "The economy and the consumer," in J. Cracraft (ed.) *The Soviet Union Today: An Interpretative Guide*. Chicago: Educational Foundation for Nuclear Science.

GOLDTHORPE, J. H., LOCKWOOD, D., BECHOFER, R., and J. PLATT, (1968) *The Affluent Worker: Industrial Attitudes and Behaviour*. London: Cambridge Univ. Press.

GOLOVINE, M. I. (1845) *La Russie sous Nicolas Ier*. Paris: Comptoir des Imprimeurs-Unis.

GORLIN, A. C. (1985) "The power of Soviet industrial ministries in the 1980s." *Soviet Studies* 3:353–370.

GOULDNER, A. W. (1959) "Organizational analysis," in R. K. Merton, L. Broom, and L. S. Cottrel, Jr. (eds.) *Sociology Today*. New York: Basic Books.

GOULDNER, A. W. (1970) *The Coming Crisis of Western Sociology*. New York: Basic Books.

GRANCELLI, B. (1974) "Il disadattamento operaio nei collettivi di produzione sovietici." *La Critica Sociologica* 30:49–69.

GRANCELLI, B. [ed.] (1975) *Operai e tecnici in URSS e Polonia*. Milano: F. Angeli.

GRANCELLI, B. (1983) "La relazioni industriali di tipo sovietico: note per una analisi." *Psicologia e lavoro* 55:3–10.

GRANCELLI, B. (1987) "Managerial practices and patterns of employee behaviour in Soviet Enterprises," in J. Child and P. Bate (eds.) *Organizations in Transition: East–West Perspectives of the Management of Innovation*. Berlin: de Gruyter.

GRANICK, D. (1960) *The Red Executive*. New York: Doubleday.

GREGORY, P. (1986) "Productivity, slack and time theft in the Soviet economy: Evidence from the Soviet Interview Project." *SIP Working Paper*, No. 15, University of Illinois at Urbana-Champaign.

GROSSMAN, G. (1977) "The 'second economy' of the USSR." *Problems of Communism* 5:25–40.

GROSSMAN, G. (1979) "Notes on the illegal private economy and corruption," in *Soviet Economy in a Time of Change*." Washington: U.S. GPO.

GROSSMAN, G. (1981) "La seconde économie et la planification sovietique." *Revue d'études comparatives Est-Quest* 2:5–24.

GROSSMAN, G., and V. TREML (1987) "Measuring hidden personal incomes in the USSR in S. Alessandrini and B. Dallago (eds.) *The Unofficial Economy: Consequences and Perspectives in Different Economic Systems*. Aldershot: Gower.

GROSSMAN, P. (1979) "The Soviet government role in allocating industrial labor," in

A. Kahan and B. A. Ruble (eds.) *Industrial Labor in the USSR*. New York: Pergamon.

GUSAKOV, A. D. [ed.] *Effektivnost proizvodstva i profsoyuzi*. Moskva: Profizdat.

HAIMSON, L. (1964/1965) "The problem of social stability in urban Russia: 1905–1917." *Slavic Review* 4:

HAINES, V. and O. SEMYONOVA (1979) *Workers against the Gulag: The New Opposition in the Soviet Union*. London: Pluto.

HANSON, P. (1983) "Success indicators revisited: The July 1979 Soviet decree on planning and management." *Soviet Studies* 1:1–13.

HENRY, S. [ed.] (1981) *Can I Have It in Cash? A Study of Informal Institutions and the Unorthodox Ways of Doing Things*. London: Astragal Books.

HIRSCHMAN, A. D. (1970) *Exit, Voice, Loyalty*. Cambridge, MA: Harvard Univ. Press.

HOOD, C. C. (1976) *The Limits of Administration*. New York: John Wiley.

HOUGH, J. F. (1969) *The Soviet Prefect: The Local Party Organs in Industrial Decision Making*. Cambridge, MA: Harvard Univ. Press.

HOUGH, J. F. (1977) *The Soviet Union and the Social Science Theory*. Cambridge, MA: Harvard Univ. Press.

HOUGH, J. F. (1979) "Policy making and the worker," in A. Kahan and B. A. Ruble (eds.) *Industrial Labor in the USSR*. New York: Pergamon.

HOBSBAWM, E. J. (1959) *Primitive Rebels: Studies in Archaic Forms of Social Movement in the 19th and 20th Centuries*. Manchester: Manchester Univ. Press.

IOVCHUK, M. I., and M. N. KOGAN [eds.] (1972) *Dukhovni mir sovetskogo rabochego*. Moskva: Mysl.

IVANOV, S. A., and R. Z. LIVISHITS (1982) *Lichnost v sovetskom trudovom prave*. Moskva: Nauka.

IVANOV, V. N. (1984) "Aktualnie voprosi sovershenstvovania sotsialnogo planirovania." *Sotsiologicheskie Issledovania* 2:35–42.

JOFFE, O. S., and P. MAGGS (1983) *Soviet Law in Theory and Practice*. New York: Oceana Publications.

JOHNSON, R. E. (1976) "Peasant migration and the Russian working class: Moscow at the end of the Nineteenth Century." *Slavic Review* 4:652–664.

JOWIT, K. (1983) "Soviet neotraditionalism: The political corruption of a Leninist regime." *Soviet Studies* 3:275–297.

KAHAN, A. (1979) "Some problems of the Soviet industrial worker," in A. Kahan and B. A. Ruble (eds.) *Industrial Labor in the USSR*. New York: Pergamon.

KAHAN, A. and B. A. RUBLE [eds.] (1979) *Industrial Labor in the USSR*. New York: Pergamon.

KAMINSKI, A. Z. (1979) "General public interest in the non-dialectic theory of planning and obstacles to participation." *Polish Sociological Bulletin* 4:5–20.

KARINSKY, S. S. (1975) "Normativnie akty VCSPS v trudovogo zakonodatelstva." *Sovetskoe gosudarstvo i pravo* 3:37–44.

KASER, M. C. (1979) "L'imprenditorialità russa," in V. Castronovo (ed.) *Storia Economica Cambridge*, Vol. 7. Torino: Einaudi. [M. M. Postan and P. Mathias (eds.) *The Cambridge Economic History of Europe*, Vol. VII: *The Industrial Economies: Capital, Labour, and Enterprises*. Cambridge: Cambridge Univ. Press.]

KASER, R. G. (1976) *Russia: The People and the Power*. New York: Pocket Books.

KATSENELINBOIGEN, A. (1978) *Studies in Soviet Economic Planning*. New York: M. E. Sharpe.

KERIMOV, D. A. and A. S. PASHKOV (1975) "Metodologicheskie problemi sotsial-nogo planirovania." *Sotsiologicheskie Issledovania* 3:22–30.

KOENKER, D. (1978) "The evolution of party consciousness in 1917: The case of the Moscow workers." *Soviet Studies* 1:38–62.

KOLARSKA, L., and H. A. ALDRICH (1980) "Exit, voice, silence: Consumer and managers response to organizational decline." *Organizational Studies* 1:41–58.

KOKHLYUK, G. S. (1976) *Trudovoi Kollektiv: Opyt, Problemi, Perspektivi*. Khabarovsk.

KOTLYAR, A. E., and M. I. TALALAI (1977) "How to keep young cadres in their jobs." CDSP, Vol. XXIX, 34:1–3 [*Ekonomika i organizatsia promyshlennovo proizvodstva* 4:26–43.]

KRAWCHENKO, B. (1977) "La classe operaia fra insoddisfazione e opposizione," in M. Cox, C. Goodey, G. Kay, B. Krawchenko, and H. H. Ticktin (eds.) *Il compromesso sovietico*. Milano: Feltrinelli. ["The Soviet working class: Discontent and opposition." *Critique* 4, 1975.]

KRAWCHENKO, B., and G. DESORLE (1978) "Workers' unrest in the Soviet Union today." *Revue des Pays de l'Est* 1:29–49.

KRONCHER, A. (1979) "Industrial accident, management and the trade unions." *Radio Liberty Research* 298/79, October 9.

KRONCHER, A. (1982a) "Economic progress is only on paper." *Soviet Analyst* 5:3–5.

KRONCHER, A. (1982b) "CMEA productive and service sector in the 1980s: Plan and non-plan." Brussels: *NATO-Economics Directorate*.

KRONCHER, A. (1985) "Soviet managers demand independence." *Soviet Analyst* 5:6–7.

KULAGIN, G. (1983) "Problems and opinions: The limits of maneuvering." CDSP, Vol. XXXV, 28:1–3. [*Pravda*, July 12: 2.]

KUROMIYA, H. (1984) "Odinonachalie and the Soviet industrial manager, 1928–1937." *Soviet Studies* 2:185–204.

KUSHPETA, O. (1978) *The Banking and Credit System of the USSR*. Boston: M. Nijhoff.

KUTSMA, M. I. (1972) "Rol pravovykh sredstv v razvitii sotsialisticheskogo sorevnovania." *Sovetskoe Gosudarstvo i Pravo* 4:39–47.

LAKY, T. (1979) "Enterprises in bargaining position." *Acta Oeconomica* 3–4:227–246.

LAMPERT, N. (1984) "Law and order in the USSR." *Soviet Studies* 3:366–385.

LANE, D. S., and F. O. DELL (1978) *The Soviet Industrial Worker: Social Class Education and Control*. Oxford: M. Robertson.

LAVERICHEV, V. Y. (1972) *Tsarism i rabochii vopros (1861–1917 gg.)*. Moskva: Mysl.

LE PLAY, F. (1877) *Les Ouvriers de l'Orient: Les ouvriers européens*, Vol. II. Tours: A. Mame et fils.

LEWIN, M. (1985) *The Making of the Soviet System: Essays on the Social History of Interwar Russia*. London: Methuen.

LINDBLOM, C. (1977) *Politics and Markets: The World's Political-Economic System*. New York: Basic Books.

LINHART, R. (1977) *Lenin i contadini e Taylor*. Roma: Coines. [*Lénine, les paysans, Taylor*. Paris: Editions du Seuil.]

LINZ, S. (1985) "Taut planning as an optimal strategy in developed economies."
Irvine Economic Papers, No. 86–7, School of Social Science, University of
California, Irvine.

LINZ, S. (1986) "Managerial autonomy in Soviet firms," *SIP Working Paper*, No. 18,
University of Illinois at Urbana-Champaign.

LIVISHITS, R. Z., and V. I. NIKITINSKY (1974) "Printsipy sovetskovo trudovovo
prava. *Sovetskoe Gosudarstvo i Pravo* 8:31–39.

LOCKWOOD, D., et al. (1968) *The Affluent Worker: Industrial Attitude and Behavior.*
Cambridge: Cambridge Univ. Press.

LOGVINOV, V. (1977) "Without an apartment." CDSP, Vol. XXIX, 1:10–11.
[*Pravda*, April 15:2.]

LOWIT, T. (1971) *Le syndicalisme de type sovietique.* Paris: Colin.

MADISON, B. (1979) "Trade unions and social welfare," in A. Kahan and B. A. Ruble
(eds.) *Industrial Labor in the USSR*. New York: Pergamon.

MAIER, V. F., et al. (1981) "K voprosy o pokozatelyakh sotsialnogo razvitia v
obshegosudarstvennykh planakh SSSR." *Sotsiologicheskie Issledovania* 4:81–92.

MALIA M. (1984) *La rivoluzione russa e i suoi sviluppi.* Bologna: Il Mulino.

MALLE, S. (1984) "Nuove forme di organizzazione del lavoro in URSS: le brigate di
lavoro." Paper presented to the Convegno dell 'Associazione per lo Studio dei
Sistemi Economici Comparati, Torino, October.

MANEVICH, Y. L. (1978) "Problems of the 10th Five-year plan: Manpower- shortages and reserves." CDSP, Vol. XXX, 16:4–5. [*Ekonomika i Organizatsia Promyshlennovo Proizvodstva* 2:75–87.]

MARCH, J. C., and H. A. SIMON (1958) *Organizations*. New York: John Wiley.

MARS, G. (1982) *Cheats at Work. An Anthropology of Workplace Crime.* Boston:
Allen & Unwin.

MARS, G., and Y. ALTMAN (1983) "The cultural basis of Soviet Georgia's second
economy." *Soviet Studies* 3:546–560.

MARS, G., and Y. ALTMAN (1987) "Case studies in second economy production and
transportation in Soviet Georgia," in S. Alessandrini and B. Dallago (eds.) *The
Unofficial Economy: Consequences and Perspectives in Different Economic
Systems.* Aldershot: Gower.

MCAULEY, A. (1981) "Welfare and social security," in L. Schapiro and J. Godson
(eds.) *The Soviet Worker: Illusion and Realities*, New York: St. Martins.)

MCAULEY, M. (1969) *Labour Disputes in Soviet Russia, 1957–1965.* Oxford:
Clarendon.

MELNIKOV, G. I., et al. (1973) *Lichnost i kollektiv.* Irkutsk.

MENDUNI, E. (1986) *Caro PCI.* Milano: Bompiani.

MICHAEL, J. C. (1979) "The independent trade-union movement in the Soviet
Union." *Radio Liberty Research* 304/79, October 11:1–12.

MILLAR, J. R. (1983) "An economic overview," in *The Soviet Union Today.*
Chicago: Educational Foundation for Nuclear Science.

MILLAR, J. R. (1986a) "The Soviet Interview Project: History, Method, and the
Problem of Bias." *SIP Working Paper*, No. 22, University of Illinois at Urbana-
Champaign.

MILLAR, J. R. (1986b) "An overview of the first findings of the Soviet Interview
Project." *SIP Working Paper*, No. 16, University of Illinois at Urbana-
Champaign.

MILLER, W. (1967) "Russians, as people," in S. Hendel (ed.) *The Soviet System in Theory and in Practice.* London: D. Van Nostrand.

MOCHALIN, F. I. (1977) "Put the decisions of the 25th CPSU Congress into effect: Branch research and consumer goods production," CDSP, Vol. XXIX, 1:10–11. [*Ekonomicheskaia Gazeta* 18:5–6.]

MOLODZOF, V. M., and V. G. SOIFER (1976) *Stabilnost trudovykh pravootnoshenii.* Moskva: Iuridicheskaia Literatura.

MOORE, B. (1978) *Injustice: The Social Bases of Obedience and Revolt.* New York: M. E. Sharpe.

MORAWSAKI, W. (1980) "Society and the strategy of imposed industrialization." *Polish Sociological Bullettin,* 4:69–81.

MOROSOV, I., and V. PROKUSHEV (1983) "And they call him Udarnik." CDSP, Vol. XXXV, 36:18. [*Pravda,* Sept. 6:2.]

MURPHY, P. (1985) "Soviet *shabashniki*: Material incentive to work." *Problems of Communism* (November–December): 48–57.

MUSATOV, I. M. (1967) *Sotsialnie problemi trudovykh resursov v SSSR.* Moskva: Mysl.

NESTEROV, V. G. (1969) *Trud i moral v sovetskom obshchestve.* Moskva: Mysl.

NICHOLSKY, A. (1981) "A note on the budget of young Soviet families." *Soviet Studies* 3:433–443.

NIKITINSKY, V. I. and V. E. PANYUGIN (1973) *Delo ob uvolnenii rabochikh i sluzhashchikh.* Moskva: Iuridicheskaia Literatura.

NORR, H. (1986) "Shchekino: Another look." *Soviet Studies* 2:141–169.

NOVE, A. (1977) *The Soviet Economic System.* Boston: Allen & Unwin.

NOVE, A. (1979) *Political Economy and Soviet Socialism.* Boston: Allen & Unwin.

OFER, G., and A. VINOKUR (1979) "Family income levels for Soviet industrial workers," in A. Kahan and B. A. Ruble (eds.) *Industrial Labor in the USSR.* New York: Pergamon.

O'HEARN, D. (1980) "The consumer second economy: Size and effect." *Soviet Studies* 2:218–234.

OLSHANSKY, V. B. (1966) "Lichnost i sotsialnie tsennosti." *Sotsiologia v SSSR.* Moskva: Mysl.

ORLAND, L. (1986) "The Soviet 1986 non labor-income decrees: Administrative law as an instrument of political and economic oppression." Paper presented to the International Conference on Soviet Law and Administration, University of Trento, December.

ORLOV, A. K. (1978) *Sovetskii rabochii v upravlenie proizvodstvom.* Moskva: Profizdat.

OSTROVSKY, E. A., and A. A. RUSALINOVA (1975) "O sotsialnikh issledovaniakh v Leningradskom proizvodsvennom obedienenii 'Svetlana.'" *Sotsiologicheskie Issledovania* 2:123–126.

OUCHI, W. G. (1980) "Market, bureaucracies and clans." *Administrative Science Quarterly* 25.

PALM, A. (1977) "Who will follow you, furnacemen?" CDSP Abstracts. [*Komsomolskaia Pravda,* Jan. 14:2.]

PARFENOV, V. (1977) "Behind the decisions of the 25th CPSU Congress: People, factories and cities." CDSP, Vol. XXIX, 47:3–4. [*Pravda,* November 26:2.]

PERLMAN, S. (1980) *Per una teoria dell 'azione sindacale.*

ROMA: EDIZIONI LAVORO. [*A Theory of the Labor Movement*. New York: Kelley, 1949.]

PERROW, C. (1981) "Market, hierarchy and hegemony," in A. H. Van de Ven and W. F. Joyce (eds.) *Perspectives on Organization Design and Behavior*. New York: Wiley.

PODGORECKI, A. (1979) "Tertiary social control," in A. Podgorecki and M. Los (eds.) *Multidimensional Sociology*. London: Routledge & Kegan Paul.

PODMARKOV, V. G. (1969) *Sotsialnie problemi organizatsii truda*. Moskva: Mysl.

PODMARKOV, V. G. (1979) "Sotsialnie planirovanie: opyt i spetsifika." *Sotsiologicheskie Issledovania* 3.

POMORSKY, S. (1986) "Perversion of Soviet administrative law." Paper presented to the International Conference on Soviet Law and Administration, University of Trento.

POPOV, G. (1977) "Scientific discussion: Economic management—Some questions of theory and practice." CDSP, Vol. XXIX, 10:10–11 [*Kommunist* 18:70–81.]

POPOVA, I. M. (1973) *Problemi sotsialnogo regulirovania na promyshlennykh predpriatiakh*. Kiev: Naukova Dumka.

POPOVA, I. M. (1984) "Tsennostnie predstavlenia i 'paradoksi' soznania." *Sotsiologicheskie Issledovania* 4:29–36.

POWELL, D. (1972) "Controlling dissent in the USSR." *Government and Opposition* 1:85–98.

Powell, D. (1983) "A troubled society," in J. Cracraft (ed.) *The Soviet Union Today*. Chicago: Educational Foundation for Nuclear Science.

PRAVDA, A. (1979) "Spontaneous workers' activities in the Soviet Union," in A. Kahan and B. A. Ruble (eds.) *Industrial Labor in the USSR*. New York: Pergamon.

PORKET, J. L. (1985) "Unemployment in the midst of labour waste." *Survey*. 1:19–28.

PUSHKAREV, S. (1985) *The Emergence of Modern Russia: 1801–1917*. Edmonton: Pica Pica.

RAEFF, M. (1984) *La Russia degli Zar*. Bari: Laterza. [*Comprendre, l'ancien régime russe*. Paris: Editions du Seuil, 1982.]

RALLIS, M. (1981) "Workers' social perceptions," in L. Schapiro and J. Godson (eds.) *The Soviet Worker: Illusion and Realities*. New York: St. Martins.

RICHMAN, B. M. (1965) *Soviet Management*. Englewood Cliffs, N.J.: Prentice-Hall.

RIGBY, T. H. (1969) "Traditional, market, and organizational societies and the USSR," in F. Fleron, Jr. (ed.) *Communist Studies and the Social Sciences*. Chicago: Rand McNally.

RUBLE, B. A. (1977) "The Soviet-American comparison: A high risk venture." *Comparative Labor Law* 4:247–259.

RUBLE, B. A. (1981) *Soviet Trade Unions: Their Development in the 1970s*. New York: Pergamon.

RUBLE, B. A. (1982) "Policy innovation and the Soviet political process: The case of socio-economic planning in Leningrad." *Canadian Slavonic Papers* 2:161–174.

RUDICH, F. M. (1980) "Proizvodstvenni kollektiv: upravlenie, sotsialno-ekonomicheskoe razvitie." *Sotsiologicheskie Issledovania* 1:76–83.

RUTLAND, P. (1984) "The brigade system in Soviet industry: An assessment." Paper presented to the Conference of NASEES, Cambridge, March.

RUTLAND, P. (1984) "The Shchekino method and the struggle to raise labour productivity in Soviet industry." *Soviet Studies* 3:345–365.

RUTLAND, P. (1986) "Productivity campaigns in Soviet industry," in D. Lane (ed.) *Labor and Employment in the USSR.* New York: New York Univ. Press.

SCHAPIRO, L., and J. GODSON [eds.] (1984) *The Soviet Worker: From Lenin to Andropov.* New York: St. Martins.

SCHEETZ, E. C. (1978) "Dissaffected workers publicly defend their rights." *Radio Liberty Research* 47/78, February 28:1–6.

SCHROEDER, G. (1979) "The Soviet economy on a treadmill of reforms." *Soviet Economy in a Time of Change.* Washington: U.S. GPO.

SCHULTZE, F., and G. LIVERMORE (1985) *The USSR Today: Perspectives from the Soviet Press.* Columbus, OH: CDSP.

SCHWARTZ, S. M. (1951) *Labor in the Soviet Union.* New York: Praeger.

SELYUKOV, F. T. (1971) *Rukovoditel i podchinionni v sisteme upravlenia.* Moskva: Redaktsia literaturi po organizatsii i upravleniiu narodnim khazyaistvom.

SERGEEV, M. D. (1970) "Osobennosti dialektiki obiektivnikh uslovi i subiektiv-nogo faktora v upravlenii sotsialisticheskim obshchestvom," in V. G. Afanasiev (ed.) *Nauchnoe Upravlenie Obshchestvom.* Moskva: Mysl.

SHATUNOVSKY, I. M. (1970) *Trudiascisia tuneiadets (zapiski feletonista).* Moskva: Sovetsakaia Rossia.

SHELLEY, L. (1982) "Law in the Soviet workplace: The lawyers perspective." *Law and Society Review* 3:429–454.

SHELLEY, L. (1984) *Lawyers in Soviet Work Life.* New Brunswick, NJ: Rutgers Univ. Press.

SHIBAEV, A. I. (1977) "Report on the work of the All-Union Central Council of Trade Unions and the tasks of the USSR's trade unions in the light of the decisions of the 25th CPSU Congress." CDSP, Vol. XXIX, 12:7–9.

SHLAPENTOK, V. (1985) "Evolution in the Soviet sociology of work: From ideology to pragmatism." Paper 404, Russian and East European Studies Program, University of Pittsburgh.

SHUBKIN, V. (1978) "Limits." CDSP, Vol. XXX, 9:4–6. *Novy Mir,* 2:187–217.]

SIEGELBAUM, L. H. (1984) "Soviet norm-determination in theory and practice, 1917–1941." *Soviet Studies,* 1:45–68.

SIKORSKY, V. M. (1977) *KPSS na etape razvitogo sotsializma.* Minsk: B.G.U.

SIMIS, K. (1982) *USSR: Secrets of a Corrupt Society.* London: Dent & Sons.

SIRIANNI, C. (1982) *Workers Control and Socialist Democracy: The Soviet Experience.* London: Verso.

SKARUPO, Z. (1978) "Cutting labor turnover and improving manpower use." CDSP Abstracts. [*Planovoe Khoziaistvo* 6:118–125.]

SLIDER, D. (1985) "Reforming the workplace: The 1983 Soviet law on labor collectives." *Soviet Studies* 2:173–183.

SMIRNOV, O. V. (1977) *Osnovnie printsipi sovetskogo trudovogo prava.* Moskva: Iuridicheskaia Literatura.

SMIRNOV, V. A. (1979) *Sotsialnaia aktivnost sovestkikh rabochii.* Moskva: Politizdat.

SMIRNOV, V. A. (1975) "Opyt ispolzovania obshchestvennoi attestatsi dlia sbora sotsiologicheskoi informatsii." *Sotsiologicheskie Issledovania* 4:117–124.

SMITH, A. (1937) *J'ai été ouvrier en URSS.* Paris: Librairie Plon.

SMITH, S. A. (1984) "Moscow workers and the revolutions of 1905 and 1917." *Soviet Studies* 2:282–289.

SONIN, M. Y. (1978) "Make efficient use of labor resources." CDSP Abstracts. [*Ekonomika i Organizatsia promishlennovo proizvodstva* 4:3–12.]

SPIRIDONOV, Y. (1983) "An economic commentator's note: Behind the penalty line." CDSP, Vol. XXXV, 28:3–4. [*Izvestia*, July 13:2.]

STAATS, S. (1972) "Corruption in the Soviet system." *Problems of Communism*, 1:40–46.

STOLYAR, I. G. (1973) *Proizvodstvennaia brigada-osnova trudovogo kollektiva.* Moskva.

SUNY, R. G. (1979) "Soviet Georgia in the seventies." *Occasional Paper* 64, Kennan Institute for Advanced Russian Studies, Washington.

SUNY, R. G. (1982) "Violence and class consciousness in the Soviet working class." *Slavic Review* 3:436–442.

TADEVOSYAN, V. S. (1980) *Ukreplenie sotsialisticheskoi zakonnosti v narodnom khoziaistve.* Moskva: Nauka.

TECKEMBERG, W. (1978) "Labour turnover and job satisfaction: Indicators of industrial conflict in the USSR?" *Soviet Studies* 2:193–211.

TENSON, A. (1980) "Seasonal migratory workers in the Soviet Union." *Radio Liberty Research* 234/80, June 27:1–3.

THOMPSON, J. D. (1967) *Organization in Action: Social Science Bases of Administrative Theory.* New York: McGraw-Hill.

TIKHOMIROV, Y. A. (1978) *Mekhanizm upravlenia v razvitom sotsialisticheskom obshchestve.* Moskva: Nauka.

TILLY, L. A., and C. TILLY [eds.] (1975) *Class Conflict and Collective Action.* Beverly Hills, CA: Sage.

TOMASIC, D. (1953) *The Impact of Russian Culture on Soviet Communism.* Glencoe: Free Press.

TOSHCHENKO, Z. T. (1970) "Vidi sotsialnovo planirovania," in V. G. Afanasiev (ed.) *Nauchnoe Upravlenie Obshchestvom.* Moskva: Mysl.

TOSHCHENKO, Z. T. (1981) "Vospitatelnaia rabota kak obiect sotsialnovo planirovania." *Sotsiologicheskie Issledovania* 2:41–49.

TSELMS, G. (1977) "Competition: The step summit of glory." CDSP, Vol. XXIX, 3:19–20. [*Ekonomika i Organizatsia Promishennovo Proizvodstva*, December, 1976:122–132.]

TUROVSKY, F. (1981) "Society without a present," in L. Schapiro and J. Godson (eds.) *The Soviet Worker: Illusion and Realities.* New York: St. Martins.

VARIOUS AUTHORS (1968) *Rol obshchestvennosti v upravlenii proizvodstvom.* Kharkov.

VOLKOV, Y., and Y. CHERVIAKOV (1977) *Trudovoi kollektiv-shkola vospitania khoziaev proizvodstva.* Moskva: Profizdat.

VOLOVOI, D. (1977) "Problems and opinions: Improving the economic mechanism." CDSP, Vol. XXIX, 45:5–7. [*Pravda*, Nov. 10:2.]

VON LAUE, T. H. (1962) "Tsarist labor policy." *The Journal of Modern History* 2:135–145.

VORONIN, Y. (1977) "The young workers skills." CDSP Abstracts. [*Ekonomicheskaia Gazeta* 4:8.]

WAGNER, W. G. (1976) "Tsarist legal policies at the end of the Nineteenth Century:

A study in inconsistencies." *The Slavonic and East European Review* 3:371-394.

WEBER, M. (1981) *Sulla Russia 1905–1917.* Bologna: Il Mulino.

WELTER, G. (1961) *Storia della Russia.* Bologna: Cappelli.

WHITE, S. (1979) "The USSR: Patterns of autocracy and industrialism," in A. Brown and J. Gray (eds.) *Political Culture and Political Change in Communist States.* London: Macmillan.

WILES, P. (1964) *The Political Economy of Communism.* Oxford: Basil Blackwell.

WILES, P. (1987) "The second economy, its definitional problems," in S. Alessandrini and B. Dallago (eds.) *The Unofficial Economy: Consequences and Perspectives in Different Economic Systems.* Aldershot: Gower.

WILLIAMSON, O. E. (1981) "The economics of organization: The transaction cost approach." *American Journal of Sociology.* 3:548–577.

WILLIAMSON, O. E., and W. G. OUCHI (1981) "The market and hierarchies program of research: Origins, implications, prospects," in A. H. Van de Ven and W. F. Joyce (eds.) *Perspectives on Organizational Design and Behavior.* New York: John Wiley.

WILHELM, J. H. (1985) "The Soviet Union has an administered not a planned economy." *Soviet Studies* 1:118–130.

WOLFE, B. D. (1964) *Three Who Made a Revolution: A Biographic History.* Harmondsworth: Penguin.

WRONG, D. H. (1961) "The over-socialized conception of man in modern sociology." *American Sociological Review* 2:183–193.

YADOV, V. A., and A. G. ZDRAVOMYSLOV (1975) "Atteggiamenti verso il lavoro fra i giovani operai," in B. Grancelli (ed.) *Operai e tecnici in URSS e Polonia.* Milano: F. Angeli.

YANOWITCH, M. (1982) *L'ineguaglianza economico-sociale in Unione Sovietica: Sei studi.* Torino: Loescher. [*Social and Economic Inequality in the Soviet Union.* New York: M. E. Sharpe, 1977.]

ZALESKI, E. (1980) *Stalinist Planning for Economic Growth.* Chapel Hill: University of North Carolina Press.

ZASLAVSKAYA, T. I. (1981) "Economic behaviour and economic development." *Soviet Review* 2:24–43. [*Ekonomika Promishlennovo Proizvodstva* 3, 1980:15–33.]

ZASLAVSKAYA, T. I. (1981) "Spontaneity and planning in social development," in U. Himmelstrand (ed.) *Sage Studies in International Sociology.* London: Sage.

ZASLAVSKAYA, T. (1984) "Paper to a Moscow seminar." *Russia* 9:27–42.

ZASLAVSKY, V. (1979) "The regime and the working class in the USSR." *Telos* 42:5–20.

ZASLAVSKY, V. (1981) *Il consenso organizzato. La società sovietica negli anni di Breznev.* Bologna: Il Mulino.

ZEITLIN, L. R. (1971) "Stimulus/response: A little larceny can do a lot for employee moral." *Psychology Today* 5.

ZUKIN, S. (1978) "The problem of social class under socialism." *Theory and Society* 6:391–427.

ZUKIN, S. (1980) Review of D. Lane and F. O'Dell, *The Soviet Worker. Telos* 43:189–198.

Index

For Product Safety Concerns and Information please contact our EU
representative GPSR@taylorandfrancis.com
Taylor & Francis Verlag GmbH, Kaufingerstraße 24, 80331 München, Germany

www.ingramcontent.com/pod-product-compliance
Ingram Content Group UK Ltd.
Pitfield, Milton Keynes, MK11 3LW, UK
UKHW021831240425
457818UK00006B/153